In the Pillared Dark

In the Pillared Dark is the story of how two unrelated incidents rock-skip across the surface of an ordinary life until, after forty years, they converge in the still waters of understanding. It is a personal history. Everything you read here is true and really happened; however, for purposes of the narrative, I took artistic license in some of the details, and, in a few places, the chronology. Also, for reasons of privacy, a few names have been changed.

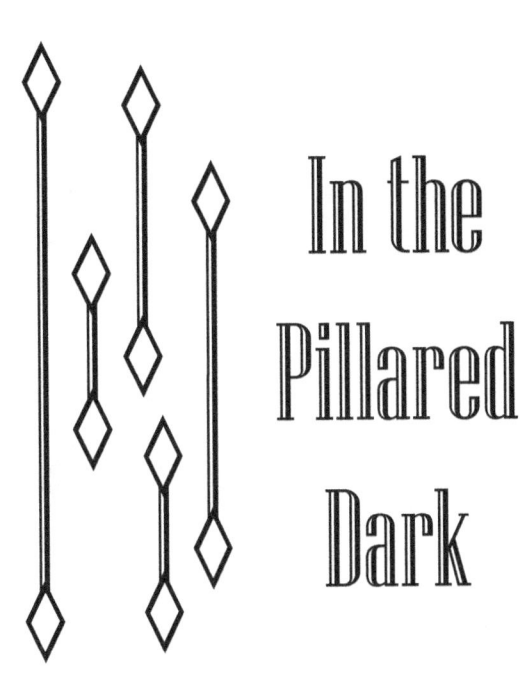

In the Pillared Dark

Lois Van Buren

In the Pillared Dark
© 2016 Lois Van Buren
cum privilegio ad imprimendum solum

All rights reserved. No part of this book may be reproduced, stored in a retrieval system, or transmitted in any form or by any means, electronic, mechanical, photographic, recording, or otherwise, without the prior written consent of the author.

This is a print-on-demand copy. Two limited editions were printed in 2013 by Thomson-Shore, Inc.: 100 copies in hardcover and 100 copies in softcover.

Acknowledgments

To those who read the manuscript in its various stages: You are the ever hopeful in search of a good book, and I thank you for believing in my potential. It helped keep me going.

To my dear friend, Elliot Ruchowitz-Roberts: Beyond the point at which I could no longer summon confidence in myself, you believed in more than my potential. You believed in my writing, in the story I wanted to tell, and in me. If it weren't for your diligent work on the manuscript, my readers would not be soon to turn this page. In point of fact, there would be no page to turn.

To Austin and Sean: I didn't always know it at the time, but growing up with you guys was an adventure I wouldn't have missed for the world. I hope you feel the same.

Finally, to two others:
> ... and the silence of the three of them had made a little kernel of sense in a world of boasting, self-excuse and rhetoric.
> – Thornton Wilder, *The Bridge of San Luis Rey*

Far in the pillared dark
Thrush music went —
Almost like a call to come in
To the dark and lament.

But no, I was out for stars:
I would not come in.

> From "Come In"
> by Robert Frost

A Note

In 1976, I took a women's poetry class with Meridel Le Sueur, whose popularity as a writer and social activist in the 1930s regained strength in the hope of the 1970s. I knew little about her except that she'd recently been interviewed by *Ms. Magazine*, struck me as a strong and wise soul, and liked to go out for ice cream after class.

Meridel encouraged us to document our personal biographies. She said they would someday be the chronicles historians would look to for insight. She said our journals would be more valuable than anything formally written about our time. I saw the truth in this, but it was not until I waded into the waters of my fourth decade, pregnant with my first son, that I began to set down my story. Here, the italicized sections in Part One are a direct transcription of tapes I made after my experience at Kent State when bullets were fired at me and my classmates there on May 4th, 1970. The rest is taken from hand-written journals, from memory, and from artifacts that sparked that memory.

Part One

The Sound of Thrush Music

Vineland, New Jersey
Late Spring 1965

As I headed out the kitchen door, the phone rang. This time its intrusion with the scene – the morning, the blue of the wallpaper, my solid sense of place – stopped me. Its interference was becoming predictable, routine, and, on this day, a curiosity I couldn't resist. I put my schoolbooks down and went back.

The kitchen phone hung on the wall near the entrance to the dining room, which was adjacent to the living room. The living room opened to the hallway which led to the master bedroom. There, a Princess extension sat on a nightstand a short reach from my mother's pillow. With painstaking stealth, I lifted the kitchen phone's receiver with my right hand while my left secured the cradle. I held my breath. Waiting another second or two, I slowly let go of the cradle and listened.

"I love you, darling," a man's voice wooed.

"Mmmm. What wonderful words to hear first thing in the morning," my mother said, still groggy from waking. There was something remote in her voice, some vagueness, as if she were mouthing words she wasn't sure of but knew all too well – the kinds of words I would hear myself speak years later, all too often, to too many men. "You can't be at work already."

"We've got to get the Morrison estimate in the mail or we won't have time to get the parts order out. You know how the old man is. Will you be here soon? If

I try to type this thing, it won't leave the building 'til Christmas."

"Is the coffee on?"

"Waiting for you."

I made up for the soundless lift of the handset by bringing it back down with a powerfully satisfying slam. Snatching up my schoolbooks, I stormed out of the house like Alice when, arms akimbo, she walked off in disgust, leaving the Mad Hatter, his tea party, and the world that, until she fell down the rabbit hole, made perfect sense. I looked up. There were puffy cotton clouds, and I could feel the warm familiar sky of that southern New Jersey day in May.

Kent State University
Kent, Ohio
May 3, 1970

There were supposed to be negotiations on Sunday afternoon in the main – in Kent Hall, I think – on the front campus. We hung out, very calmly. Everybody waited to see what was going to happen in those meetings, but I don't think anything did. I spoke with a couple of the National Guard. They were from Akron, which is only ten miles from Kent. They were also college students, same age, or a few years older. I put flowers in the muzzle of the rifle of one of them. We flirted. He was cute. I remember being impressed with the fact that he was as young and naive as I was, and that he was just doing what he thought was right, like kids doing what their parents tell them to do. He didn't know, I don't think. I don't believe he really knew that guns kill. Not really.

1 Something had been said

Walking along the side yard, past the garage, and toward the street where the bus stopped, I fixed my eyes on the Thunderbird my mother would pick me up from school in that afternoon. Since his crew-cut days, Daddy talked about buying a Thunderbird. "Four hundred horses under one little hood! Can you believe it?" By the time he could afford one, Ford had changed the look from a sporty two-door coupe to a larger "personal luxury car." He didn't care. He bought one anyway. Then Ford, in Daddy's words, "pulled a dirty trick on me" and came out with the Mustang. A hot little maroon four-on-the-floor – the call of the wild – ended up in the garage nestled beside the Thunderbird, and from 1964 to 1970, we owned a series of each.

The T-bird became Mom's car, the family car, the one that brought home the groceries, the one we sat next to each other in when I got out of school. Merging with street traffic, she settled into the unconscious rhythms of driving before concentrating on her argument.

"Lois. Please. What you thought you heard this morning. He's a dear friend, and that's all."

Brooding as only a fifteen-year-old can, my retort was pristine. "Don't 'please' me, OK? I know what I heard."

"Listen to me. Try. Can't you try? You'll understand someday. Honey, look – one man can't do it all and shouldn't be expected to. Your dad's an excellent provider."

"Oh, yeah? What else do you need, Mother?"

Slowing for an intersection, or possibly, to find the right words, she attempted an explanation. "I can't talk to your dad. He never wants to go anywhere. I have to do the asking, and then he only goes because I nag. Then he pouts and can't wait to get home to his TV shows. It gets to me."

"He is who he is. You should know that by now."

"I do know that by now."

In those days, cars had little vents under the dash on both sides that opened manually via a nifty knob that, when pulled, let outside air blow in. The pleasure of watching it make a billowing, half-balloon of my flowered shirtwaist, not unlike that famous image of Marilyn Monroe, did not elude me. As I savored the coolness on my thighs, anger seeped into my body. I could feel the freshness of spring under my dress, the fire of betrayal in my cheeks.

"You know you'll never change him. What's going on, Mom?"

"I haven't committed adultery, if that's what you're thinking."

We arrive at feelings, and when we think we are sure of them, we label them and put them aside in a bowed box or atop a shelf for later, not knowing or caring or asking when later will be. It's how we keep going. It's how we carry on.

I hated her.

Something had been said

◊

It's not like my dad never cheated on my mom. He did. As a matter of fact, the only time I ever saw her cry was a year earlier on the night we drove around town looking for him. She had an idea about where we might find him, and sure enough, there he was at the doughnut shop. The wraparound windows made it easy to spot him. It didn't look to me like he was with anybody – he was just sitting there, mindlessly stirring his coffee as he watched the counter girl wait on someone. Apparently, that was all Mom needed to see. She cut a big, wide U-turn and took off for home. She went straight to bed and cried herself to sleep. Daddy didn't come home that night, but he did return the next day and never stayed out all night again. Something had been said, but it was a long time before I knew what.

2 Climbing into each other's skin

That summer, the summer right after the phone stopped me dead in my tracks, I got a job at the trucking firm where my mom worked. I knew "he" was somewhere, but never suspected how nearby somewhere was. I had it in my head that he was one of the auditors from corporate who passed through every now and then. I never met any of them and no evidence pointed in that direction. In fact, evidence pointed in the opposite direction. "He" must have been someone on the inside, not a visiting auditor. But that obvious point didn't occur to me. I preferred imagining mystery man in suit and tie, debonair, refined, graying at the temples and ready to whisk my mom away to a life of cultured prosperity.

Years later, when I was married, and when my husband Patrick and I were running a business together, I developed a crush on Ian, one of our employees. Things started getting a little scary, so Patrick and I parked along a seaside drive not far from our home outside of Santa Cruz, California, to talk about it. Putting his arm around me, he tried to guess who the lucky guy might be. Pat imagined it to be my accompanist.

"Who is it?" he ventured.
"It doesn't matter."
"Have you . . . ?"

"No, no."
Sigh of relief.
"Is . . . is it Stephen? I thought it might be Stephen."
"My accompanist? No. God, no." I smiled inwardly, relieved he was way off base. I could see where he'd think that. Maybe Pat needed to imagine the man luring his wife away as a highly worthy rival in the same way I got carried away with the fantasy of my mom's lover. A classical pianist, comatose to the world beyond his piano as he feverishly rehearsed for his next command performance, would do just fine.

There's a picture of me at a piano, dating from when I was seven years old. An upright, it was painted mint-green and was the kind of piano that came with a round, spin-top piano stool. In the photo, my fingers are about to come down on the keys, and I'm in the process of swiveling toward the camera, all smiles. When, in fifth grade, the music teacher laid out – in glorious display – the band instruments he had for us to choose from, I chose the clarinet. In high school, I came to recognize the sound of the French horn whenever I heard it in whatever piece of classical music I happened to be listening to, and I knew I had to be a part of that sound. So to the consternation of the woodwind teacher, I gave up the clarinet and took up the horn. I never stopped playing piano, though. I played it for solace; I played the horn for beauty.

Patrick had childhood stories of ferrying a saxophone back and forth between school and his family's hilltop home, a drudgery which probably didn't help instill a longing to become a musician, but may have afforded him time to ponder the lives of those who did. Perhaps he imagined my accompanist and I romantically drawn together by irresistible musical forces.

Climbing into each other's skin

But no, Stephen and I were working on Dukas's "Villanelle for Horn and Piano," and it was true, we were meeting more than usual, but not to steal a kiss. We were rehearsing for an upcoming concert with a Santa Cruz chamber group.

Pat was as wrong about the fellow he imagined I had a crush on as I was about the one I imagined my mom was having an affair with.

July and August at the trucking firm went by with numerous filing, alphabetizing, and ho-hum receptionist tasks. Mom was a cheerful teacher. She knew her job, and her peers respected her. Unlike many women of the '50s, marriage did not keep her at home. She became a bookkeeper after graduating high school in 1943, continuing on in that line of work until she retired in 1983. "I was always good with numbers," she once told me. I liked seeing her at work, especially the way she pushed the buttons of the adding machine with the eraser end of the consistently sharp pencil she held between her index finger, her third finger, and her firmly anchored thumb. She was professional.

Daddy didn't use an adding machine, but I was intrigued by his use of a pencil, too. He was a milkman and part of his job was to keep an accounting of everything he took in. He had a small, black, soft-covered, three-ring ledger with a page for each of his customers. The pencil he used was short and stubby. I enjoyed watching him figure long columns of numbers. He'd talk to himself. "Let's see. Carry the 1. Plus 7 = 8. 8 + 1 is 9. Plus another 9 = 18. Carry the 1 again." He'd looked up, smiling, whimsy in his voice. "Mrs. Morelli better treat me to some of those cookies she's making with all this butter she bought." He wasn't talking to himself, after all. He was talking to me, including me in his work, and I loved it.

My parents met because of a pencil. It was early 1942, when they were in their teens. My mom was working the lunch counter at J.J. Newberry, the local five-and-dime. My dad delivered ice. One day, she accidentally stabbed his palm with her pencil as he spun the receipt pad around so she could sign for that day's delivery. Laughing with embarrassment, she tried to make up for it by practically rubbing his hand off with her apron. As the story goes, he'd already looked up at her and fallen in love. Then she looked up at him; and to the day he died, my dad had a lead speck stain in his hand to prove the propitious incident true.

And one night during that summer I worked at the trucking firm, one clairvoyant night, I took up my own pencil. But not for the purpose of adding or subtracting or signing my name to a receipt pad. It was 4 a.m. and I'd awakened with a start. Rolling out of bed onto the hardwood floor, tangled in my full-length, pink and violet rose-covered nightgown, I blindly grabbed a sheet of paper and began writing.

Morning revealed page after page of pubescent, pseudo-philosophical babble. I awakened to a girl whose only possible answer to the question "Who am I?" was "Go and find out." Finding out, I knew even then, would at first determine what values to embrace, and at last define the person I was to become. I took it all very seriously.

"It *is* possible to think too deeply, you know," my mom said one day when she took me aside to talk about my newly detected predilection for piercing through others to learn about myself. "Stop staring at everybody. It's unnerving. You look too far in." It did get tiring.

◊

Later, when I was in my early twenties and living on my own, I learned to create fun diversions for finding out who I was. Once, while visiting a friend in Boston and with nothing to do while I waited for her to get off work, I took a walk to see what I could see. Observing a Playboy logo high on the corner of a drab, seemingly windowless, brown brick building, I stopped. It was autumn and overcast. The sharp lines of the structure against the white sky made its utilitarian architecture look two-dimensional, as if some weekend art school student had painted it onto God's canvas. Wearing a drab, brown overcoat myself, I cocked my head, pulled at my chin, and mused, "Why not?"

The club was an elevator ride to the top floor. The door opened into a darkened lounge with comfortable couches and a handful of middle-aged men wearing business suits, cocktails in hand, commingling with Playboy bunnies who were hopping happily, congeniality as much a part of their makeup as their mascara. One of them, playing hostess, hopped over to me and proffered, "May I help you?"

The initial shock of her costume made me gulp. "I'd like to apply for the position of bunny," I stammered. Position? Maybe not the best choice of words.

"Oh, good," she said. "You're in luck. It so happens we're taking applications. Wait here, and I'll bring you one."

She went through what looked like a hidden door while I scanned the premises. Everything was manly. The walls were paneled with walnut or some other rich wood. The furniture was a russet-colored leather; the mahogany bar was trimmed with brass and glass and garnished with bourbons-on-the-rocks in short, stout tumblers. A closer look at the bunnies' outfits brought my visual sweep to a standstill. I tried not to gawk.

Dear Lord! Stiletto heels, fishnet stockings, a high French-cut silky black body suit with dismembered collar, bowtie and cuffs, topped by rabbit ears and finished with a bunny tail. A little, white, powder puff bunny tail. Of course! Everyone's seen pictures of Playboy bunnies. But to see one in the flesh was like viewing an original Picasso after a lifetime of seeing only photos of his work in coffee-table books. Everything about these suddenly living, breathing girls appeared, like the actual Picasso paintings, so much more vibrant. And everything from their stiletto heels, their raised hips, their boosted butts, lifted boobs, and frozen smiles appeared so . . . pushed up. By the time the hostess reappeared with an application, I was feeling sick. Zombie-like, I filled out the form and handed it back to her. She disappeared behind the secret door, re-entering in a minute or two to proclaim, "The Bunny Mother wants to speak to you." The Bunny Mother? Oh, my God.

"Mom" was older and larger than her offspring, wore a tailored suit and was earnest about her parental responsibilities. She had me sit across from her, leaned forward on her forearms in a nurturing sort of way and proceeded with the interview. After some routine questions, we progressed swiftly to the next level. Evidently, the shabbiness of the over-sized Salvation Army coat I wore did not disguise my ample breasts.

"Let me show you around," she suggested.

I pictured myself in my soon-to-be new work clothes sitting on a Hefner look-a-like's lap. That did it. Time to get out of there. Heedless of making a bad impression and losing a potentially illustrious career, I gave her a

Climbing into each other's skin

blank stare and mumbled a lame excuse about having to meet my friend. Out on the street, the surrealism of the scene took hold. The overcast sky behind the Playboy logo thickened, and rain clouds opened. With a plea of "Somebody, please explain these people to me!" I lowered my head, opened my umbrella, and moved on.

◊

The darker hue of self-awareness that flourished during my teens was especially intense during my sophomore year of high school. Somehow, probably by default, I was elected co-president of the Southern New Jersey District of the YMCA Tri-Hi-Y youth association. The main purpose of this organization was to teach teens leadership skills, morals, and civic responsibility by modeling various aspects of the political process. We play-acted at being politicians, and, together with a male counterpart, Gabe DeLorea, who was also a friend from school, I sat on the Area Cabinet composed of representatives from New Jersey, Maryland, Delaware, the District of Columbia, and Puerto Rico.

To accomplish another important purpose of the Tri-Hi-Y clubs – character development – we were matched with a sister city, Newark. Newark was in the northern part of the state and was the largest city in New Jersey. Vineland was large too, but not in population. It was New Jersey's largest city in area – farmland acreage. Newark kids were street wise; we Vinelanders were backwoods hicks. They were seventy percent black; we, seventy percent White, Anglo-Saxon Protestant. They were underprivileged; we, middle-class.

The two groups met regularly in encounter groups, more popularly known at the time as "sensitivity meetings." Consigned to a fitting context – beanbag chairs, pillows, carpet, fireplace – we were supposed to sit and talk about our feelings. That way, the theory went, we'd tap into each other's experiences and become "sensitive" to the other guy's plight, improving our own moral rectitude in the process.

Harper Lee used that phrase – "moral rectitude." Through the splendidly succinct Atticus Finch, she also coined the aphorism, "You never really understand a person . . . until you climb into his skin and walk around in it." She must have realized that the better known version of the Cheyenne proverb, "Don't judge someone until you've walked a mile in his shoes" didn't work as well for her narrative of the South in the '30s. It didn't work as well for us, either. The only way we could hope to develop character was to climb into each other's skin, not each other's shoes; and since Negroes were already subjected to a disproportionate amount of life inside the skin of the white man's culture, Gabe and I and the other Tri-Hi-Y'ers from our hometown had a tremendous amount of climbing to do. The Newark faction knew it. Man, oh man, did they know it.

"Touch my hair."

"What?"

"Go on, girl. Touch my hair. Bring your hand on over here. Come on."

"That's OK. I'm all right where I am."

"What's with you? You 'fraid of finding out about somethin' different from yo'self? You 'fraid you might like it? Come on now. Gimme your hand. That's right."

"Oh . . . Oh. It, it's – wow – it's, it's not . . ."

"You damn tootin' it ain't. It ain't nuttin' like yours, and I'm glad it ain't. Yours is all stringy and slippery and waxy and gits all over ever'thing. Mine's soft and stays put, and I don't have to do anything to it if I don't want. Unless I'm tryin' to make it look like yours. Which I ain't. Ever again. Catch my drift, girl? Now look over here in the mirror, honey. Lookit that. You so pale. You better not go out in the sun. How you stand it? Lookit that nose. It all skinny and thin. How you breath out that thang? See mine? It wide and flat and look proud to be on my face. Yours is lookin' like it tryin' to hide under dem freckles. An' lookit dem lips. Hey, Charlene, take a look at this white sista's lips. Sweet Jesus!"

These urban youth had recently ascertained they were not Negro, but black, and black was beautiful. They were enlightened to the importance of racial dignity by Black Power Movement activists such as Huey Newton and Stokely Carmichael. Consequently, as they became empowered by Black Nationalism, they saw the wisdom in guiding us small-town neophytes into breaking out as well. Through their hands-on, show-and-tell approach, they invited us to join them in learning what it meant to be black in America. Their freely distributed lessons on discrimination and bigotry in a democracy that included the clause "All men are created equal" in its mission statement were a revelation like no other. The scales fell from my eyes, and I couldn't get enough of this newly perceived truth.

◊

Thursday night, April 30, 1970: In the middle of the film festival that had been going on all week, an announcer interrupted from the projection area above us and said, "Nixon has sent troops into Cambodia." I thought it was a part of the show. I thought it was a joke. Then I realized it was for real, and my feelings changed immediately from playful to shock and hurt. This is interesting because, just the other night,

THE SOUND OF THRUSH MUSIC

something was on the radio about how every American remembers where he was and how he was affected by the announcement that Kennedy had been shot. I remember seeing stunned teachers and crying girls in the hall, but it had no emotional effect on me whatsoever. I remember walking out of the building (school got let out), not knowing whether to be proud of myself for that or ashamed. I was thirteen. Here, at twenty, I was emotionally involved in politics and in the ownership of my country – my country. Something like Nixon going into Cambodia, a decision of such magnitude, was a shock to me. It depressed me to a great extent.

The atmosphere of the auditorium where the movies were shown had been quite the party. We were acting like kids, throwing popcorn and paper airplanes, hissing and booing, applauding, shouting out comments and laughing out loud. "Bambi Meets Godzilla" showed. It was a huge hit. I remember it so well; it's a classic. It sent our already high spirits over the top, but when the announcement was made, the movie projector was turned off. I'm not certain of that, but I know I went home and went to bed, and the next morning got up and went down to The Hub, the place where everybody hung out on campus. I was still depressed about this latest news of the war. I ran into a professor, a young woman professor, and I said, "What are we going to do?" She said, "You can start by handing these out." She handed me a single sheet of paper – a declaration of how some professors on campus opposed entering into Cambodia, and how they were going to bury the U.S. Constitution on the commons, near the Victory Bell, at noon. This was Friday.

Climbing into each other's skin

I felt like – "Well, I'm doing something." I talked to her for a while and took the stack of paper, and – oh, she said to me, "You know, something else you can do to influence people about what's going on in this country is to play your music loud so they hear it. Play it so people can hear the words. Maybe they'll listen and understand what's happening." I passed the flyers to a bunch of people and even slipped one under the dorm mother's door. I really liked the Jefferson Airplane album "Volunteers" so when I got back to the room, I put it on and played it loud: "If you smile at me, you know I will understand, cuz that is something everybody, everywhere does in the same language."

◊

Instruction about the black man in America came from my parents early on during the dinner-table tradition of family bonding. It went something like this:

"Got a joke for ya."

"OK, Daddy. Let's hear it."

"Austin!"

"Lena! Good gravy! Can't I ever say what I want in my own house? Send that steak over here and shut up, will you? To the moon!"

"It's all right, Mom. Daddy's jokes are funny."

"Don't talk with your mouth full, sweetheart."

"How do you keep nigger . . . "

"Austin!"

"All right, all right – *colored* kids from jumping on the bed?"

Silence while we watched his knife and fork performing their evening ritual. As the meat went down the hatch, precisely timed with an eye-twinkling smile, he hit us with the punch line.

"Stick Brillo pads on the ceiling."

This sort of gem was polished often during my grade-school years. Farther back, these kinds of precious stones, though more rough-cut, were also more firmly set. The most memorable teachable moment came when I was little more than a toddler.

Because he was a milkman, Daddy got up every morning at 1:30, returning home in the early afternoon just before Mom left for work. She didn't work for the trucking company during my preschool years. She was a part-time receptionist and bookkeeper in an appliance store. Daddy, ever tired, babysat while he watched TV in the cramped 10-by-10 room at the rear of the house he'd converted from a bedroom into a den. It contained a gray upholstered sofa and chair, separated by a low corner table where Mom kept her magazines and a candy dish that sat on a white crocheted doily my grandmother made. A bulky, box television set typical of the 1950s sat on the floor opposite these pieces of furniture. Daddy's habit was to zone out in front of the TV, reclining on the couch or the rug, lying on his side with his head propped up in his hand.

On this day, he must have been in the mood for spending some quality time with his daughter.

"Hey, you. Whatcha got there?"

"Teddy."

"Looks like he's gotten over that washing you gave him."

"You want to hold him?"

"Sure."

"Here, Daddy. Here he is."

"Where're you goin' there, little girl?"

Climbing into each other's skin

I distinctly recollect waddling toward the candy dish, a feeling of bulk hanging around my bottom, probably plastic pants over triple-thick underwear. The dish was made of cheap cut-glass with a dome cover that obscured its contents. But I knew what was in there – my favorite: licorice baby dolls.
"I want some candy."
"You know you have to ask."
"Daddy, can I have some candy?"
"Ask for them right."
"Please?"
"You know what I mean."
"Daddy, may I have some candy, please?"
"Ask for them right if you want some. What's their name?"
"Please can I have some baby dolls?"
"That's not what they're called."
I knew what he wanted me to ask for, but I also knew, probably from my mom, that it wasn't a very nice thing to say. Thumb in mouth, I toddled around the room a bit longer, keeping my eye on the candy dish.
"I know, Daddy, but can I have some?" I began to plead.
"No, you may not. Not until you tell me what they are. Now what's their right name? And get that thumb out of your mouth."
With the instantaneous sucking sound of the ejected digit, I exclaimed, "I'll be good. I want Teddy back now."
"I thought you wanted some candy."
Lachrymose, the tears spilling over, I asked properly for the candy I wanted so badly. "Daddy, may I please have some n-n-n-nigger babies?"
I got them, along with a warm hug and a smile, a "Daddy do love his little girl," and a legacy.

THE SOUND OF THRUSH MUSIC

◊

These object lessons from my father were not the only way I learned about the black citizens of our community. Perspicuity frequently seeped in from townsfolk. Interesting tidbits of information floated about, like the truth about all the tiny, paper-like flecks in Cedar Lake, a popular public swimming hole just outside of town. When you noticed them, you weren't supposed to say anything. You were to simply put on your poker face and turn and step quietly out of the water without looking around because you knew those flecks had nothing to do with the trees on the perimeter of the lake. No, those flecks weren't debris that fluttered down from those great overhanging branches. They were tiny pieces of "nigger skin" that came off in the water because "those people don't bathe at home."

These fine insights into how the other side lived also came from over-the-fence conferences between neighbors that might go like this:

"You know how black absorbs heat, right? Don't you think they get awfully hot in the summertime?"

"Maybe that's why they're so damn lazy. Maybe the heat and the black make 'em naturally slower. I guess it's not their fault, but God, their laziness galls me."

"Hmm. They're big, and they got a lot of muscle. You can say that for 'em."

"Yeah, and they're good at basketball."

"Yeah, but they aren't very smart. Why, do ya think?"

"Only God knows the answer to that."

"Why in the heck do you think he made their palms and the bottoms of their feet white?"

"I wanna know what's with the watermelon and fried chicken."

Climbing into each other's skin

My favorite query to flummox a young mind was whispered between parents on an idle summer's eve as families promenaded about downtown, licking after-dinner ice cream treats, the hands – and ears – of their loving children securely held between them as they observed a couple across the street: "Can't she get a white guy?"

By the time I was president of Vineland's Tri-Hi-Y club, my standard reaction to racist comments had become one of silent consent. When, after Sunday-night service, my church friends conspiratorially giggled, "Over there! Ten o'clock." "Ten points." "Quick! Get the shotgun," as they singled out every black pedestrian walking along the main drag we were cruising, I said nothing. When someone added, "Only five for the little kid," I didn't speak up.

If I'd continued down that path, the one of least resistance, of quiet acceptance, I might have graduated from the University of Racial Prejudice, maybe not with flying colors, but a graduate nonetheless. As it was, those wise and munificent Newark high-schoolers entered my life at a pivotal moment, unlocked the doors of my xenophobic prison and introduced me to the Afro-American, a person who was part of an assembly of individuals not unlike myself, living in a world filled with a new race of people I was learning about, the only race, the human race.

Yet, even with all they taught me, it was with trepidation that I stepped into the house of a black boy and observed that his room contained the same accouterments as mine – an alarm clock, a laundry basket, an old Teddy bear. To see that he had a bookshelf filled with titles I'd read in the past – *Far From the Madding Crowd*, *The Picture of Dorian Gray* – and the book I was currently enjoying – *Catcher In the Rye* – and a book I would soon be devouring – *Soul On Ice* – and then, yes then, to find that his kisses contained a tender softness I could never have imagined, was a gift of water for a desiccated soul.

    Two opportunities for travel and exploration presented themselves during my term as Tri-Hi-Y president. The first was a conference held in Washington, D.C., to model a government general assembly. Student attendees became delegates, officers, senators, congressmen, pages, reporters, lobbyists and the like. We debated legislation in committees and on the floors of a makeshift U.S. House and Senate we created. Regrettably, I don't recall anything about any of it.
    I do remember our accommodations, though. We got to stay in one of those old, majestic hotels reminiscent of Victorian English country inns. The period décor included crystal chandeliers in the lobby and wallpaper scrolled in royal blue and gold. The steep staircase, lined with fine landscapes, rose to guest rooms. Ours was equipped with sleigh beds covered in velvet and needlepoint, and there were alcoves that looked out over the city. Heavy, ornate curtains hung on one wall, and the bathroom had an old, chipped, white porcelain washbasin, its cracks adding to the allure. I roomed with Evelyn, one of the intimates crucial to the vitality of the Vineland Tri-Hi-Y and the girl who would marry Gabe, my co-president. We enjoyed acting like girlfriends, giggling and telling secrets. She was experiencing some anxiety about her relationship with Gabe, and consulted me. We discussed our opinions of sex before marriage. I got the feeling she'd already given in because she was worried

Climbing into each other's skin

he didn't love her when, it appeared to me, he did. She was a sweet, sincere, sad-eyed girl, and I truly liked her.

As a memento of the conference, I took the room key home. It was brass attached to an oversized green plastic tag stamped with the words "Drop in any mailbox." I kept it in my jewelry drawer, shoving it from side to side whenever I rooted around for a necklace or bracelet. After a year of this and reading, almost daily, "Drop in any mailbox," I decided to go ahead and do just that. The small jolt of guilt and furtive thrill I received from dropping – legally, no less – a bare naked item, no envelope and no postage, into a United States Postal Service receptacle would have made any adult chuckle. Grownups, I would learn, also took pleasure in these perceived secret rebellions because they are, after all, sometimes all that happens in a day to make you feel as if you're getting something for free.

Gabe and Evelyn and I got something for free during that conference weekend. At the end of the day on Saturday, everyone in Washington seemed to have gone home, and nobody, but nobody, was anywhere when we stumbled onto a series of subterranean corridors under the Capitol Building. We ducked under a neatly handscripted "Do Not Enter" notice strung with a burgundy, velvet-tasseled cord across an ivory tiled stairway. Since such directives didn't apply to teenagers, the sign was not a concern, and we scurried down the steps two at a time.

We found ourselves wandering through a maze of hallways that went this way and that, intersecting with others going here and there. Marble statues and busts of pony-tailed guys at every turn gave an aura of mystery and mansion. At points along the hallway, there were rooms – offices and a library – with glass panels through which we could peer, faces pressed against the glass, into sumptuously executive interiors. At several junctures, these tunnels joined, encircling white cupola-like stone domes ten feet above our heads. Our voices resonated and echoed as we jumped up and down beneath them hollering, "Whoop!" We laughed and whooped and couldn't have been happier. When we came upon a stairwell that brought us into the glistening sun, we found we were some blocks away, lost. We didn't care because it felt so special to have glimpsed some inner sanctum that only privileged citizens were privy to.

The second opportunity for travel and exploration was a character-building retreat at Springfield College in Springfield, Massachusetts. We were to tour the college during the day and get to know each other better in the evenings via sensitivity meetings. The Newark kids weren't there this time, so rather than concentrate on cultural differences, we got more deeply involved with each other as individuals. This was achieved by spotlighting a single member of the group and delving into whomever he or she was, or appeared to be, to the rest of us. We used others' impressions to gain insight into ourselves, thereby hopefully gaining the leadership perspective we were in the YMCA to attain.

Having participated frequently in this process, I was familiar with the procedure. Emotions surfaced, since all types of hidden fears, inner ghosts, and negative personality traits were made apparent to the person in the spotlight. It became a purge for the poor bloke at the center.

On Saturday night of this retreat, my peers turned toward me in a way that said my time in the center was overdue. As we sat in our comfy circle, Gabe and the others, including our leader, Jim, I could tell, had been cooking this up behind my back. Jim got the ball rolling.

Climbing into each other's skin

"So, Lois, let's talk about you tonight. Would you be comfortable with that?"

"Yeah, sure." *I* didn't have anything to worry about.

"Good. Evelyn, would you like to start? I believe you have something you'd like to say."

"I do." She turned stiffly toward me, with the air of a doctor interviewing a new patient about what ails her. I began to get nervous. "I really like you a lot. I want you to know that," she said. Oh, brother, here it comes. "I think you do know that, but there's something that's been bothering me. I'm sure you don't mean to do it. You probably don't know you are."

"What do I do?"

"You . . . treat me differently depending on who we're with."

"I do? No I don't."

"Sometimes you ignore me, like you don't want to be seen with me."

"What? I do not."

"Yes, you do. If we meet somebody you want to impress, I'm all of a sudden not there."

"Come on, Evie. You know better than that."

"I know I feel like I'm not good enough for you except when nobody else is around. Then all of a sudden, we're best friends."

Jim interrupted, "Larry, did you want to say something here?"

"Evelyn's right. You're so into yourself, you don't even know it. What I've noticed is that when I give you a compliment, you don't thank me. It looks like you're thinking, 'Yeah, Larry, you're right. I'm beautiful, smart, and talented. Ho-hum.'"

Oh, stupendous. Here was another Tri-Hi-Y'er I'd spent a year with turning against me. In disbelief, I blurted out, "Hold on, you guys. You're blowing me away."

Jim interrupted again, "Lois, why don't you take a minute to register these comments before responding? Everybody in this room cares about you. We want you to know what we see so that you can understand your effect on those around you. Tell us what happens inside you when you get a compliment or are out with friends and meet new people."

I came swiftly and sharply to attention, like a soldier saluting a superior officer, all the while shaking in her boots. *People don't think about themselves, about who they are. People simply are. If what I am isn't good, I can't help that. What do you want me to do? Kill myself?* My mind was racing.

I wanted to shout, "Leave me alone!" Instead, I said, "I don't say anything when you compliment me because I don't know what to say. Because what you're saying isn't true. There's nothing about me worth complimenting. You may not know that, but I do."

"So," Larry came back, "you're telling me I'm no good at judging someone? That what I think isn't valid?"

"No! I'm telling you *I'm* no good. Not *you're* no good."

"But that's not what you say. You say nothing."

Jim explained. "When somebody doesn't speak, it's usually because he's thinking something he'd rather not say since it wouldn't be polite. So he doesn't say anything at all."

"Oh, God. It's the opposite. I'm not better than anybody. I'm worse. I don't answer because I'm embarrassed."

"You coulda fooled me," snapped Evelyn. "You use your looks to get the attention you want. It's fun for you and you pull it off every time. At our expense."

"Evelyn's right. That's precisely what you do," Gabe put in.

Climbing into each other's skin

"All right now," Jim intervened. "Lois, I want you to try and see how your actions look from outside yourself. Are you willing to do that?"

"Yes." I was starting to cave in. Not give in, but cave in like a collapsing parachute as it touches the ground. "Am I really like that? I don't mean to be, but I guess I am. I'm a jerk."

Gabe came back with, "You're not a jerk. You're a great person, but you come off as a snob. A nice snob, but a snob. Nobody can get anywhere near you. You're closed off. Hidden. Secret. You let us pour out our hearts to you, and you listen. It's the best part of you, and we love it, but you never let on about yourself. Like, you've never said anything to us about your mom. It's gotta be killing you inside."

"What? What about my mom? There's nothing about my mom." Was this what they'd been waiting for?

"Lois, everyone knows your mom is cheating on your dad," said Evelyn.

"She is not. My mom and dad are happy."

"Oh, please," came back Carolyn, another of our cadre who, up until then, was mute. "She goes to lunch with him all the time. They think no one sees, but my dad says it's disgusting."

"How's your dad know so much? From experience?"

Unshaken, Carolyn continued, "We all know. Don't act like you don't. Why are you so defensive?"

"Oh, no you don't. You guys aren't going to do this to me. Are your lives so perfect? Are your parents perfect? I am not a snob. I am not vain. How can I be when I don't even like myself? I HATE MYSELF! Get it? My mom is not cheating on my dad! Yours is!"

With that, I flew out of the room. Tears streaming, I ran until I found the campus chapel, an unlocked place where nobody would find me.

I remember that small room. It was ovals and curves, no squares, few rectangles. The lighting was candle dim. The pews were made of hardwood with an aisle down the center. The carpet was sanctuary red. The altar was backlit. A murmur beckoned that I could not – did not – want to refuse. Was there someone there with me? I curled up on a bench and quieted down, allowing myself to be wrapped in an atmosphere pervaded by the heavenly. My eyes burned. My lids were heavy. *How did they find out? How could they know?* My life was ruined. I wouldn't be able to go to school on Monday. *How could she, the awful she, do this? I'll think about it tomorrow. But not now. Now, I'll* . . . After a while, long enough for Shakeapeare's Queen Mab to drizzle a mist of dreams over me, I awoke to the sound of the heavy chapel door chafing across the carpet and Gabe whispering, "Lois, are you in here?"

For some inexplicable reason, whenever I think back on the Tri-Hi-Y period of my life, I see a scene that couldn't have occurred the way I remember it, but I believe somehow did. I was with my first boyfriend, Fred. We were walking into one of the more ritzy restaurants our hometown had to offer, the kind of place you'd expect to see everybody during the holidays or on special occasions.

The woman I babysat for, Mrs. Freiberg, is seated with a man. Their table for two faces the door; they see us come in.

"Now, there's a beautiful girl," he remarks.

"That's Lois Van Buren. She watches Alex for us."

"You know her?"

"Oh, yes. And you're right, she is beautiful. It's a shame about her mother."

"That's not Lena's daughter, is it?"

"Yes, it is."

"My God, it is. Now that I've placed her, she's the very image."

"I've seen Lena and her 'friend' eating lunch here. Funny to see Lois. How young they are! Her boyfriend must be trying to impress her. He's a nice looking fellow. I wonder if he comes to the house after I leave."

The next time I babysat for Alex, Mrs. Freiberg told me she saw Fred and me at the restaurant, and that her dinner date remarked I was one of the most beautiful girls he had ever seen. But I already knew he said that. I also knew where they sat and what she was wearing – a black Jackie Kennedy dress – and how comfortable they seemed with each other. But how could I know this when I never saw them? Or did I see them? Why wasn't it her husband? Why did that seem perfectly natural?

> Certain things they should stay the way they are.
> – J.D. Salinger, *The Catcher in the Rye*

3 A new normal

Nothing more was seen or heard of extramarital indiscretions. Home life became like the recording of Rachmaninoff's second piano concerto, which I could practically hum by heart. Onto the turntable the album would go, filling the air with a sound that kept me company. I'd see Mom and Dad as I passed through the house on round trips between my room and the kitchen, and just as the soothing alpha waves generated by the music filled the air, my parents' presence surrounded me with a comfort I could take no notice of.

It is possible that Daddy's atonement for his part in the indiscretions came in a decision he made in the middle of one of those hundreds of passing-ships encounters. I'll never know what motivated him, but one afternoon in the fall of my junior year, he stopped abruptly, and without warning, hugged me long and hard and told me how much he loved me. All my life, his expression of love had been a half-smile that leaked out the side of his mouth, bringing my universe to a momentary standstill. To hug, to speak of love – this was out of character, and I was taken aback.

That tentative smile, certainly not unheard of, was just as wonderful. One time, two of them happened on the same day. It was Christmas 1957 or '58. We were on the floor by the tree, opening presents, when Daddy pushed the biggest one in my direction and said, "Here, open this." I was used to seeing my mom's handwriting on the to-from tags taped to all my Christmas presents, and I was used to all my Christmas presents coming from both her and my dad, so when this gift's tag bore just his name in his handwriting, I stopped. His name, in his handwriting. I looked up, and there was the smile. I unwrapped the present to discover he'd given me a beauty shop doll play set that had a salon-style hair dryer, two mirrors, flowered walls, a checkered floor, and a shampooing station with a sink that worked. Delighted, I looked up a second time, and there it was again.

The father's hug and the words of endearment that didn't come until the beginning of my junior year opened the door to the child within me. I gave way and so did he, and in that instant our relationship changed forever. As he held me, I asked, "Daddy, how can you do what you do day after day after day? Don't you get tired of the same old thing? You get up so early and go to work. Then you come home, watch TV, eat dinner, go to bed, and the whole thing starts all over again."

He stood back, pausing before he spoke. "I'm a cog in the wheel. You've seen gears. I've shown you how they work. I'm like one of the teeth in a gear wheel. If I weren't there doing my job, the wheel wouldn't turn smoothly. The machine wouldn't run right." Again, I was startled.

In John Knowles's *A Separate Peace*, Gene, the narrator and protagonist, states, "Everyone has a moment in history which belongs particularly to him. It is the moment when his emotions achieve their most powerful sway over him, and afterward when you say to this person, 'the world today' or 'life' or 'reality' he will assume that you meant this moment, even if it is fifty years past.

A new normal

The world, through his unleashed emotions, imprinted itself upon him, and he carries the stamp of that passing moment forever."

Before me stood a man who dropped out of school at the same age I was that very moment – sixteen – so that he could become a Marine and go fight for a belief he did not need to analyze, but that he intuitively knew would someday give the girl now in front of him the luxury of ignoring her parents on her way to get a bowl of ice cream and some cookies, hurrying because she left textbooks open on her desk and the phone off the hook. And though she would soon leave home and immerse herself in the explorations of her generation, an understanding expanded with each hug they shared thereafter.

Daddy had never spoken much about World War II. I knew he was a mess sergeant and "saw a little action" in the South Pacific, but that was about all. As a child, I'd sometimes rummage through his Marine Corps memorabilia stored in the attic, running his memories through my fingers over and over, wondering what they could possibly mean. Among the items was a heavy lapel pin – a half globe resting on a rope-entwined anchor and topped with a spread-winged eagle, the design I later learned was the standard USMC insignia. There was a sort of yearbook with lots of action pictures of men at war and the equipment they used – airplanes, ships, tanks and weapons. There was a sword I knew was Japanese, and there were discharge papers substantiating he'd been in battle.

When my curiosity about my dad's past was running deep, I'd descend the attic stairs and go to my parents' bedroom, where, from my Mom's bottom dresser drawer, I'd pull out her ribbon-tied stack of letters from him. Thoughts of one never far from the other, I'd soon be absorbed in wondering about the history of both my parents. How did my mom feel about censors reading private conversations between sweethearts? How did the censors decide what to cut? What secret information could my dad have inadvertently told the enemy? Some of the pages looked like a string of paper dolls. I'd look through the cut up sheaves searching for hints of myself, but the closest I got was their shared fantasy of someday having twins.

The breach in my relationship with my mom had, by the spring of my sophomore year, simply normalized. Because she worked, my after-school chore was to make supper. She'd call at four o'clock to check in and tell me what she'd taken out of the freezer and her plan for it. I thoroughly enjoyed learning how to cook. Blissfully ignorant of the detrimental consequences of using Crisco and MSG, I scooped and sprinkled to my heart's content. Typical dinner fare was taken from a menu of American staples that included pork chops, macaroni and tuna casserole, rib-eye steak, spaghetti and meatballs, and liver and onions. The only meal I didn't attempt was rump roast with peas, mashed potatoes, and gravy. That was my mom's specialty, and it wouldn't have been right to take that away from her. Maybe our relationship hadn't normalized, but had simply found a new normal.

◊

At noon – this would have still been Friday, May 1st, I – I went over to the commons to see the burying of the Constitution. There was a speech or two, crowds of people, and that was that. The day went on. I don't remember what happened. I didn't go to any classes if I had any.

A new normal

The next thing I remember is being with my friend, Julio, in his room, his dorm room, and asking him if I could do some LSD. Julio had been a little rich kid in Cuba, chauffeured to school, apparently. His parents weren't keen on Castro's world view. They ended up living in Miami, bitter, trying to maintain their culture, wishing they were back in Cuba – minus Castro. Julio promised me he'd make me some fried bananas some day. Anyway, I told him that I wanted to try LSD, so he gave me a hit. I took it and then sat on the bed for a while. He wanted to know if I was coming on. I didn't know what to look for or what was supposed to happen. He told me to look up at the fluorescent light. Then he said, "Is there anything different?" I looked up at the lights. Again he said, "Is there anything different?" I said, "Yes, I see rainbow colors coming from the fluorescent light." He said, "Yeah, well, you're starting to come on."

After a while, we went out – over to the apartment of a guy we knew. Gosh, I'm seeing all these people and streets and places run through my mind, but I can't remember the names of any of them. It was this one guy. I never got his name. I know he was blond and wanted to go into law, and I was attracted to him. He had an apartment with this other guy. It was an upstairs apartment in one of those big, old houses that get split up into rooms for students. There were a bunch of people up there, and – I don't know. It was my first trip, so I don't know what everybody else was doing, but Vincent was there. That I know. It was possibly the first time we met.

Well, the trip was real good for me. I went through a lot of emotional turnover. At one point, I was crying – a happy crying, when you're feeling the fullness of life and all that jazz, very wet tears as I recall. The guys thought that – I had no idea what a bad trip was – and these guys thought that I was having a bad trip. They were concerned about me. I reassured them, "Oh, no. I'm just happy."

Farther along in the evening, the blond guy – he must've gone out at some point – ran up the stairs calling, "The revolution's started! The revolution's started!" We had been talking about the injustices we felt were going on. We were talking the way rebels might, so when he came up the stairs hollering like that, I thought, what's this? It can't be. Everybody was excited, so we went down to see what was going on.

As we were walking to town, Vince picked a hedge flower and handed it to me. I watched it, and it changed a multitude of times. I hallucinated that flower to be many flowers. I remember that vividly – its changing shape, changing color. It was night-time dark, but I could see the changes and the colors clearly as we walked. We got downtown, heading for a bar.

The majority of the crowd had gone into Kent to raise some Cain. There was a lot of running and yelling and whatnot, and the cops were out. We didn't stick around because we were so high on drugs. So here my first trip on acid was also the first night of riots at Kent State – going out into the streets and experiencing, not being involved, but experiencing through observation, things that had a great impact on me, on all of us. That's how my weekend at Kent started. I don't remember much because I was tripping so strong, except that the hills on the way back to campus were velvety green like painted lawns.

A new normal

◊

In contrast to the security of my home life, student life in South Jersey in 1966 was rock-n-roll blaring from car windows punctuated by call-ins to the Philly AM stations with lovesick dedications. It was French fries from White Castle, cross-town rivalry between Vineland's nameless chicken mascot and Millville's Thunderbolt, and rowdy after-prom parties in Ocean City. There were couples, and there were lonely hearts, and there were lengthy and abundant phone conversations about each. Mine centered on either Fred or Robin. Fred saw me through my freshman and sophomore years. Robin would escort me through my stint as an upperclassman.

Fred was my Romeo. Our make-out sessions included one spirited and fervent scrubbing of condom lubricant that had squirted out of its wrapper onto the mod sixties pumpkin-colored couch in the family room. Muffled giggles brought my mom out to see what was going on. I quickly sat on the washrag while Fred smiled up at her.

"Sorry, Mrs. Van Buren. We were laughing about something that happened at school."

"You should go home, don't you think? It's late."

"Yes, Ma'am," he acquiesced, while I, Cheshire grin in place, remained on the wet spot, learning that rule – that the girl always gets the wet spot – early on.

For a long time, far into my marriage, I was plagued with a recurring guilt dream about Fred. It was the way I broke up with him. We were in the Thunderbird, and I kept saying "Get out." He kept pleading. I told him I didn't want to go to the same college and I wasn't ready to marry anybody. He cried. Tears. I made a man cry tears. It was horrible. "Get out! Get out!"

It's the only recurring dream I've ever had.

Robin "The Bird" Daplyn and I were less the Shakespearean tragedy and more the matter-of-fact Homer and Marge Simpson. Romance for Robin was a box of Cheerios, a quart of milk, and a bowl and spoon. Pleased with himself, he once presented this breakfast to me in bed when his dad and step-mom were out of town. At the same time, he stressed the gravity of the sign he had placed above his headboard the year before: *Dead men tell no tales.* "Dead men tell no tales, Lois. Dead men tell no tales. You want some sugar?"

My mom said that Robin was the one to marry.

"How do you know?" I asked.

"I know because you don't go running to the mirror and fuss whenever he comes over. You don't care what you say to him."

"Oh," I replied.

"And," she added, "you're willing to hang up on him and then call him right back and tell him what you think of him. I've seen you stick your tongue out at him, too." She smiled.

Fridays at 5 p.m., without fail, Robin called, sounding like he was chewing on a carrot, Bugs Bunny style, but instead of saying "What's up, Doc?" he'd say something terse like, "Be ready at 6:30."

"Where're we going? Are Lorraine and Mike coming with us?"

"Not tonight. We're doing something special."

"Like what? Going to the sand dunes in Avalon without a blanket again?"

"Very funny. No, tonight's the night we find out which is faster, the Mustang or the Thunderbird."

A new normal

"What's the plan, Stan? How're we going to get them both out of the garage without my parents hearing? You know the Mustang's faster so why bother?"

"Ah, the challenge. Don't worry about it. Just be ready at 6:30."

"I can't wait."

◊

Daddy taught me how to drive a manual transmission one afternoon in early April of my junior year, about four months before I took Robin up on "the challenge." The sky was cloudless and dry. Exiting the school bus, I made my teenaged slothful way toward the front porch. He met up with me as he was closing the screen door behind him.

"Come with me," he said.

"Where are we going?" I asked as I followed him back down the narrow walk.

"*I'm* not going anywhere," he replied. The Mustang, I noted, was parked close to the street, at the lower end of our sloping driveway.

"Get in," he said in his brusque way. "No, not that side. How are you going to drive from over there? Get in the driver's seat."

I did. There was no use arguing with my dad. Wasn't it obvious that the latest lesson in driver's training had begun? He got in on the passenger's side.

"OK," he began. "Is the emergency brake on?" He looked. "Yes, good. See that pedal on the far left? That's the clutch. Press down on it all the way with your left foot and hold it there. Good. Now look over here. See this? See how it wiggles? That's neutral. Start the car."

This he knew I could do from my lessons on how to drive the Thunderbird.

"The first thing you have to learn is how to keep the car from going anywhere with just the clutch and gas pedal. Here, look at my feet." I did.

"Clutch, gas pedal. Brake pedal in the middle. All right now. Step on the brake pedal. Take the emergency brake off. Like this. Look. Pull up first, see? Now you try it. That's right."

I was getting nervous.

"Now you have to put the car in first. I'll show you. Is the clutch in all the way?"

"Yes, but my calf is starting to hurt."

"You'll live. Let off on the brakes. It's going to roll back."

"Daaa-d." I hit the brakes.

"That's OK. Don't fall apart. Trust me. Now, when I say so, give it a little gas at the same time you let up slowly on the clutch. If you keep the two pedals balanced just right, the car will stand still. Try it."

The car lurched forward and stalled.

"That's all right. It's going to take a couple of tries. Try again."

Bump. Stop.

"Again."

Another jolt of inertia.

"And again."

Jerkity-bump. Stop.

"Easy, honey! You have to be gentler than that. There. Good. Now let the clutch out all the way. There you go. Nice and slow. Watch it. You don't need to mow the lawn. I did that yesterday. Clutch in. Step on the brakes!"

Relief. I saw he knew what he was doing when he had us start at the bottom of the drive.

"Now look here." He explained neutral, the four gears, and reverse. I listened intently.

A new normal

"Did you get all that?"

"I think so."

"Did you or didn't you?"

"I did."

"OK. Here's some money. Go to the store and get me a pack of Luckies."

I gaped at him, stupefied. Why, I don't know. That was my dad.

"Close your mouth before the flies get in." He got out of the car and walked to the house without so much as a glance back.

Fortunately for me, more so for everybody else, there were practically no cars on the streets in our neighborhood at that time of day. The store was a short two-block, five-minute round trip. It took me forty-five. When I got back, I handed him the cigarettes.

"Where's the change?"

"Oh." I handed him the change.

Without taking his eyes off his afternoon television show, he concluded the lesson.

"How about the keys?"

"Oh, yeah. Here."

"From now on, put them on the kitchen table so they'll be there when I go to work in the morning."

By the night of the big race between the Mustang and the Thunderbird, I'd become competent in running through the gears and thought of myself as a qualified handler of a standard transmission.

◊

Well, we – there were four or five of us, girls and guys – stayed up all night. Early, very early, Saturday morning, we saw a guy in uniform running with a cup of coffee in his hand. We followed him and hid down low behind a hill. We then crawled over the rise and saw what looked like an encampment. We couldn't believe our eyes. We felt special that we were the first to find them out, like we were in a juicy spy novel, and we were the spies. We also felt indignant in our rebel righteousness.

That was the first evidence of military presence in town because of what had happened the night before. I don't think riots had gone on, but apparently what did happen prompted the military to be called out. There may have been windows broken. Remember, I was in a psychedelic world of my own and made sure to stay on the fringe.

I must've slept during the day on Saturday because I don't remember much. The campus was in, oh, turmoil's not the right word. Everybody was kind of anxiously hanging out to see what was going to happen. Jerry Rubin had spoken the week or a couple of weeks before. He was a well known radical back then. I didn't understand why he would want to come to a party school like Kent, but he did. He spoke outside. I remember the image of him – fist in the air. He was perturbed with the United States government. My friends and I were talking about the coincidence of him being there so recently. The black kids, if I've got this right, had a rally of their own going on on Friday, but when all this happened with Nixon escalating the war and everybody grouping up and having something to say about it, they decided they were going to stay out. They were a strong community, and the black student leaders elected to stay out of the whole business. Let the white kids deal with this. It was their world that had created this mess. That was the word passed around, and we respected it. As far

A new normal

as I know, that's what happened. OK, so I must've slept for a while.

◊

Robin picked me up in his stepmother's rust-bucket sedan, as usual, and we went to the movies. The latest Bond flick, "You Only Live Twice," was playing. Robin said nothing about what we were really supposed to be doing. Good girl that I was, I said nothing, too, but if I live to be 150, I'll never cotton to this idiosyncrasy of men. I've gotten better with it, but only through assiduous Zen-like effort. Girls need to talk, damn it. Nonetheless, it wasn't until after the movie, French fries, and scant yet vigorous necking in "our" spot at the end of the unimproved, deserted section of Vine Road that he finally got down to the evening's assignment.

"I'll walk you to the back door like always. While you're messing with the key and going in, I'll quietly open the garage door." Apparently, we went to the movies first, not exclusively to waste time, but for Robin to get a few pointers from Agent 007.

"Go to your room," he instructed. "Stay there for ten minutes. Lie down. If you need something to do, think of me. Then sneak out." Robin was a very funny young man. This is the part about men that keeps me coming back. "Don't forget to grab both sets of car keys on your way to the back door."

"Got it. Then what?"

"Women. Jeez. Then we slip out the garage, down the drive, and onto Oak Road. We go to where it meets with Tuckahoe, turn around, and . . . How much more do I have to spell it out for you?"

THE SOUND OF THRUSH MUSIC

◊

Like all thoroughfares in Vineland, Oak Road was barely wider than a country lane. Robin let me start out in front. "The weaker vessel handicap," he informed me. He believed in the Thunderbird's engine power, and the Bird soared by right away. I believed in the Mustang's stick shift, so I, astride my steed, dug in my heels and galloped past. This set up a risky game of tailgating, flooring it, passing, and then cutting back in too close. Robin flipped on his turn signal each time for emphasis. "Oh, cute. Nice touch, Robby," I commented out loud.

Ignoring the speed limit and double yellow lines, we continued this series of stunts to see who ended up in front before we entered town, where we both knew we'd have to slow down and appear to look well behaved. Robin was too often in the lead, which really made me mad, so, forgoing all restraint, I romped on it and banged down into third to power up before I threw it into fourth and took off to catch him and go for the finish.

Suddenly, he wasn't playing the game so aggressively. By the time I realized he'd slowed for the approaching railroad crossing, I knew it was too late for me. I'd forgotten to anticipate a fact known to all Cumberland County drivers: railroad tracks are built on a rise, a hump, with the road generally narrowing for twenty yards or so on either side.

The need for control took charge. Aiming for center, I fearlessly flew over the tracks, ferociously switching from slamming gears to slamming on the brakes. The Mustang spun a three-sixty and then stopped in the middle of the road, just short of the point of misfortune. She stood stock still, nostrils flaring, eyes glaring, her muzzle pointed in the direction of home. My heart

A new normal

pounded. I watched as the T-bird's taillights became a blur. Then I saw brake lights, and then headlights. That was it, the end of the race. I dropped my head onto the steering wheel. My dad's poor car!

In a daze, I waited for Robin to come back. Our headlights face to face, he got out, ran to my door, leaned down, opened it and said, "You OK?"

"I don't know."

"You scared me."

"I scared me."

"I forgot about the tracks and knew you would, too."

"Let's go home, Robin. Follow me. Don't take your eyes off me."

We limped back. When we got to the house, we silently steered the two weary racers back to their resting places, the Mustang to her stall and the Thunderbird to his perch. Robin walked me to the door. He told me that when he looked in the rear-view mirror, he saw the Mustang's headlights, then didn't see them, and then saw them again. He said he thought I was a goner. We exchanged a warm and tender good-night kiss. His lips explored my cheek solicitously as they wandered an unhurried, meandering voyage to my earlobe. Into the curve of my hair, he exhaled, "The bird won."

◊

Both Fred and Robin had received an informal yet binding oral contract plainly stating that going steady was against Lois policy. My feeling on the matter was that diversity in masculine attention served to enrich the cultivation of a refined young woman which, assuredly, they'd want me to be. I guaranteed them there was nothing to fear from an extemporaneous date now and then. This left me conveniently available for the infrequent boyfriend pro tem, and in the spring of my junior year, Adrian Abbate filled the bill. His level of admiration for the splendor that is female was renowned; my attraction to his expertise in the game of sexual repartee was inescapable.

He spent the three months of our ad hoc "date" devising ways to get my bra off, claiming heroic triumph over most girls in this arena within two weeks. I was his Scheherazade, telling him tale after tale as we sparred in every space allocated to teens for that purpose: the back porch, the back row of the movie theater, the back seat of his car, the back den, the back bedroom. I finally decided that if he wanted my bra that badly, he could have it.

His birthday was coming up. I thought it would be funny to put this craving of his in a box and present it as a gift. Taking special care to wrap it with pink frills and paper filigree, I delivered it publicly at the party I took the trouble to give, ostensibly to celebrate his birth, but expressly to carry off this inside joke. No sooner had he untied the ribbon, taken a peek under the lid, and shown everybody the contents, than the backfire blasted throughout my being. I wanted to shout, "No! No, everybody! You've got it all wrong!"

How could I be so stupid? Giving your bra to Adrian Abbate? He knew the intended gist of my innuendo right away, but he was the only one. Quick on the draw, and in the time it takes to blow out birthday candles, he took full advantage of the situation. With all eyes on us, he sidled up to me and said something dumb but effective like, "Let's go to the casbah, dah-ling. I have something for you, too."

A new normal

◊

"Yes, well, the apple doesn't fall far from the tree," was my mom's comment when I related this episode to her the next day.

"Huh?"

"Like father, like son. Adrian's dad had the reputation for being a womanizer when I dated him."

"When you *what*? You dated Adrian's dad? Mom, how could you?"

"What do you mean, how could I? I did! Just think, Lois. You could be Adrian's sister." The facetious comment fell flat.

"Oh, my God, Mom. Why didn't you tell me?"

"Don't use the Lord's name in vain, please."

This was more than I could take. No more ad hoc dates for me. I called Robin.

◊

Late Saturday afternoon, I heard rumors that there was going to be another gathering. I don't remember if these things were planned. I don't think they were. It was just a group of people. We didn't know what we were going to do. We were a bunch of students saying, "Hey, we don't like what's going on." We gathered on the commons. The ROTC building was in eyeshot, and somebody got the bright idea to burn it down. We thought that would be kind of fun, so a bunch of us started to do that. There were varied attempts that didn't work. There was a motorcycle parked near the building, and a couple of us thought, "Well, gee, you know, we could siphon some gas out of that tank and splatter it all over the building. That would help get it started."

Nothing was working, but the fire department came out. Somebody must have called them. The National Guard were still not showing their faces, but the fire department came out and tried to put the fire out that was barely started, if that. I don't remember any flames. We cut, tried hard to cut, the fire hoses. It's pretty tough stuff. I believe we pulled off some slashes and slices. It was definitely one group against the other. Students and firemen.

There was an older woman who – maybe she knew more than we did – was very upset because of what was going on. Maybe she had been in some protests. Maybe she knew the possible consequences. There was a photographer. I don't know who or where he was from, but his camera was bigger than a Brownie. He was trying to take pictures of what we were doing when some of the students put him down, struggled with him for the camera, got him to the ground and took it. I don't know if anyone hit him or not, but the older woman was very upset. She kept calling out, "Let's keep it calm. Let's keep it calm." I remember seeing the pain in her face and the concern, and this affected me. You have to realize I was only twenty and had never experienced any sort of violence before. I was still innocent to all these sorts of things.

Well, we kept trying to cut the fire hose. There was a long line of people all holding on to it, trying to do something with it – keep it from the firemen, anything to disturb their efforts. It was heavy; we were clumsy, and our efforts didn't seem to be panning out, and the idea was dropped. The building still hadn't started burning, so the crowd decided to go downtown and march. Whoever had the loudest

A new normal

voice and was the most aggressive person could get the crowd to do what the crowd did. I remember the mass of people following the person who could yell the loudest. A friend of mine said, "Well, while everybody's attention is on this crowd downtown marching, why don't we stay back and get this building going? This'll, you know, let 'em know we mean business."

◊

 Truancy became a predominant modus operandi of upperclassmen. The weather dictated it, and Vineland's proximity to the seashore informed its locale. With outstretched bodies, we girls sacrificed ourselves to the sun god Ra as we lay on beach blankets in the sand in the bikinis for which our male chaperones paid obeisance to Ra.
 A particular day remains with me, quintessential because of the sensation of ecstasy its sun-bleached azure conjures up. My friend Lorraine, her two cheerleader friends Cheryl and Jan, and I drove to the sacrificial ceremony being held that day at Ninth Street Beach, Ocean City. Cheryl was at the wheel and AM 560's jingle, "Much more music WFIL," was calling us to worship. There was a contest going on that had to do with selecting all-time favorite hits. Whenever someone called in his or her pick, the DJ played it. Whichever Golden Oldie got the most airtime within any given hour won a position on the short list. It was a great ploy by the station's managers for keeping us tuned in. Not that we, the teenage listening audience, cared that we were the target of an advertising gimmick intended to reap the harvest of a capitalistic endeavor. We were too happy listening to

Smokey Robinson singing "Ooo, Baby, Baby" over and over again.

Taking the lead, Lorraine started to croon. Jan and I followed suit, and before long we were all vociferously anticipating the next caller's vote. Whenever other girls from around the state verified what we knew to be true, we'd scream, "Motown!" at the top of our lungs. Then, with our hair streaming out the car windows and our faces lifted to the pleasure of the radiant warmth that burned crimson beneath our eyelids, we wailed Smokey's heart-wrenching lyrics.

◊

The cheerleaders had their effect on me. In the autumn of my senior year, I went so far as to support the hometown team by taking a shot at vying for homecoming queen. *That* was a delusion of grandeur and an anomaly that only hindsight could give clarity to. For a girl who would soon discover, and then surrender, to the reclusive, creative, cerebral side of her nature, representing eleven bulging-with-testosterone football goons was a joke. Maybe losing that contest pushed me into a subconscious decision about which path to take. Maybe that disappointment turned my aspirations toward the bohemian life I intuitively knew I was meant for.

I had been writing poetry since the night I fell out of bed in my pink and violet flannel nightgown, and though my poems turned from those of the prim, collegiate, angel face I put forward, to lines emanating from a hidden darkness within, everyone got used to seeing them in the English Department's annual poetry magazine. They made me an enigma, keeping me half in the in-crowd, half in the out. The cheerleader crowd trusted my looks but were apprehensive of what went on in my head. The

A new normal

superficiality of my looks kept the intelligentsia back, yet that crowd was intrigued by my similes. Vanity kept me vacillating between the two. It was an ongoing conundrum, but the yearning to enter the confines of the beatnik coffeehouse won out. By January of my senior year, I gravitated toward the Vietnam War protesters, the pot smokers, and the avant-garde. Pom-poms and school colors were discarded and the radio dial turned from AM to FM, a subversive act of the newly formed Underground itself.

As graduation neared, the importance of social standing waned. I needed to get into college, and it wasn't happening. I'd applied to the New England schools I had grandiose ideas about, but got accepted to none. In desperation, the guidance counselor pulled out a list of scholastic institutions in need of students.

"Colleges advertise for students?"

"You bet. Let's take a look. Hmmm. Here's one. Have you ever heard of Kent State University? It's in Ohio."

4 A particular moment in history

"Mom, Dad. You don't have to stay. I'll be all right."

"We want to stay. Let us carry your things." This came from my mom.

"No, that's OK. I can do it."

"You've been saying that since you were four years old." This, from my dad, and not the first time I'd heard it.

"And now look," my mom added. "She's eighteen and still can't wait to get rid of us."

"Come on, you guys. Don't be that way. I'm just excited."

Excited wasn't the word for it. I was ecstatic, thrilled, and otherwise out of my wits with exhilaration at being an eight-hour drive from home, in a strange place I never heard of and where nobody ever heard of me. Mom was right. I couldn't wait to get rid of them.

"What floor are you on?"

"Sixth."

"Top floor, huh? I hope the rooms up there are bigger than the ones down here."

"Austin, leave her alone."

"For cryin' out loud, Lena. You leave *me* alone."

"Please, Dad."

THE SOUND OF THRUSH MUSIC

"Two bunk beds? Four of you are expected to cram yourselves into each of these excuses for a room?"

"Daaa-d."

"Austin! Don't be a killjoy. Let's go."

I entered the elevator, set my bags down, turned, pressed the sixth-floor button, and looked out at my parents. As the doors began to close, I saw that my mom was crying. The portrait made by the two of them, standing there in my direct line of sight, was perfectly framed by the elevator doors. Dad was on the left, Mom at his side. They were slightly turned toward each other – four feet in shoes marking out two sides of an equilateral triangle. His chin was lowered, and his muscular arms were at his sides. Her elbows were bent close to the waist; her hands clasped a crumpled Kleenex. They cast a sepia tone redolent of the photographs in the parlor hall of some grandmother's house – those photographs that got smaller and farther away, receding into the plaster as you ran past on your way out. If you didn't forget, you'd ask about those old pictures when you came in from playing. Wait. Was my mom clenching a nosegay of violets? Was that an eyelet lace collar? Was Daddy holding a brown Borsalino fedora with a wide hatband he nervously turned unceasingly through his thick fingers? He didn't wear hats! I shook my head and looked at the girl next to me as the elevator door closed.

"Hi, I'm Corrine. Cory, for short."

"I'm Lois."

"Where're you from?"

"New Jersey."

"Really? Me, too. Where?"

"Vineland."

"Never heard of it."

A particular moment in history

"It's South Jersey. Tomatoes and eggplants and people who run and hide if you smile at them on the street. Wish I'd never heard of it."

"I know what you mean."

"Why? What town are you from?"

"Lambertville."

"Never heard of it." We laughed. "So, are you rooming in Korb?

"Yeah."

"What floor are you on?"

"Sixth," she replied.

"Oh, wow. Me, too."

"I got here this morning," Cory said. "Wait 'til you see the showers. And come here. Check this out." Exiting the elevator, we proceeded to her room, which was at the end of the hall.

"Look out there," she said. "Across the way. See? That's the boys' dorm on the other side of the quad."

"Where? Oh, yeah. Look!" I put my bags down and pointed.

"What? Oh, jeez," Cory said. "Are those binoculars?"

"Looks like it. What shall we do? Moon 'em?"

"You ever mooned anybody?"

"Once. From the rear window of a '56 Chevy. You?"

"In front of the garage when my boyfriend Robin was backing down the driveway."

A true friendship in the making, we turned our backs to the window, hung our pants around our knees, and bent over.

A half-hour later, returning from the first floor vending machines and absorbed in our own chatter, I spied my first roommate. She was holding the door of our room open with one foot while shoving a capacious and cumbersome trunk over the threshold with the other, strenuously nudging her way in. *Oh, my God.* I couldn't believe what I was seeing. *She's black!*

"Let me get it," I proposed, interrupting my conversation with Cory.

In those days, the shock that such an appalling room assignment would have inflicted on a small-town Caucasian like myself often resulted in an appeal to the R.A. and a phone call home. But *my* heart skipped a beat. Having a black roommate might lead to having a black girlfriend, and having a black girlfriend had been a secret wish of mine since the Tri-Hi-Y days. She, justifiably, would be dubious of such a wish. Black girls knew their position in the food chain, and any attempt at chummy kinship coming from some honky chick would be seen as a cheap maneuver to keep her in her place. Ignorantly, I thought a friendship with a black girl would, in one fell swoop, advance all forms of social struggle toward peaceful reconciliation.

"Is this your room, too?" she asked.

"Yeah. I've been here for hours. I haven't claimed a bed, yet. I thought I'd wait."

"OK. I'll take the top bunk over there."

"Great. What's your name? Here, I'll lift that for you. Where're you from?" If enthusiasm breeds suspicion, this girl had good reason to be skeptical.

"I'm from Akron and my name's Charlotte," she stated. But her wry smile jeered, *Wanna make something of it?*

My reply was sad proof of my lack of cultural sophistication. In possession of neither the cunning it takes to recognize the obvious, nor the perception necessary to identify myself as the adversary, I said, "No kidding? I lived across the street from a girl named Charlotte. She and her sister Suzanne and I did everything together. We

A particular moment in history

trick-or-treated and made angels in the snow and bicycled all summer. Stuff like that."

Is it possible that, in the long run, any overt harm administered by a full-blown bigot might be less menacing than that covertly issued by one who thinks she's come to the Lord on that score, been redeemed, and now loves and understands everybody, red and yellow, black and white? The right thing to do would have been to let Charlotte make the first move. If a friendship was to be, let it be her idea. Instead, I persisted in my brash exuberance. "Oh, I'm sorry. I'm standing right in the doorway. If you need the bathroom, it's down there on the left."

She was already gone.

I tarried. When she didn't come back, I decided to show Cory a picture of Robin. On my return, the two remaining roommates, Denise and Estelle, had showed up. They were both black. *O Fortuna, velut luna, statu variabilis, semper crescis aut decrescis* - the opening line of *Carmina Burana* come to life! "Oh, Fortune! Like the moon, you are changeable, ever waxing and waning!" My eyes, suddenly incandescent, and my mouth, open and breathing in a gasp of wonderment, gushed forth with plausibly the most idiotic statement I have ever made. As four parents, a few siblings, and all three roommates looked on, I let fly with girlish glee: "Oh, wow. I was hoping for one black roommate. I never dreamed I'd get three!"

In horror, their eyes shot back the incandescent gleam; their mouths collectively mimicked the gasp of wonderment, but they kept their thoughts to themselves. Now I understood what Jim, the Tri-Hi-Y leader, meant when he said people often don't speak because what they have to say wouldn't be polite. However, my new roommates' actions soon spoke louder than any impolite words they may have been thinking. They took it upon themselves to teach me what it meant to be in the minority, and for the next few months, school was hell.

My bed became a repository for items tossed aside when getting in after a long day. Hooded sweatshirts, cardigans, books, notepads, purses, and the wrapper from the candy bar eaten on the way up to the room could be found in a heap in the center of my mattress. Unfortunately, none of these "Honey, I'm home" things were mine. My own effects could be found on the floor. I'd pick them up along with all the other errant belongings and place them atop their respective owners' bureaus, whitewashing my feelings of dejection with a thick coat of affability. In acknowledgment, I could count on hearing remarks along the lines of, "How's my things always gettin' put on the dresser when I know I put 'em on that bed nobody sleeps in? I swear. We must have us one o' them poltergeists."

Whenever the phone rang, Estelle lunged for it. If it was for me, she'd canvass the room, terminating her search when her eye caught mine. With a duplicitous glint, she'd assert, "No, somebody by that name was supposed to move in here, but she never did. So you got yourself a wrong number." Click.

I persistently brushed off these debilitating offensive moves. In the end, it was our differing schedules that gave the girls a real leg up, and what finally caused me to plead no contest.

Early each Monday, Wednesday, and Friday, I slogged along the narrow, concrete walkways of Kent State's gently sloping Midwestern landscape until I reached the phys ed department's swimming pool. Campus buildings were far enough apart that the trek often became a fantasy I still entertain. Imagining myself a bonnie lass hiking the highlands of Scotland – a country girl given to

A particular moment in history

wandering hill, moor, and narrow glen, with nothing but the panorama of heather and sky and the thin horizon between them to distract her – was an enjoyable morning reverie for the sleepy student bound for class.

The after-class experience wasn't as beguiling. Shivering on the entire return trip to the dorm, my frozen hair always made me think of how Estelle would lay her head down on the bright, white ironing board so Denise could iron her hair straight.

I'd get back about the same time they were beginning to stir from their slumbers. Since Charlotte, Estelle, and Denise didn't have to be present in any lecture hall until ten, they didn't have to get up until nine. This meant they didn't have to go to bed until well after midnight, and so, on Sundays, Tuesdays, and Thursdays, they made sure not to. At approximately 10:30 on those nights, they outfitted themselves not only with the binder paper, pencils, and prescribed texts needed, but also the hot chocolate, fingernail polish, make-up, *Seventeen* magazines, and recent love letters that their long study-cum-gab sessions relied on. These thrice-weekly vigils were replete with the latest LPs, a record player, and plenty of light.

It was the light that did me in. It was one thing to be ensconced in an olfactory mix of cocoa and Revlon's Nude Pink, and another to be surrounded by shrill sounds of uninhibited laughter acting as backup to The Fifth Dimension, but the latter was a lullaby compared to the relentless stabbing shards of light emanating from the ceiling lamp. Holding the pillow tightly over my head as I burrowed deeply into the sheets did not keep the brightness from piercing through. I could see it, not with my eyes, but with my mind, as it filled my head with an abominable antecedent to the white light we are told we will someday greet.

THE SOUND OF THRUSH MUSIC

Hence, on Mondays, Wednesdays, and Fridays, I wearily got ready for my second class of the day as the not-so-silent majority lazily awakened and jokingly reviewed the prior evening's proceedings while feigning total oblivion to my presence. By December, without ever mentioning to the dorm resident assistant my real reason for wanting a change, Corrine and I successfully petitioned to room together.

◊

These sufferings were not tolerated without dispatches to the home front. The telephone relationship between my mom and me developed into a well-rehearsed three-act play that opened with a mutual exchange of pleasantries, moved into a deeper discussion of my problems, and ended with copious amounts of welcomed maternal guidance. More often than not, however, Mom wasn't home so Dad answered. His telephone etiquette was dependent upon which TV program he was watching. Deficient in decorum, he talked too much or hardly at all.

The "too much" consisted of monotonous reiterations of anecdotal blather I'd politely listen to, stoically adhering to mannerly conduct while painfully aware that the non-stop prattle only meant that none of his favorite shows was on. The "hardly at all" consisted of grunts and silences that meant one of his favorite shows was on, and that he had either fallen asleep despite himself or was wide awake and steeped in his dedication to following the lives of any number of formulated television characters. Dr. Kimble's fugitive re-run whereabouts, the antics of Hogan's heroes, or the hillbilly seductions of Billy Jo of Petticoat Junction's Shady Rest Hotel captured his attention more than anything going on with me. Regardless of which way the conversation went – too much or hardly at all – my needs were met with a perfunctory, "I'll tell your mother you called."

◊

"Hell-o." The perky, upbeat bounce of the word was my cue to prepare for *la hora del cuento* – story hour.
"Dad. Hi. It's me."
"I know who it is."
"Is Mom there?"
"No. She drove up to Cherry Hill to go shopping."
"When isn't she driving up to Cherry Hill?" I asked.
"How she can spend every other damn Saturday shopping for nothing is beyond me. I've given up asking questions about what you women like doing."
"Come on, Dad. You know you love us."
"Can't live with you. Can't live without you. That damn dog of hers threw up again. He waits till she's gone and my coffee's made, I got my sandwich how I like it, and I'm going in to sit down. It's unbelievable. He knows when my ass is exactly five-and-a-half inches from the cushion. It's your mother's way of torturing me. Women. You're all the same. I sold the Mustang."
"You what?"
"You heard me."
"Who to?"
"Robin's cousin, Todd."
"Oh, right. He was interested in buying it." Todd was a heartthrob. I'd had a crush on him since we met, but he was too old, and he was Robin's cousin. When the three of us were alone on the beach in Sea Isle City, appraising the seashore's twilight and our impending futures, it was he who predicted Robin and I would never make it if I went away to college.

" . . . I was talking to Cholly at the hardware store the other day."

"Yeah?" I almost forgot that Dad was still jabbering away. God, I loved the way he said Cholly for Charlie.

"I didn't have Todd's number, so he gave it to me. I called him up, and he came right over. He was chompin' at the bit to get that car. You should've seen him trying to hide it. I knew I made the right choice when I bought that baby. Got a good price. He's got a good car, too, if he doesn't ruin it trying to make it better than it needs to be. I hate seeing what you nutty kids do to things. You're not happy unless you're wrecking something. Souped up Mustangs. It's lousy."

"Dad?"

"What?"

"I'm going to miss it."

"You're not here to miss it. What are you worried about? You'll see it when you get home. When are you coming home?"

"Christmas."

"OK. Well, I'll tell your mother you called."

◊

"Hell-o." This time, a guttural ribbit hinted at eyes struggling to open and focus. Their reaction time was too sluggish to correct for the absence of lucidity. Background fumbling noises confirmed it. There's no hiding the recently napping voice.

"Dad? Did I wake you up?"

"No. What d'ya want?" Ribbit.

"Is Mom there?"

"No, she's out."

"Where?"

"Where else?"

A particular moment in history

"Oh. How's everything?"
"Same as always."
"I got the highest mark in class on the biology exam."
"Good."
"What are you watching?"
"The Fugitive."
"Did he find the one-armed man yet?"
Pauses increased. They were fast becoming the identical twin to radio's occasional dead air – that unexpected break in the action that makes you hold your mental breath. It might be a hole through which our galaxy has just fallen. Worse yet, those few seconds could be the preface to CONELRAD cutting in for important instructions about a Soviet air raid imminent in your neighborhood. But then the announcer returns, the earth wobble passes, and you start to breathe again.
"Nah. He's still looking."
I looked at the clock. It was only halfway through the hour, and I didn't want to experience the feeling of being shoved aside for David Janssen once the commercial break was over. It was time to sign off.
"OK, Dad. Well . . . "
"I'll tell your mother you called."

◊

Uncommonly depressed after one of the hardly-at-all conversations, I embarked on a pilgrimage to the downstairs vending machines for the absolving saccharine ministry of a Snickers, a 3 Musketeers, some Hostess cupcakes, and a carton of milk. After too many "I'll tell your mother you called" promises and not enough of the sympathetic counsel those mother-calls bore, I despaired. I wanted to tell her I decided to move out of my room and in with Cory. I wanted to tell her of the latest round of agonizing tribulations. I wanted to ask her what she thought. I wanted her to tell me I was doing the right thing. I wanted. I wanted. I wanted. But I'd not received. *What is it? What's going on?* I continued probing. A bag of Wise potato chips and a Dr Pepper got in line behind the chocolate. *There really is something I'm not getting.*

The gloomy mood granted access to the filing cabinet of the subconscious. The junk food spurred the incentive to go in and extract whatever it was that was bothering me. I gingerly pulled open the top metallic gray mental drawer. From a swollen manila folder marked "Anytime Now" liberated words began flitting about like so many wool-eating moths. Some of them were my dad's. Some were my mom's. All were pieces of telephone parleys of the last few months. " . . . said she'd be back at four." "You know, honey, I'm home after church on Sundays." "She actually bought something." "Oh, I like to putter around the mall, I guess." "I'll tell her you . . . "

I sank into the snack room's dilapidated couch and stared at the linoleum. The thought struck me that my mom was not a big fan of shopping. Hadn't she habitually opted to give me the funds to buy clothes, rather than chaperone my apparel-stockpiling excursions? Then the manila folder fell open, releasing its many pages. *She's not a shopper at all.* I was getting somewhere.

Dropping more coins in for the salt and bubbly – what the heck, a Milky Way – I began retrieving the loose pages from the office floor of my mind. Images rose up, swirling. They were older than the word moths that had escaped, and they were somewhat smudged: the passenger's seat in the Thunderbird, the kitchen counter next to the phone, my books on the table, the little trap door. Then these images were promptly displaced

A particular moment in history

by more flying words, just Mom's this time: "Good provider," "Can't be everything," "When you're older."

As swift as the freedom you feel when you kick your shoes off at the end of the day, elucidation flooded over me. It was like the greeting of a Rocky Mountain waterfall at the end of the spur trail you can't resist because the sound of the waterfall is more deafening than that of the river it is part of. The truth rang out in my head like a shot. *She hates shopping!*

Totally unaware of the bustling dorm life going on around me, I plunked back down into the scratchy cushion. *Men think women are nothing more than frivolous creatures who fill their time with empty-headed activities like painting toenails, baking cookies, and shopping.* I tore open the candy wrapper. *They've got us pegged to the point of such predictably that they needn't give it another thought. Well, surprise, surprise. We're smarter than you think.*

I could see my dad on the couch. *Sometimes,* I thought, as I pictured my mom at the mall, *people – even women – use the human penchant for stereotyping to their advantage.* Bending down for the fallen candy wrapper, I stopped short, sucking melted chocolate through my teeth. "Jesus." My thoughts hit the surface. "Damn. Damn her. Still?"

◊

It was really only Corrine I had to talk to. In her, I had a confidante, someone who gave me room to communicate my perception of the world. I could tell her my feelings without fear of losing any sense of self or reputation. In fact, here in Ohio, as of yet, there was no reputation. Cory and I were away from home, together in the foxhole, where trust is the ante and not the bet. Like showing your poker hand through the blunder of a recognizable bluff, you shouldn't give the truth of your life away through distracted moments of weakness. The only thing we had to lose by prematurely showing our hand was a close friendship. In the vernacular of the 1970s, we could "let it all hang out." How freeing it felt to be on my own!

◊

We snuck up onto the hill above the building to get a look at what we could do without being seen. There was a big trash can, a dumpster, that we could see looking down from the hill – not far from the ROTC building. We figured we could get the trash in that going with a rag soaked in gasoline from the motorcycle, and then push it into the building to see if that would do the job. I don't know if I helped push or if we watched a few others do it, or if the whole thing was an idea of ours that was never implemented. All I know is that a few hours later, the building was ablaze.

During those hours, we must've gone downtown because I remember returning to the hill to find the burning building, and because I remember seeing people looting parking meters on the sidelines of a marching crowd I was part of. This was wrong, and I knew it would not help our cause. A guy Cory and I knew from the dorm who had literally starved himself to get out of the draft was one of the leaders. We were worried for him. He was reacting to the – I'm sure he had to go through a lot of real struggle to starve himself to keep out of the draft, so he hated the government, and he was getting it out on them by leading this crowd of people downtown, creating a path of destruction as he went. Where have I seen words, something like – "riding high on a sea of people"? It was like that. You had no choice but to move with it.

There were some cars that found themselves there with us, in the wrong place at the wrong time, you might say. They were in the street with us as we marched along. One was close to me, to my left, with a family in it. I caught the mom's eye, and she hurriedly locked her door and had her kids do the same thing in the back seat. I was shocked at the fear on her face. I would not hurt her. How could she think that I would hurt her? We were both Americans. Then I saw Charlotte and Estelle watching me as the crowd marched by them, urging me on with big "Right on, girl!" smiles on their faces. Estelle had an Afro. I gave a big smile back and a peace sign. They shouted some encouragement, and I knew everything was all right between us.

Then I remember standing on the hill. It was night now, and the ROTC building was in full blaze. It was really a pretty sight, the fire itself. It was like a big bonfire, but nobody brought marshmallows. We all stood there and watched. There was a tree that had caught on fire nearby. Cory and I tried to put it out kind of heroically. People didn't pay much attention to us. They didn't care about the tree. I remember that. So we watched the building burn. I think the tree fire burned out soon on its own.

By this time, we were under martial law. There were posters stating this, saying that the campus and the town were both under martial law. You couldn't stay out after a certain time, and you couldn't form in groups. I don't know what other restrictions – nobody paid attention to them. Also, we – whoever "we" were – I remember the feeling of having student representatives, but I couldn't tell you a thing about them. We were trying to get Governor Rhodes and the president of the school – I forget his name – to negotiate, but I don't know what the goals were. I don't know if it was to get Nixon back out of Cambodia, or what.

Everybody, both "sides," were mesmerized by the ROTC building fire. After it was not more than a pile of burnt shambles, we were herded back to the dorms. A crowd of us got caught in The Pit, the central area of one of the dorm complexes. We ended up staying there because we weren't allowed to leave. It was a situation that paranoia is made of; it was jammed full, but instead of freaking out, it turned into a party with music – guitars and percussion and all. It was fun, and it was scary.

I slept in Julio's room Saturday night. Whether it was part of the dorm complex we got stuck in, or we were finally allowed out to go to bed, I don't recall. All night long, helicopters flew very close. They shined their searchlights in all the dorm windows and kept shining them in all night long, keeping us awake with the lights and the loudness of the helicopters. We really thought we were at war, but it was a toy war. It was fun and games to us, but obviously not to them. We didn't realize that it wasn't Cowboys and Indians. That's the unfortunate part.

◊

It wasn't long after becoming roommates that Cory and I became a team, going everywhere together, confiding and debating in passionate nonstop dialogue. Gobbling up on-the-spot invented philosophies and emitting at-long-last unrestrained speculations, we got so deep

A particular moment in history

into our inner world, we were myopic to what was going on in the one outside.

Thursday nights were different, though. These were set aside for a jaunt downtown where we went outside ourselves long enough to focus on Joe Walsh, who was making a name for himself in the local music scene. With two saved-up dollars apiece and an anticipation that put speed in our step, we all but skipped from campus to the cellar club where he played. We submerged for hours, listening to his special brand of guitar, watching for the infamous beer bottle ever present in the back pocket of his jeans. When we emerged, refreshed, jazzed, and ready for more discourse, we'd walk back to Korb Hall, once again engaged in the bildungsroman we were living.

On one of these late-night walks, the topic of home came up. Cory and I discovered we had more in common than rural New Jersey, a taste for rump roast, high school band practice, and boyfriends left behind. We both had parents who fought. We talked about this all the way home, where, after a brief hiatus to allow for the completion of bedtime ablutions, the chat continued. Then, like Forrest Gump's feather, it wafted from upper bunk to lower bunk during that unruffled interval before sleep makes its final diaphanous descent.

"God, Cory. What other junk did you have to listen to?"

"My mom's a lot younger than my dad, and she never lets him forget it. She puts him down about it every chance she gets."

"Like how? What's she say?"

"She tells him his ways are old and what he does is old. She doesn't like the way he wears his socks. She doesn't like his socks! She says they look dumb when he crosses his legs and everybody can see his garters. It embarrasses her."

"She told him that?"

"Yeah. She shouldn't've married him if she doesn't like him being old."

"So what's he say?"

"That's what he says: 'You were fine with the age difference when we got married. What'd you do? Lie to me?' That's when the shouting begins."

"Yeah. My mom always complains about my dad's driving."

"Oh, that's a good one."

"You'd think they'd figure it out after twenty years. 'Austin, you drive too close. Why do you have to drive so close?' I get so sick of it. Their other broken record is about going out. 'You never tell me what you want to do. I always have to ask you. Then you fight me when I suggest we visit your mother.' And my Dad says, 'I don't fight. It's you who fights. I don't want to go visit my mother. Why make a federal case out of it?'"

"It's so familiar," Cory empathized.

"His two best are 'Go pound sand' and 'Don't let the door hit you in the ass.' Oh, and then he shuts her up by saying, 'Anything you want, Lena.'"

"What's 'Go pound sand' mean?"

"Who knows? I've been trying to figure it out since I was three."

◊

A striking feature of the natural world in Kent was its black squirrels. Much like a speck that needs to be plucked from a garment, a black squirrel on a tree trunk attracts one's attention. Noticed within the first day or two of most visitors' arrivals, they were soon the

A particular moment in history

subject of inquiry. Evidently, they were conscripted from Canada by a groundskeeper in Kent, but any reason he may have had for their recruitment was absent from responses given to the inquisitive. The black squirrels did what all squirrels do: hop about and run in jaggedy-raggedy spurts up and down trees and across limbs. In fact, they're really just gray squirrels sporting black coats.

When snow fell, the most outstanding setting for this contradiction of color was in its antithesis, that is, the squirrels' onyx black against winter's alabaster white. Cory and I got to experience this when we went sledding on the serving trays one of the cafeteria ladies let us use for sleds. Nostalgia in her smile, she made us promise to always return them by dinner time, which, because we respected her kindness, we always did. Once, our ardor for the speed and recklessness of the sport ruptured a tray smack down the middle. When we returned it, sheepishly, the cafeteria lady's smile remained unaltered. If anything, the longing it held shone brighter, sanctioning not merely that day's amusement, but the delight of an entire winter's open-air experience.

The hill where we used the trays was on the front campus, below Kent Hall, which housed the administrative offices. I remember feeling the watchful eye of authority behind us as we rocketed past trees on our way to the bottom. Cory had more chutzpah than I. Starting out on the fresh, virgin layer of frost, she was the first to leap onto the shiny chestnut of her melamine sled. I'd follow. We'd meet up at the lower end, trudge back to the top for another try, and before lunch we'd have four or five icy-slick runs to choose from.

The black squirrels were there with us. The little guys' funeral garb was so stark against the snow that they resembled one of those eighteenth-century silhouette cutouts, much like Dolley Madison in her oval frame. We saw them as we whizzed by, ourselves in the oval frame of carefree youth.

◊

Sunday morning, I think it was, a parade of Army tanks and – tanks! – Army tanks, Army trucks, a convoy going slowly down the main street outside of Julio's window, parading past Kent Hall – to show their strength, I guess. It must be what the military has to do so that you see they are there. We were calling it the Boy Scout Jamboree, but it was no Boy Scout Jamboree. It was the National Guard in town, taking over.

Sunday was pretty quiet. I remember getting tear-gassed over the weekend, but it was so chaotic that I'm having trouble separating which time was which. All of the running on campus took place in the same area: the commons, the hill above it, and some open field that must've been right there. I remember running, feeling chased, and getting gassed by vapors. Some people said it was pepper gas. I helped put Vaseline under people's noses so it wouldn't burn so much, and I carried a supply of wet rags to hold over our noses. I remember running. People right next to me – all around me – running. Running. It was possibly on Saturday night, we literally stampeded a fence down because we were surrounded by "them" – police, firemen, National Guard? Who knows? "Them" – on three sides. Our only way out was on the fourth side, which was the fence. I experienced . . . group paranoia. When we saw we were in jeopardy, and the only way out without fighting was

A particular moment in history

through this fence – well, we stampeded it down. It was a cyclone fence, too.

In the evening on Sunday, a large group of us ended up at a central intersection downtown or near the entrance to the campus, maybe. We were having a sit-in. We sat and waited for the governor or mayor or some official to come and talk to us. Nobody ever did. After a while, it seemed to be a ploy to keep everybody in that one place. I wanted to give one of the National Guard some flowers when some friends of mine said, "No, don't do that. They might think you're going to harm them. You'll be antagonizing them." A few people had tried to make advances during the weekend and had bayonets shoved at them, so I'm glad I heeded the warning.

We were all sitting in the street there – right in the middle, where all the corners met. We sat for what seemed like hours. Again, we were waiting and waiting and waiting, and nothing happened. Later – it was night now, I was sitting cross-legged, and as I looked around, I started noticing there were National Guardsmen all around us, at the back edges of the scene. So they were doing it again. Ah, I see. I remember this feeling of them doing it again, so the fence thing must've happened on Saturday. They were surrounding us very quietly. When I noticed this, I mentioned it to somebody, and I guess a few others were noticing it, too. We freaked and ran. Everybody took off. Mayhem again.

◊

My first year at Kent State, as well as most of the second, went merrily by, a superbly orchestrated postponement of responsibility. Nothing was forced on me.

No unreasonable restrictions were set. All expenses paid, I was free to roam terra firma supported by adults, yet not encumbered by their supervision. I didn't even have to do the vacuuming! It was the lull before the storm of real life, a tempest (as the cafeteria lady must have known) protracted by the eventual necessity to obtain food, clothing, and shelter all by one's self. Until then, I could display the ignorance of youth with casual panache, fusing my three worlds – the natural, the academic, and the social – into one utopia.

High school as compulsory and college as choice, in itself, made the academic experience of higher learning more agreeable. The large amphitheater-like lecture hall gave it an Ivy-League distinction that made me feel erudite. I loved to pause above the tiered rows looking down on a lectern, where stood the typecast professor whose every word imparted knowledge voraciously recorded by a hundred-plus pencils taking notes at well-worn, graffiti-chiseled, and love-carved desk-seats. My grades, not always exemplary in high school, ardently reflected this mental image, and I ended up on the Dean's List, putting a nice touch on the transformation of fantasy into reality.

Socially, whatever your lifestyle – jock, sorority, straight or hippie – the party was omnipresent, and Cory and I made an effort to attend the festivities every chance we got. By the beginning of my second year at Kent, I was a full-fledged flower child with bell-bottoms and a homemade braided suede neck band. For a while, I hung bells from my belt buckle. "So I always know where I am," I'd say.

I'd experimented with smoking dope once in high school. I'd heard about the stuff and, curious enough to seek it out, wrote to a friend who'd already graduated and was living in St. Louis. She was gung-ho on the idea

A particular moment in history

of my tuning in and turning on, so on her next flight back to Vineland, she brought a half-dozen joints with her. Transporting and possession laws were stricter back then, so she placed the doobies inside six separate Tampax applicators from which she'd removed the tampons. She then carefully cut each tampon into three pieces, threw away the center section and used the end sections as plugs to hide the deadly marijuana cigarettes. When she showed me what she'd done, my affection for mutiny kicked in. We lit up and had a blast, but that was it. She returned to St. Louis, and I didn't have the nerve to pursue the curiosity further while living in my hometown. But after Cory and I met that first day in the elevator, it didn't take long to ask, "Have you made any connections, yet?"

And oh, so easy they were to make! Confidently relegating the cloistered Lois of poetry, literature, and classical music to dormancy, I plunged headlong into the workings of the drug culture. By March 1970, pot, hard rock, friends, and the causes of the counterculture defined who I was. Then, a few months later, I met up with my particular moment in history.

> *Now for Monday: there was another speech and rally scheduled on campus despite the injunction. I don't know what the demands were. I don't remember. I don't know what we expected to have come out of this or how we were planning to end it. It ended itself, of course.*
>
> *I went down to the commons to hear the speeches and people speaking their mind, when all of a sudden, we were running again. Again. There had been fireworks going throughout the weekend, and*

we were getting so used to tear gas that this is what I was expecting – another repeat – but I heard some pinging, and I felt some whooshing go by my head. I looked to the left and saw a car window shatter. I looked to the right and saw a person fall. Then someone yelled, "They're shooting. Get down!" I felt something in my leg and dove under a bush. Then there was silence.

My initial reaction was panic. I wanted to find Corrine, who was my loved one. I wanted to find Cory. I wanted the security of another loved one with me. I was calling for her. She was calling for me. Everybody was calling for friends. I was wringing the heck out of the rag I'd been using all weekend to protect my lungs. I was wringing it out of nervousness. I was in a rage. I learned what rage is. In those few seconds, I was totally stripped of everything I had believed in. I wanted to blindly shoot anybody who was behind me because behind me was where Nixon was, where the National Guard was, where my country was and I hated them. I experienced pure hate. I experienced the ability to kill. I could have killed if I'd had a gun in my hand. There's a chance that I would have been – I WOULD HAVE BEEN shooting blindly. I turned and stared in the direction of the onslaught. The only thing I remember seeing at that moment was the movie screen of my mind. It blocked out everything my eyes might have been looking at, and on it was a movie of me in third or fourth grade, with all of my classmates, standing and reciting the flag salute. It's a moment that stands by itself. Everything else stopped. This place that had brought me up and that was supposed to be mine, on my side, that I was a part of, turned and said, "No, you

A particular moment in history

are not a part of us. You're against us, and we have to shoot you down." Everything I believed in was scourged from me. I can't think of the word. Scoured. Scorched. I think I mean that – scorched. Fire and harshness and scrubbed – ripped out clean. Some combination of that.

These were the immediate minutes right after it happened, and although people were crying and yelling and calling to each other, there was a strange silence throughout the whole area.

I watched one of the four die. I didn't realize what was happening. There were some people stooping over her body. I remember a guy taking his hand and wiping out her mouth. I remember seeing some guts or flesh or something pink and white like that fling from his hand. Maybe she had vomited. I don't know what it was. He tried to give her mouth-to-mouth resuscitation. Her shirt – t-shirt – was not all the way covering her body, so her stomach was exposed halfway. I was watching her stomach. It was not a person I was watching. It was a biological entity. It was a body. It was a stomach trying to keep its life. She was pumping very hard to breathe, or maybe that was him pumping his breath into her. I don't know. I don't think so, but I remember the impression that this was not a person. It was a biological thing trying very hard to stay alive, and somehow that biology was her essence, her soul, and was the part I didn't want to see end. But it didn't work. The guy lifted his head and said, "She's gone." My first inclination was that she'd fainted. Then I realized, "No, she's dead." It was the first dead person, other than people at viewings, that I had ever seen. Have ever seen. It left a heavy burden on me.

THE SOUND OF THRUSH MUSIC

I watched a friend of mine named Scott taken away on a stretcher. He had been shot in the neck. A number of us had been calling to some flaky girls watching from second-story windows. We were shouting to them to call the ambulances, but I guess they were too afraid to help us. It's hard to realize that we were the enemy. We were foreigners to them. I couldn't grasp the fact that they didn't realize I was an American, and I was part of them. That was real hard for me to compute.

Come to find out, I had been injured somehow – shot in the leg, a ricocheted bullet or something. Maybe a stone kicked up or a bullet skimmed my leg. I'll never know. I was in shock and it had to be pointed out to me. A guy came up from behind and said, "Hey, you've got blood soaking through your pants." We looked and a glob of blood spilled over my boot when we pulled the pant leg up. He helped me get to a bathroom to wash it. I was wearing cowboy boots, square-toed Frye's. He said he saw I was limping and came over to give me a hand when he saw the blood. We washed the wound, but it became infected, and I had a scar from that for a while.

Well, those of us left behind after the ambulances drove off tried to have some kind of civil talk-it-out, but it was no use. We disbanded. It didn't last very long. We gave up. I went back to the dorm. An all-points type bulletin went out stating something to the effect of, "Everybody must leave campus. The campus is closed. Everybody go home; take only as many belongings as you can carry. Don't go into town. You'll be contacted over the summer." We were then instructed which route to leave campus by. Nobody wanted another shooting to take place, so

A particular moment in history

everybody followed orders. Cars were packed with people. Cory and I got a ride. I remember I had an Acme bag full of clothes, and so did she. It was a real scene. We got out of town a few miles in this crowded car, and then we hitched the rest of the way home to New Jersey. That was it for the year at Kent. Exams were sent through the mail. Grading was done through the mail. And, of course, it made the national news.

5

Life does not stop at the crossroads – a moment merely precedes the hours, days, and weeks that supplant it

The summer after the shootings was spent reacting to the trauma. Disillusioned by democracy and alienated from those who had never been stung by it, I went deeper into the woods of the hippie. I became what was known as a freak. My bell-bottoms got so long they left frayed lengths of edging dragging beneath my shoes – when I wore shoes. My t-shirts were dirty, torn, and tie-dyed with plenty of Rit Dye. I did not bathe daily, nor did I use deodorant. I did not shave. I did not interact with my parents. I did not have a job. My room was a fright, piled high with clutter and wallpapered floor to ceiling with enough posters to open a head shop ("Should A Gentleman Offer a Lady a Joint?" "I Want You!" "War is Not Healthy for Children and Other Living Beings."). I ingested a lot of psychedelics and smoked a lot of cannabis. I wore a bra only because it hurt not to. I listened to Deep Purple, Black Sabbath, Led Zeppelin, and The Who. Aching from rejection, I donned the loosely fitting cloak of the spurious expatriate, a bastard thirsting to be invited back into the fold. I was the walking personification of apathy.

"Lois."

"Hey, Robin."
"How ya doin'?"
"I had another nightmare."
"Lay it on me, girl."
"Oh, nothin' different. It's a drag. I'm there watching. She's lying on the street in front of me. There are other people, but it's like they're frozen, and it's just her and me, but I can't do anything for her. Kind of like you felt when you couldn't do anything about your mom dying of cancer. I know it's not the same, but . . . "
"Bummer."
"Yeah. Hey, it was a gas hanging out with you guys yesterday. That crusty old dude with all the writing on his truck was boss. He really believed you, me, and Duane were the Mod Squad."
"Too bad you're not blonde."
"Yeah, well. Tough."
"You coming over to G's with us tonight?"
"Yeah, I'll be there. Anything to cut outta here. Can you pick me up? I don't feel like asking them for the car."
"Sure. Mr. G said he'd be back at 9:30."
"OK. I'll wait for you outside. Were you able to – uh – procure?"
"Oh yeah. Procured the cure, baby. We got us some primo bad-assed stuff."
"Far out. I'm definitely up. Who got it – you, or the G?"
"The Big G."

Mr. G was Mr. Guyton, our high-school geometry teacher. We went over to his house to smoke ganja, drop acid, and listen to the album "Tommy" over and over again, until we felt like Tommy's journey from the Darkness to the Light was our own: *Don't want no religion/As far as we can tell!/We ain't gonna take you/Never did and never*

Life does not stop at the crossroads

will!/We're not gonna take you/We forsake you/Gonna rape you/Let's forget you better still!
"If they only knew."
"Life is but a joke, my friend. See you in a few," I said with a coolness that did not belie my apathetic state of mind.

As if to test how apathetic I was, an incident took place a few weeks into July that gave additional endorsement to the pursuit of indifference.

Because I was waiting for news from Kent about final exams, I was always first to the mailbox. On this day, it contained a card for "L. Van Buren." There was no return address. *Hmm*, I thought, looking over the apricot colored envelope as I sauntered toward the house. *I wonder who this could be from? It's not Corrine's handwriting. Which of my lame girlfriends would be sending me a card? I suppose it could be for Mom, but – I seriously doubt it.*

I decided that the sender's feckless use of the initial "L" legitimized my opening the envelope, so, with no qualms, I tore into it. The card had an embossed drawing of a basket of spring blossoms of the buttercup, scarlet pimpernel, forget-me-not, and primrose variety, with the words "Thinking of You" printed above it in Italian calligraphy. Inside, the flowers tumbled out of the basket, strewn willy-nilly around a stanza that read something like:

> *The flowers of the field*
> *To my heart do yield*
> *In trembling, blushing attitude*
> *This humble gift of gratitude.*

It was signed, "A Secret Admirer."
"Jesus!" Repressing the urge to commit harikari right then and there, I stomped up the front steps, through

the front door, and across to the patio where my mom was relaxing in her lounge chair.

She casually looked up from her daily devotional, a publication called *The Upper Room*, and said, "Oh, did you get the mail? I was so engrossed in my reading I didn't hear the mailman drive up."

Noticing what she was so engrossed in increased my fury. The choir leader-Sunday school teacher-Christian? The hypocrite was more like it.

"I just picked it up," I bristled.

"Anything interesting?"

"No. There are a couple of bills, something for Dad from the ski club, a letter for me, and . . . " With the determination of the resolute, punctuated by a scowl of disgust, I dropped the card in her lap. "Here. I think this is for you."

◊

Animosity between my folks and me had been quietly simmering all summer. Finally, a week before I returned to Ohio, it bubbled its way to the top and boiled over. The deference given to cordially dishonest communication spewed out a thick, lava-hot stew of emotion.

"Couldn't you sit at the table and eat dinner with us, for once?"

"My friends are waiting for me, Dad."

"Let them wait. We need to talk."

"What about? I've gotta go."

"Honey," my mom said, "if they're your friends, they'll wait."

"Mom, nobody likes waiting. It doesn't mean they're not my friends."

"What do you do when you go out?"

Life does not stop at the crossroads

"What, Dad? This is what you want to talk about? What do you care? It's none of your business."
"It *is* our business. We're supporting you."
"So. Everything is money, isn't it? *That's* what you care about –"
"Be careful, little girl."
" – And if I'm making you look bad with what I do when I go out."
"Watch it!"
"You don't care about me. You only care about yourselves and what everybody else thinks!"
"Lois, how can you say that?" Now my mom got in on it. "With the way you treat us?"
"What?"
"Who's the one who doesn't care about anybody but herself?" It was Dad's turn to ask the blistering questions. "Who's the one who only cares about money? Try living on your own for a while. You'll find out what's to care about money."
"*How* do I treat you?" I was still back on what my mom said and wasn't going to let her get away with it.
"You ignore us. You don't so much as give us the time of day," she answered.
"What's that mean?"
"We have nothing in common anymore," she continued, ignoring my question.
"So, why should we make conversation? Just to talk? How phony. That is so phony. Especially you." I stared into my mother's eyes. She stared back for one hard second. She knew what I meant.
"Don't speak to your mother like that. Do you hear me?"
"Why shouldn't we make conversation, Lois? It so happens we're family, you know."

"Not much of one."

"That's enough!" my dad roared.

"Not much of one?" Mom cut in. "Whose fault is that? You're really making me mad."

"Let *me* tell you how you treat us." Dad was at fever pitch. We were now three pit bulls in wire cages thrown in the back of a rusted-out pickup truck. "You ignore us as if we were invisible. You come and go as you please. We let you be and try not to say anything. Have you looked in your bedroom lately? It's a garbage dump – dirty clothes everywhere. And what's on those walls? What the hell *do* you do when you leave this house!?"

"Austin!"

"Garbage dump!"

"If you don't like the looks of my room, don't look!"

"We don't say anything about your hair or the way you dress." Mom tried to calm things down with reason. "We don't ask you to do anything. You could at least show a little respect."

"Oh, brother. I respect you. How do you want me to show you respect? I leave you alone, don't I? Isn't that enough?"

"No, it's not enough. Your father and I would like to see you once in a while. You could come out of your room and sit with us sometimes."

"What, and have you nosing into my life?"

"Hey! Watch it I said."

"So what don't you like about my hair, Mom? And what's wrong with the way I dress? Is it because I don't look like you?"

"Lois, please. We don't expect you to look like us, but you could try to be neater, couldn't you? You're so pretty, and you hide it under that straggly hair and those awful clothes."

Life does not stop at the crossroads

"What, Mom? Are you going to try and make everything all sweet and wonderful? What else don't you like about the way I look? Let's hear it."
My dad couldn't resist. "You're a damn pig!"
"Austin!"
"That's what we don't like about it!"
"You could take a bath now and then, honey. Your feet... Why don't you wear shoes?"
"Because I don't want to. That's why, Mom. Look, Robin is waiting. Please let me go."
"Fine, then, go. Go for good, why don't you?"
"Austin, please."
"All right, I will. As soon as school starts, I'll be out of your hair."
"Good, but don't come back here cryin' when you need something."
"Don't worry, I won't. I'll do fine."
"What? Are you kidding? With all those kooky friends of yours?"
"Will you two stop, please?"
"I'm sorry, Lena, but I can't stand by any longer and watch those nitwits she calls friends, with their greasy, long hair and asinine clown outfits, parade through my house. Where'd they all come from? The Funny Farm?"
"Lois, your dad is worried for you. We don't want you to go back to Kent. Don't you see? Stay home and go to Glassboro or Montclair. We'll buy you that TR-6 you want."
"That goes to show how much you don't know me anymore. I haven't cared about cars in years. You aren't worried for me. You're worried for yourselves. You're worried that people might notice we're not the perfect little family."

"Oh, your mother and I know who you are. You're selfish and ungrateful, and you've been living under my roof all summer long, doing whatever you damn please. We haven't asked you to contribute to this household one bit. You haven't lifted a finger to do anything except eat the food I work to buy and lay out there tanning yourself on chairs I bought – on the patio I built!"

"Gee, I didn't know I was a paying renter. I guess I forgot to sign a lease. How much do I owe you? Huh, Dad?"

"You owe me respect."

"Lois, your dad works hard to give you the things you have. The least you can do is acknowledge that."

"I do acknowledge that, but he doesn't acknowledge me – who *I* am. And who my friends are. And we're NOT asinine and greasy! But YOU'RE a couple of old fogeys who have no idea what's going on in the world! And that's a fact. I'm going back to Kent, no matter what you say." My screaming became a choked, high-pitched squeak. "I don't care!"

The tension between love and understanding reached an impasse, and for the moment, love didn't conquer. I got kicked out of the house.

So much for my utopian life.

In the aftermath of the shootings, many of us spoke at various colleges and universities around the country. I was asked to speak at Douglass College, the girls' part of Rutgers. It was a real fiasco – a humiliating experience for me. Because of what happened at Kent, other schools were marching and protesting and doing their thing and having different people speak, so I went and spoke at this school. It was

Life does not stop at the crossroads

quite a crowd of people who came to listen. I'd say the hall held 400. They were overflowing into the aisles and out past the exit, which made the place abuzz with people. I didn't have anything prepared. I didn't know what to prepare. I was told to just go up there and talk about what happened.

I got booed, literally booed. Hissed at and booed. It was a horrible experience. I cried. I was telling them my impressions of what happened. I was telling them about all the drugs that were in town and that most of the people I knew Friday night were on drugs. Like I said, this was my first LSD experience, so it was very much a part of the whole thing for me. But they booed me. I was just telling them what I saw. Me, not anybody else. They were trying to ask me these stupid news commentator questions, and I was totally humiliated. I think I got about halfway through my impressions of the weekend when I couldn't stand it anymore, so I went back to my seat on stage and sat there and sobbed. They didn't like what I had to say.

While I was sobbing, some girl went up to the podium and tried to head up a bumper sticker committee. I thought this was really ghastly. It made me very cynical; I felt like jumping down her throat for that. Here they were, booing me – all 400 or how many the hell it was – for telling them what happened to me as I saw it, and they were trying, in their snootiness to what they felt they knew, to get a goddamn bumper sticker committee together. What good were bumper stickers going to do? They thought they knew what went on. As if they were the ones that were there, and I wasn't. Well, I was there, and they didn't want to hear what I had to say, so they booed me back to my seat. A friend who had accompanied me to New Brunswick was in the wings. She got my attention and shushed me off the stage when she saw I was so humiliated and crying. I really cried when I got off the stage. She told me later that the audience felt sorry for me and gave me a standing ovation. That made me want to puke. They should've realized that I was there. At the shootings. And that I was emotionally involved.

For many years afterward, it was uncomfortable to talk about, and whenever I did, it took a day or two to recover. If the memory of that one isolated weekend could rattle me like that, how can a soldier go to war? How dare we send him?

Part Two

The Call To Come In

It so happened that John Lennon was wrestling his way through some thorny patches with his parents, too. In April 1970, Paul McCartney appropriated the break-up of The Beatles by making the first public announcement of their irreconcilable differences. This upset everything, or more likely, brought everything to its logical conclusion. John and Yoko ran screaming – Primal Therapy screaming – onto a collision course with their pasts, where John confronted his mom and dad, though not his folks, per se. Few of us ever do that. What we crash into are the feelings we had, as children, that grownups condemned as too childish, even for children. We were not to be coddled under any circumstances. "Grow up!" they instructed, as we tried to explain what really happened at school, or after school, or at the park, or at a friend's house, or anywhere our feelings may have been hurt. "Stop that!" we were told, as we cowered by the master bedroom door, our entreaties turned whimpers as they fought with each other yet again. "Grow up!"

So we did, alone in the private places of our hearts, where we left behind all those childish emotions to dissipate throughout our bodies, not to disappear, but to assert themselves later on in behavior explained away by others as disposition.

John and Yoko were disposed to explaining their opinions on social and political issues in unprecedented media campaigns. This behavior propelled them into the limelight. It seemed an eternity since the notion that going to war with the Commies in Hanoi might not have been discreet strategy, but where would we go from there? The Lennons had a few recommendations on this and other controversial subjects pertaining to the human condition. Eventually their convictions trickled down to all of us in one way or another. For me, it took until October of that year.

6 Zealous in the cause

Sitting in Hahn's Bakery in downtown Kent with Vincent, bestower of hallucinatory hedge flowers, the brisk fall air made me feel like ordering a cup of tea.
"What kind would you like?" the waitress asked.
"Well, what choices do I have?"
"There's Tetley, Ceylon, English Breakfast, and Constant Comment."

Her words were too faint to hear all she said, but, unwilling to swallow my pride and ask her to repeat the list, I internally assessed what I thought I heard: *I like English Breakfast, but I'd want it with cream and sugar. That's too much like fattening. Tetley'll make me too buzzed. Ceylon is bitter. I'll try that last one she said. I've heard of that. Good name for a tea.*

"So what'd you decide?" she asked.
"I'll try some of the Instant Karma, please."

Pencil ready, but not moving, she looked down at me. I knew I'd said something wrong. I looked at Vince. He looked at me. He looked at her. Then he said, "Not much we can do when that choice is offered. Make it two."

As we finished our tea, Vince asked if I had something to write with. "Yes. In my bag." He leaned in. "Here ya go," I said, and handed him a pen. He wrote

something on a napkin as he hummed, *"like the moon and the stars and the sun."*
"What are you doing?"
"Leaving the waitress a tip."
"No, you're not. You're writing her a note."
"I'm writing her a note and leaving her a tip."
"Why? Can I look?"
"No." He drew my attention from the booth by taking my hand and leading me out the door, but as we exited, I pulled away, sprinted back, whirled the napkin around and read: *For you, superstar. Shine on!*

Vincent and I had become sweethearts shortly after my return to Ohio for fall semester. We ran into each other at The Hub one day and by the next, we were deep into a world all our own – a planet that revolved around poetry, nature, and hobo housing. You might say our relationship was Emerson in essence, Guthrie in practicality, and whether our intention was to recite or to rest, we never failed to ask a tree's permission to sit beneath its boughs. Auden to Yeats, we discerned that all purveyors of lyrical meter were, at one time or another, inspired to write about nature and its indelible seal on the heart of man – *Our uncle, innocent of books/Was rich in lore of fields and brooks/The ancient teachers never dumb/Of Nature's unhoused lyceum* – that sort of thing.

I was back in school but with no support from home. I was able to pay tuition with what I made as a car hop at a local joint called Lujan's, but didn't have enough for housing. Vince, for some synonymous reason of youth, also didn't have much money, so though our afternoons were spent under lush, deciduous trees romancing each other with verse, our mornings were spent running reconnaissance for a place to stay that night.

Zealous in the cause

We scrounged for sleeping sites. University towns, we correctly surmised, were rife with options for places to crash: sympathetic dorm girls going home for the weekend, acquaintances with floors, friends with couches, friends pulling all-nighters, and friends staying up all night doing drugs. It was a simple matter of organizing the Rolodex.

Vincent and I held on as long as we could, our relationship a time out of time, which is the best time, but a time that cannot last. We were a twosome on holiday, visiting the inhabitants of the Yellow Submarine; calling on Mole under the river bank; picnicking with Pooh, Piglet, and Tigger; and immersing ourselves in hypotheses with the Little Prince on Asteroid B-612, having a lovely time, but then anxious, excusing ourselves because we had to get back to the world of the narrator and move on.

Actually, because of a passing comment Vince made, it was just me who gave the excuses. During an otherwise mundane conversation, what I heard hit me like an H-bomb and put an abrupt end to our relationship. White girls were the only ones who ever gave him trouble? What a thing to say! How about the black girls in his life? It didn't matter which color gave him trouble – that wasn't the part I heard. It was the fact that he was apparently in the habit of dating only white girls. Shouldn't he have been in the habit of dating only black girls? Come to think of it, he should have been dating a black girl at that moment, but I'd dismissed this, presuming we'd found each other as a result of our mutually enlightened awareness of the unimportance of color. In the same way that he was my only black guy, I should have been his only white girl. Maybe it wasn't me he wanted. Maybe it was my whiteness.

Fair or not fair, there was no reasoning at play here, only anger. I felt betrayed and suddenly had no desire to be Vince's girlfriend anymore. Poof! No more Piglet. No more Little Prince. I moved on.

◊

Not long before I had my first sip of Instant Karma tea, a lanky, meek, and somewhat reserved stranger breezed through Kent. Rumor had it he was from California, traveling the country to share information on how to be a proponent for change in America's political structure without initiating an out-and-out revolt. Campus uprisings had their place; they helped get us out of Vietnam, but our nation's youth were now dying right here – four in Ohio, two in Jackson, Mississippi. We needed to be done with the madness of our parents' era. War was not the answer; we were on the cusp of the Age of Aquarius. We no longer put our trust in government men who, unwittingly or by part and parcel, were pawns of those who increased their wealth through the war machine, having convinced themselves and our parents they were nobly making the world safe for democracy. The lyrics, *We are leaving/You don't need us*, danced on our lips. But how could we leave? How would we do that? The visitor from California, it seemed, came to show us.

Haphazardly penned flyers tacked to utility poles specified a meeting to be held at the Unitarian church. Anyone interested could attend. I went, as did a dozen others. The slender man had come to teach us how to assemble a food cooperative. As he spoke, we saw truth in the ideals he fostered. He was, as were we, beginning to look to a slower, less complicated life for a solution to our society's afflictions. We, like he, looked for something new in the old. We looked to our immigrant

Zealous in the cause

grandparents and great-grandparents, and to what we saw as the simple life, the period before the industrial ushered in the suburban – when family farms dotted the landscape, small manufacturers produced most of the goods, and mom and pop stood behind the counter.

We would not allow ourselves to become part of the rat race, working nine to five for thirty-five years. To us, the gold watch was a booby prize. We dreamed a new American Dream, a dream for all people, one that took thousands West, some literally, some figuratively. We were to be the new frontiersmen and women who sought not escape, nor land, nor gold, but an ideology and a mantra, soon to be caramelized into the maxim, "Think globally, act locally." The stranger left town gratified his message had not gone unheard.

I became a buyer for the newly formed food co-op. I also typed up the price sheet. Orders were taken during the day on Thursdays, compiled that evening, and at 4:30 a.m. on Fridays, Norm, our fearless leader and price haggler extraordinaire, dispensed caffeine pills (the standard issue of what we called speed), and he, his wife Holly, and Mark and I sped our way toward the Cleveland Farmers' Market ready to bargain.

The object was to bypass the chain supermarkets and their processed products. If we bought directly from the farmer, we could deliver fresher vegetables at lower prices. Mark drove the rented pickup, Norm carried the clipboard, and Holly and I squeezed in for support.

Arriving back at the church basement about the time a rooster's crow gets annoying, we'd meet up with Ed, Paul, Theresa, Kathleen, Rob, Jimmy, and Anne, who were setting up for the day's distribution of fresh, inexpensive produce. It felt good to be surrounded by confederates like-minded in the hunch that acquiring the basics of survival is tantamount to controlling one's life. These resources were elementary to the pioneer who was to endure the wilderness without getting eaten by grizzly bears, scalped by savage Indians, assaulted by winter storms or . . . clobbered by corporate moguls. We'd start with food gathering. Next, we'd build our own homes, something we often talked about.

In the meantime, cheeses and bulk items, including grains, beans, flours, oils, and butters, got on the order list. Soon, we were contracting with natural foods companies like Erewhon and Hain. When we reached our appointed goal of seeing housewives shop with us, we celebrated. We landed a front-page article in the newspaper, and the co-op gained popularity. Going back to the land became the push toward the future.

◊

Zealous in the cause and indefatigable in its labors, I spent most of my time at the co-op. Despite that, there were plenty of moments to till the soil elsewhere in the garden of my life. I started playing piano more. I'd been entrusted with keys to the Unitarian church, so after the practice rooms on campus closed for the day, I could go there. I'd discovered that as I worked out the notes and fingering for Bach's two and three part *Inventions*, I could also work out many of my personal problems. I spent time opening the lines of communication with my parents. Mom and I were having heart-to-hearts again, even though she still wasn't there much when I called. By now, the old homestead must have been filled floor to ceiling with mall purchases.

The lion's share of my elsewhere moments, however, were set aside for one Pete McGuffey, a guy who, like so many other men, necessitated the development of the Women's Liberation Movement.

I met McGuffey through Cory when circumstance brought us together again in late November. After I'd broken up with Vince, but was still homeless, she found herself in need of a place to live, too. She asked if I'd like to share rent on a house she'd found within walking distance of the bar and music scene. I didn't drink, but I got a kick out of goofing around with my friends who did, and I relished going into the clubs and keeping tabs on how the local bands were doing. The house, a well-known, off-campus residence, was divided into two units. We took the upstairs with the fellow who was already living there: McGuffey.

Within a week of moving in, Cory decided to do a semester in Mexico, leaving the already nicknamed Guffers and me to go it alone. An Oberlin College couple in a similar situation made it to the cover of Life Magazine in November with the headline, "Co-ed Dorms: An Intimate Revolution on Campus." Fine for them, but Guffers and I found ourselves on the cutting edge unintentionally. Our co-ed cohabitation was purely circumstantial, and its awkwardness cascaded into an unequivocal love-hate relationship. In his estimation, I was a bookish prude with a stick up her butt. As far as I was concerned, he was a lecherous male chauvinist pig. The guy expected me to do the dishes. He left them in the sink for days!

Monitoring the moves he made on chicks was nauseating, but that didn't keep me from taking pleasure in pronouncing them so. His pet scheme used to clinch the deal was particularly repulsive. He'd get Miss Flavor-of-the-Night seated in the overstuffed chair and then pull out his guitar, a twelve-string. (He *was* a devious S.O.B.) He'd sit close to her on the ottoman all cuddly-like, bringing her to the edge of the chair cushion. He'd hit her with some James Taylor; she'd get starry-eyed, and then it was all over. In the bag. I took to standing behind Miss Flavor, making faces at Guffs – fourth-grade gestures of the cross-eyed, tilted head, neck in noose, tongue dragging, finger down throat, ejaculation imitations variety devised to piss him off.

I had to figure out how to make lemonade out of this lemon. Maybe I couldn't do anything about McGuffey, but I could advance the principles of feminism in my own way. I'd launch a one-woman show to prove to men that women were a lot more than a lay in the hay. Like Count Dracula or the school teacher in the movie *Looking for Mr. Goodbar*, my nights would be different from my days. I'd prey on gullible men, stalk them, bring them home, and . . . *not* have sex with them. How perfect would that be? I'd get them into my bed, no doubt about that, but instead of nookie, we'd have fun staying up most of the night, talking and laughing and sharing secrets. They'd be so enthralled that by the next morning, they'd skate away, appreciating so much that there's more to a woman than her body that they'd consider becoming eunuchs to avoid temptation. As it turned out, only three men became entangled in my snare – my three little piggies, as I've come to think of them.

Butch, owner of the straw house, was a railway worker. Train tracks ran behind many of the downtown establishments, and when he wasn't at work, Butch was at Walter's Tavern, where I met him. He was older, in his thirties, one of those guys you see leaning up against the bar the way you might envision Ernest Hemingway or John Wayne, one boot on the footrest, swirling his drink, ruminating, as if he and the whiskey just had a consultation and were both evaluating the last statement. Getting

Zealous in the cause

Butch into bed was a cinch, and my plan of using the platonic versus the physical as a means to an end worked. But to be honest, thinking back on his snoring, maybe the credit should be ascribed not to feminist wiles, but to Jack Daniels.

Garrett, constructor of the house of sticks, was more of a clear victory. He was a student from Cuyahoga Falls who, with dogged tedium, hitchhiked to and from his classes at Kent every day. We knew each other from The Hub. Over hamburgers one afternoon, I told him that if the weather ever got too bad, he was more than welcome to stay at my place. He took me up on it the next inclement evening.

After allowing my latest victim time to arrange a quilt and pillow to his liking on the living room sofa, I went to check on him. I knew it was cold out there because the radiators didn't function well except for in my room, insider information I artfully exploited. "This is silly," I coyly demurred. "You'll catch pneumonia out here. Why don't you come sleep in my room where it's warm?" Diffidently, he trailed after me and, prince of a lad that he was, set himself up on the floor next to the bed. I told him that was stupid, and why shouldn't he be in comfort, like I was? He didn't argue, for chivalry knows when to submit to prudence. We talked and laughed and shared secrets, nothing more. We fell asleep in the vicinity of 2 a.m., he aglow in the divine of the upper chakras, I smugly adjusting this new feather in my cap.

As I reveled in the glory of my greatest success to date, Brad, the third little piggy, came into view. I knew him from Korb Hall days. He had been on the dorm maintenance crew and never shied away from some merriment with us girls whenever he came 'round to replace a light bulb or unclog a shower drain. We bumped into each other downtown in front of one of the local clubs, The Kove. He was wearing a fringed suede jacket, boots, and a ten-gallon hat.

"Been down to hear 15-60-75?" I asked. "Best blues band in town."

"Yeah, I know, but I can't get in."

"Why not?"

"I'm too young."

"What? How old are you?"

"Sixteen."

"Sixteen? Whoa. I didn't know that. Far out. What are you doing out here? It's freezing."

"My parents and I don't get along."

"So."

"I'm staying with my brother."

"And?"

"He's got a girl over. I could tell he wanted me to take a hike, so I split."

"Ah, I see." My wheels churning, I mentally rubbed my hands like a comic-strip villain.

"So?" he mimicked.

"Oh, sorry – spaced out for a minute. I don't know, it's cold out here. What are you doing later?"

"Diddlysquat."

"You wanna come over to my place?"

"Where's your place?"

"Brady Street."

"Yeah? I knew some people who lived on Brady Street."

"Probably the same house. I don't know anybody who hasn't known somebody who's lived there."

"What number?"

"One-twenty-four."

"That's the one."

Zealous in the cause

"Told you. Later?"
"Nah, thanks. Why are you smiling?"
"No reason – the way you said thanks."
"Oh, uh. OK. Well, I'm gonna hang out for a while and then go home. I'm leaving for Montana tomorrow to live with my sister and need to get an early start."
"No kidding? Montana? Gosh. Wow. I'm glad we got to see each other again."
"Me too. Well, see ya."
"Bye."

But sometime after midnight, a bashful rap-rap-rap came on my bedroom door. I was asleep.
"Lois?"
"Who is it?"
"Brad."
"Brad? How'd you get in?"
"Your roommate is still up."
"Oh. Well, what are you doing standing there letting the light in? Get in here and shut the door."

I soon discovered that the libido of a sixteen-year-old boy is not to be tampered with. Brad broke free of my conspired snare, and there was no way I was going to blow down his house of bricks. I'll never forget that cowboy hat. He wore it. I wore it. The lamp next to my bed wore it. I cracked up watching his boots in pantomime wearing it, whinnying as they pranced across the room, the hat working its way back to my bed and coming to rest on the bedpost.

That year, I received two Valentines, and with the exception of the bouquet of bare-root fruit trees my husband gave me in the second year of our marriage, they were my most memorable. One was a package postmarked Missoula, Montana. It contained a pair of red satin bikini underwear that had a pink and white cupid appliquéed on the front with the words, "Be Mine," on a banner flowing across the little angel's nakedness. The other was from an anonymous suitor. It sat on my dresser, unnoticed at first, but obviously, patiently waiting for me. My inquisitive, "What's this?" was answered as I reached out to take the gift. It was a black rose and a sympathy card. I held them for a long moment, staring at the flower and mulling over my name on the envelope. I went into McGuffey's room. Within a few minutes, I found what I was looking for in one of his notebooks. His L's were unmistakable.

◊

The food co-op kept up its momentum until March, when, due to a truly insidious case of cabin fever, Norm and I conveniently remembered an important component of the co-op's charter. Members were to rotate jobs so everybody knew both managerial and worker-bee tasks. This made it so we all had a stake in ownership, and so that anyone could step down without fretting over the co-op's continued operation.

Norm and I were burned out. We'd heard that the Rockies were astounding and that Boulder was the place to set up a base camp. Our strong reaction to this information rapidly elevated our cabin fever, which then metastasized with great vehemence into spring fever. I'd already stopped attending classes, so it wasn't but a few weeks into Lent before our trip to this magical land became a self-prescribed panacea. Norm, Holly, and I bundled ourselves and our gear into their chartreuse VW Bug and hit the road.

When we got to Boulder, I became a believer in love at first sight, because at first sight, I fell in love with the Rocky Mountains. We were numb for days from the

Zealous in the cause

sheer beauty of them. Young, rugged, invigorating, and random; immaculate, imperial, high, vast, and chaste; full of color, sturdy and robust; immutable in strength and ever changing in scope, they were everything that was right with the world. Yet we, saddled with the constraints of our physiology, had to do what was needed to stay alive to enjoy them. Norm and Holly perused the classifieds for jobs and a place to rent. I made a call to Vincent.

We had parted ways along about Thanksgiving, but that following Easter when, despite Norm and Holly's proximity, I found myself absolutely on my own, in a way I'd never found myself before. I remembered Pooh and Piglet – and Vince. I dialed. His roommate, Clarence, answered. He told me that he and Vince were no longer roommates. Vince was living in Cincinnati with his mom and had been since our break-up. Ouch. The insinuation smashed into the bull's eye: I was the reason for his departure from Kent. A fleeting image, an abbreviated half-thought, breath let out – what could I do about it? Here I was in Colorado. I'd never been on my own, not really. All that adult supervision I'd blithely shed was like taking off the morning's sweater to welcome the noonday sun. But suddenly feeling all alone in Colorado was like realizing I'd forgotten my mittens and parka in the attic just as a gust of glacial wind blew open that sweater in what was now the season of blizzards.

Against his better judgment, Clarence gave me the number to Vincent's home in Cincinnati. Hearing his gritty baritone, I wept and sniveled until his offer to come to my rescue made me feel better. He honored the pledge and spent the next two weeks quitting his job, buying a backpack, gathering up some cash, saying good-bye to his mom, and hitch-hiking out to Denver where I picked him up.

By the time he got there, however, I didn't need him to be. After he made me feel better, well . . . I felt better. While he was busy in his preparations for my delivery from the pit of despair, I was busy peeking over the creased corner of the handkerchief I was using to blot away the tears, and I liked what I saw: Keith. Blue-eyed blond-haired Keith. Vince saw him, too, shortly after he arrived, and when there they stood – The Nordic and The African – Mark Twain's "curtain of charity," drawn to hide Tom Sawyer's ignorance in confusing David and Goliath for two of Christ's disciples, would have been an act of generosity drawn across the likes of me, too.

The rest of that embarrassing scene notwithstanding, Vince and I embarked on a safari to California we'd mapped out in that phone call during which he so successfully consoled me. He'd traveled all that way, after all, and, though it appeared otherwise, I *was* still in possession of some decency.

◊

After just a few tractor-trailer rides from bored or lonely truck drivers, we found ourselves ambling down Wilshire Boulevard near UCLA.

Maybe we were tired from the trip, hypoglycemic from the lack of carbohydrates, or stretched from the strain of the unsavory truth, but what started out in the morning as banter, by afternoon exploded into a horrendous argument about my shortcomings. It's the only top-of-your-lungs screaming fight I can remember ever having with anyone other than my parents.

Its frame is solidly etched: The street, flanked on both sides by a row of trees, was chiefly empty of cars.

Zealous in the cause

The concrete sidewalks were swept and clean. Pedestrians were dispersed here and there, an occasional one or two pausing to observe our ruckus of flailing arms, angry facial expressions, and boisterous diatribe. The content of the argument – its outline, anyhow – is also embedded in my brain. Vince told me I was everything I was most afraid of being: priggish, pretentious, and persnickety (a real Miss Priss), selfish, self-centered, demanding, concocting, and spoiled (Scarlet O'Hara epitomized) – all the adverse attributes a girl could hold title to. It was all true, and I denied every bit of it. Then, like a practical joker who creeps up from behind, the urgency to fill our bellies and find somewhere to sleep gripped us and quelled the energy fueling the altercation. We laid our weapons down and declared a truce.

Savvy in obtaining temporary lodging, we tapped into the local network within the hour. By nightfall, we were being served a yin-yang balance of short-grained brown rice and steamed peas. Our hosts were macrobiotics who, by a bizarre fluke or perhaps uncanny kismet, were conducting a cease-fire of their own, producing an aura in their snug bungalow electrically charged with palpable tension oddly infused with harmony. They explained that by extending benevolence to us, they hoped for a distraction to diminish the strain. Hearing the latest tidings of travelers, they thought, might make their last night together more bearable. If my father had been there, he'd have said to them, "Looks like you thought wrong."

The tension between Vince and me was infused, not with harmony, but with my seeming predilection for discord. Like them, Vince and I were to split up the next day. In going through our finances, we determined that I had two fives and some ones, and he had some quarters and dimes. He asked if I'd lend him part of my stash. I flat-out refused, considering his request an affront. Didn't he know I'd be entirely on my own (which he was supposed to have rescued me from) and needed every penny? Vince's rationale didn't persuade me: that Vince was on his own, too, and that it would only be fair if we each started out with the same amount.

Indifferent toward our dinner partners, who calmly ate as we quibbled, we rudely continued sparring until one of them sighed, and the other began clearing the table. The remainder of the evening was occupied with housekeeping or reading, each of us on a foam pad in detached parts of the communal living space, a solitude our hosts had not predicted.

At six the next morning, I awoke to a peaceful drone coming from across the room. Timidly, I craned my neck out from under the pillow until I could see the stouter of the two housemates sitting cross-legged on his mat, eyes closed, back straight, and wearing an incredibly serene countenance. I'd never beheld anything like it. He appeared to be sleeping, but he was not. His mouth was shut, yet it was clear that the vocalization originated from him. He, I deduced, must be meditating. Fascinated, I watched for approximately twenty minutes as his demeanor of placid repose delicately permeated the house. When he plopped over onto his side and into a fetal position, I thought I saw him bounce ever so gracefully, as if he were Tinker Bell landing on a pillow of Jell-o. He covered himself and slept. So I did, too. Later, after we all breakfasted on cooked millet, the corrosive miasma that was I surfaced, woefully empty of the nirvana of the dawn's meditation. Grumbling over a one dollar bill I felt coerced to relinquish, I huffed, impatiently waiting for Vince to finish packing. Unceremoniously bidding adieu,

Zealous in the cause

he and I were soon off, having figured we'd walk to the freeway entrance together.

A foot apart and a light year between, we sullenly paved our way, until, after about fifteen minutes, the thrum of our treading was cut short by the sound of bare feet padding toward us. Instinctively we stopped, angled in toward each other and twisted back to see the more ascetic of the two roommates in his drawstring pajama bottoms and tunic top, jogging toward us, carrying something. Panting, but without a word, he held his cupped hands out to Vince. In a huddle, the three of us watched as Vince's hands received the few scrunched up dollars and mixed coins. Nothing said and no more done, the Good Samaritan retreated from whence he came, and the trance of our ill-humor transmuted to hypnotic amazement.

Vince and I cautiously raised our heads to look at each other. Our eyes, portals to the soul, locked for a moment. Not frightened, we remained as fixed as bronze sculptures, steadfast and unflinching, and we were again one. It was like drowning and seeing your life pass before your eyes. Everything we had been together stood before us; some word was spoken. Then a car pulled up, and the spell was broken. The chasm reformed, broad and incisive, and the valley walls rose. I climbed in and have not seen Vincent since.

Twenty-five years into the future, I began to step back into that moment, and allow it to become part of the wisdom that defies time. Gradually, the chasm becomes narrower and the valley walls are slowly closing. Someday they will merge, but I expect when they do, my life will pass before my eyes.

THE CALL TO COME IN

◊

The car I climbed into held a girl and two guys traveling from Vancouver. They were on their return trip and agreed to drop me off in San Francisco en route.

She was petite, with auburn hair that hung loosely to her shoulders. She was dressed in jeans, a brightly colored top, and bangly-dangly jewelry. She may have been a Libra, if what I'd heard about Libras as flirtatious, scatter-brained, and gullible was accurate. Both fellows were equally as typical in appearance, but different in character. The one sitting next to me claimed to be a writer of Gothic poetry. He was certainly morose enough for it. The other, the driver, seemed optimistic and out going. He was crippled, but this astonishing fact did not come to light until he asked for his harmonica. The poet stretched forward and fetched it from the glove compartment. He then fit the instrument into the withered and, until now, hidden right hand of the driver. He gently curled the deformed fingers over the harmonica. I was rendered speechless, and to this day, I don't know how that boy did it, but the barrage of blues that surged from his harp explained why harmonicas are called mouth organs. Without the pedals, stops, keys, or knobs of a cathedral's pipe organ, his sound was as sublime as a performance of *St. Matthew's Passion* on Good Friday, and as we navigated up the coast, he played on and on, saturating us and our tabernacle on wheels with song.

We stopped at Isla Vista to read a letter from Angela Davis that was supposed to be fastened to a bulletin board there. Like most college-aged kids, we were faithful to our antiheroes, and it meant a lot to us to see this artifact – possibly a leftover from the rally held in January for her release from jail. That night, we camped on the beach, sitting around a fire and improvising rhyme.

Somebody in Santa Barbara had given us the phone number for making connections in San Francisco, so the next day, we quickened our pace, pressing on to get to that famous City by the Bay before sundown. I started to feel like I was in California. Calling from a pay phone located somewhere on Van Ness, we got the address to where we would spend the night. Our concierge, a burly dude in Black Panther attire, met us at the bottom of a long set of rickety stairs outside the three-story building where we were to sleep. He unlocked the door, showed us in and said good-night.

Furnished with a wooden straight-backed chair in the corner and a double bed in the center beneath a hanging, unshaded single bulb, the room was a desolate composite that could have been a scene in a film noir. Our compadre the Libra went to see about the nightlife. The poet went to get some Chinese take-out.

When we were stopped at Isla Vista, I learned our driver's infirmity persisted beyond his hand. While he was grappling with getting the key out of the ignition, I had bolted for the bathroom. On my return, I saw he hadn't gotten out of the car yet. He was sitting sideways in the driver's seat with the door open, strapping on a leg brace. I knew right away he was a baby boomer who succumbed to polio before Dr. Salk had a chance to develop the vaccine that made a whole generation of parents breathe a sigh of relief. I was blown away that he could simultaneously play a harmonica and drive a car while trampling a disability. I was also mortified that I was too obtuse to notice the extent of his condition. I could have helped out. Luckily, Libra was standing by to hand him his crutches, which were not the wooden variety

THE CALL TO COME IN

you rent at the hospital supply when you sprain your ankle, but the leg brace's more stylish companions made of heavy-duty aluminum, the kind that cup the arms below the elbows, drawing the hands down to clamp onto rubberized handles perpendicular to the frames. Now in our five-star hotel suite, he asked me to assist him in removing his vestments. I obliged. He guided me through the experience, and together we lay his contorted body down.

When Mr. E.A. Poe's spirit-heir returned, the three of us shared not only egg foo yung and chow mein, but the double bed. My feminist goals an unnecessary enterprise of the past, we talked, laughed, and shared secrets well into the night.

Before we nodded off, the cripple, who was no longer a cripple to me, said, "Hold my hand."

"Can I do that?"

"Why not? It's not a hook, you know."

"Else you'd have heard us calling him Captain Hook," the poet quipped.

"Ha ha."

I took the hand, and it was true. It did not bite, but neither was there the pressure of a reciprocating squeeze. Instead, there was a tingling that moved up my arm, merging with the blood already circulating. In tandem, they orbited my body. I lay on my back, tummy sunken in, feet and legs rag-doll limp, no pillow under my head. A smile took over as my mind emptied. The poet rested on the other side of me. To complete the highway of happiness coursing through my veins, I took his hand, too. "How can I keep from singing?"

That's the last I remember until morning, when we went our separate ways. They continued on to Canada, and after a brief stop in Berkeley, I hitchhiked back to Boulder and the blue-eyed blond.

◊

Flat as a can of Sprite left open on a refrigerator shelf, the romance between Keith and me lost its fizzle before the leaves changed color and the air turned chilly. We spent what was left of that spring madly in love, so much so that we moved in together undeterred by, or maybe because of, the fact that living with someone outside of marriage in 1971 was not accepted mainstream practice. Our first "home" was an old Airstream in a trailer park in Grapevine, Texas, where Keith had taken a summer job working for his dad's cement silo manufacturing company. "Welcome to a Growing Grapevine." In August, we moved into an apartment in Marietta, Ohio, Keith's hometown.

We never said it, but what doomed us to failure was our difference in opinion over the baby. I wanted it. He didn't. I was so elated to be two months pregnant that I ignored the looks of the sad nurse and disapproving doctor as I left the doctor's office. I bought a crisp, hard, cold, and juicy Red Delicious and ate it as I bounced along back to the apartment. It was a beautiful day. When an old man smiled and said, "Good morning," I believed my child was blessed. But when I reached the apartment, the look on Keith's face couldn't be ignored. Deflated as a popped balloon, I slumped down onto our waterbed, bouncing again, but more like a seasick sailor than the happy girl I'd just been. A child sans father, sans family, wouldn't do. I agreed to have an abortion.

The operation was legal in only a few states at that time. I chose to take the train to a hospital in New York – devoted entirely to abortions – because Cory was staying with her parents in New Jersey, and I knew she'd be more than willing to come and get me when it was all over. The girl I roomed with was a secretary from somewhere in Iowa who'd gotten knocked up by her boss. She wept and wailed the whole time. I took the ordeal in stride, but that deflated feeling returned when I looked out the passenger window of Cory's car and watched the slick wet black of the city's pavement and the glistening raindrops reflecting the red and green of the traffic lights. As we accelerated through the Holland Tunnel back to the Garden State, I heard only silence.

A year later, I saw a poster of an embryo at eight weeks. It had fingers and toes. If I had known, if I was educated, if the consequences had been drilled into me, I would have used protection. Better than that, I'd have been a little more select in my choice of partner.

7 More like Siddhartha

Hitchhiking between Ohio and Colorado became the canopy under which I took refuge for the next four years. Like the migrations of so many birds, my migrations seemed to be defined by the pull of the seasons. I spent my autumns and springs in Ohio; my winters and summers in Colorado. When I was twelve, my dad named me "The Wanderer." "Because," he said, "we never know where you're going to wander in from." My Kent and Boulder friends said it was because they never knew *when* I was going to wander in.

Ohio evenings meant the Johnson Road farmhouse, meeting place of my Ohio friends, where we played Scrabble and browsed the *East-West Journal* and *Mother Earth News*. It was a time for making meals from vegetables grown in the garden; trying our hand at grinding corn for bread and chicory for coffee; picking lamb's quarters, elderberry blossoms, and baby cattails; and drying coltsfoot for smoking. It was a time for gathering black walnuts from an old orchard, making beer, and swimming naked in the pools at the abandoned quarry. It was a time for sitting on the porch watching the bees come into their hive while daydreaming about beekeepers and ashrams. We idolized Hanuman. We hunted ginseng.

Colorado evenings were spent at the Pioneer Inn in Nederland where my Boulder friends and I played poker, shot pool, and danced. We browsed no magazines. We ate pizza, blue-cheese burgers, and steak and baked potatoes. We rode horses out of Central City up to the Continental Divide, and we talked about going down the Green River on a raft to look for pictographs. We stood in line all night to buy tickets for a Grateful Dead concert. We hiked the mountains. We hunted dried bones.

These two places and these friendships meant everything to me, but I couldn't decide between the two selves they represented – the homesteader or the frontierswoman – or to which north to set my inner compass, magnetic or true. Thus I became a loner.

I kept trying to go to school. I re-enrolled at Kent State, and after a few months, when that didn't work out, I applied and got into the University of Colorado at Boulder. I also worked a myriad of part-time jobs, doing everything from pumping gas in Colorado to factory work in Ohio to answering the phone for the Leanin' Tree greeting card company when I was again back in Colorado. Vulnerable to any viable suggestion for adventure, Cory baited me with a month in Mexico. She wanted to practice transporting barbiturates that she could buy over-the-counter in Mexico, but were prescription in the United States, creating a fruitful market for the American street vendor. "Now that I know the language," she said, "I've got this idea. I'm going to hide it inside shells - conch shells, if I can find them - and then seal the hidden inner part of the shell with melted paraffin." I went along for the ride. We had an extraordinary vacation, staying in a palapa high above a beach near La Cruz, north of Puerto Vallarta, where horses had free range. We collected shells and we bought some paraffin,

More like Siddhartha

but when we got back to the Rio Grande, Cory couldn't go through with it. We threw the shells – and their contents – into the river.

Not considering myself aimless, but more like Siddhartha – seeking – I knew life's treasures were already in my possession. The treasure chest, however, was unfortunately locked up tight. It was the key I needed, and that was what I sought. I wanted to travel. I also wanted the down-home lifestyle, but I didn't know how I'd get that home-baked bread on the table. I considered becoming a photographer for *National Geographic*, but that was too far-fetched. What I really wanted was to play horn in a symphony orchestra, but I was already too old for that. I didn't think a Bachelor's degree would get me anywhere; a Master's might, but I didn't have it in me to go that distance. Even if I did, I had no idea what to study. The quandary hung in the air like the smell of green cabbage in the cook pot.

Four events from those years became recurring memories that kept popping up, but never in any particular order. They reminded me of the moles in the carnival game Whac-A-Mole, where each time you hit one mole head down, another pops up somewhere else. Pesky was the word their regular occurrence brought to mind, but their importance, I'm sure, shed light on my psyche or maybe that of my generation. What that insight might have been, I never fully determined.

1. The FBI visits my parents – twice, ten years apart

When I was nine, a certain neatly jacketed, thinly necktied, courteous man periodically came to the house to see my dad. I always answered the door and greeted him before leading the way to the TV room where Daddy dismissed me, shut the door, and didn't come out for anywhere from ten to twenty minutes. It was very hush-hush, but not troubling, because the man was amiable and because my dad would never do anything wrong. This went on for some months. Then, as cryptically as the appointments began, they stopped. Several weeks later, when it was my parents' turn to host Pinochle Night, my dad divulged what it had all been about: Our mysterious guest was a G-man on his weekly rounds to collect intelligence from my father, an informant for the FBI.

"Neat-o!" I exclaimed as I sat on Daddy's lap, captivated by what he'd just said but still trying to figure out what trump meant. Before I had a chance to ask a question about that all-important card game concept, questions about Daddy's startling revelation began flying around the kitchen table like miniature animated pterodactyls zeroing in for an attack.

"Austin! You could have gotten shot! Why didn't you tell me about this?"

"Aw, Lena. It wasn't like that."

"Why did they pick you?" Aunt Edith wanted to know.

"Because I'm a milkman."

"What's that got to do with it?"

"I'm the only person out there at three in the morning besides drunks, prostitutes . . . "

"Austin!" I loved it when my dad said whatever he wanted.

" . . . and crooks, and the FBI'd have to pay them and hope to get an honest night's work out of 'em. With me, they knew what they were getting."

"Pay them to do what?" Uncle Bill asked.

"To spy."

"Spy? Go on. You're pullin' my leg."

More like Siddhartha

"Hell if I am. They suspected that one of my customers was involved in criminal activity and wanted me to watch them."

"Wow, Daddy. Like Spy vs. Spy. Ya think they were communists?"

"Lois, you're as bad as your father. I'm sure they were *not* communists," my mother harrumphed.

"Well, they were something," my dad replied.

"What'd you have to do?" Uncle Bill was excited. This was the juiciest story he'd heard all month.

"Keep an eye on the house. Look for unusual activity. Keep track of who or what came and went."

"Who or what? Like what who or what?" My uncle was really into this now. The card game stopped, and all eyes were on Daddy.

"I don't know. Cars, packages, license plate numbers, envelopes, descriptions."

"Did you help catch them, Daddy?"

"That's classified, honey. But I can tell you they moved out, and yesterday, the agent stopped by to say, 'Thanks for everything'."

"Oh, Austin!"

"Oh, Lena!"

So it was ironic when, during my years of commuting between Ohio and Colorado, the FBI knocked on my parents' door, the very one I answered as a kid. They were looking for a fellow they said was a buddy of mine, an alleged member of the Weather Underground, the violent offshoot of the radical Students for a Democratic Society. The Weathermen believed negotiating with the government to bring about change was a waste of time, and they made their point by starting riots and bombing buildings. They always called ahead, though, and except for a few of their own, nobody ever got hurt. Even so,

Dad and Mom didn't see the humor when the FBI called about my friend's whereabouts. I told them the Bureau didn't have to go all the way to New Jersey ferreting out my presumably seditious friend. All they had to do was open the Kent, Ohio, phone book.

2. I speak with a friend about the shootings

On a bleak February night in Rollinsville, Colorado, the snow and the howling wind got folks pondering the arctic, the Eskimos, their igloos, furry hoods, and walrus blubber. Some brave souls, more in need of human contact than fearful of winter, ventured out to the Bluebird Cafe to listen to an acoustic guitar, drink a beer, and chat awhile. I was among them, as was my friend Scott, who'd been shot at Kent. Although he, too, was now living in Boulder, we seldom saw each other, so it was nice to catch up. The ale, the warmth of the fire, the mellow music, and the ambiance of those who gathered formed an elixir that stimulated an internal inventory of the serious.

"Do you ever think about what happened?" I asked.

"May 4th?"

"Yeah." Conversation hung back like a shy kitten. After we tended to our empty beer glasses, I said, "I saw you, you know."

"Saw me where?"

"On the stretcher."

"You sure it was me?"

"It had to be you. You turned your head and looked at me. We looked at each other. How else would I know you were hit?"

"I don't know."

More like Siddhartha

"You were getting carried to an ambulance." We paused as we each envisioned our separate versions of the emergency crew working its way through the crowd. "What happened to you?"

He hesitated, as if calculating how much to let out, how much to allow himself to feel the pain. Then he said, "Like everybody else, I was running. You know what it was like. We ran. Then I felt a prick. Like a bee sting. No more than that, in the back of my head, at my nape. I put my hand there, just like you would if there were some sort of insect landing. Not to slap at it – just to swipe it away. Then something made me bring my hand to my cheek. There was a depression in my face, and my finger slid into a hole I felt there. It made me sick. That's when I knew."

"I remember hearing you were getting taken care of, but I worried about you. I thought to go see you at the clinic, but it got so crazy right after, having to leave campus and all."

"It's OK."

"You were flat on your back with your fist up in the air." I smiled at him. "You looked like a revolutionary."

"I remember." We shifted our gaze to the glowing embers. "We were revolutionaries, whether we meant to be or not."

"Do you think we learned anything?"

"Nothing we needed to know."

"You're right on that."

There was nothing more we wanted to say. The elixir, having taken us to a place we normally wouldn't go, kept us wrapped in a blanket of liquid warmth until it was time to go home. Ready to face the cold, we hugged and said good night.

THE CALL TO COME IN

3. I make pear sauce and meet Bonnie Raitt

Late one spring, the elusive underground Weatherman and I spent an afternoon canning a batch of undoubtedly treasonous pear sauce. In the low-slung kitchen of our beloved Johnson Road farmhouse, he taught me what he knew about making and preserving fruit butters. He showed me how to wash, peel, quarter, core, and press. Then he coached me on how to add sugar and spice, to boil and stir the mixture, to prepare the Ball jars and lids, and to process the sauce using a pressure cooker.

It was an all-day affair, and like everything you do when you're under thirty, it required accompanying music. He had a Bonnie Raitt album he wanted me to hear, so as we set out on our cooking adventure, we set the vinyl spinning. The next thing we knew, the afternoon coalesced into a marvelous holiday with no name. We washed; we listened. We peeled; we read album covers. We quartered and cored; we talked about the lyrics. We pressed; we listened some more. We added the sugar and spice; we danced with our dishrags and spoons. We boiled and stirred; we looked at cover photos. We prepared the jars and lids; we danced with each other and sang. We processed the pears, and we processed the music.

A year or more went by. During one of my tours of duty in Boulder, I saw a handbill announcing that Bonnie was playing at Tulagi's, the local jazz venue. The covers of her albums I bought after the pear canning venture had edges so worn and bare that cardboard shown through as if mice had chewed their way in. The albums themselves also showed signs of constant use, especially since I loved to lip-sync all the songs.

More like Siddhartha

I was aware that a career in music would be tough to pursue, regardless of age, but even so, I'd been thinking more about going down that path. I respected Bonnie as a female vocalist and slide guitarist, and thought she'd be a good person to confide in about the rigors of going professional. Resolving to ask her advice on the subject, I bought a ticket to the show. At intermission, I boldly knocked on the Green Room door and was received by a lilting, "Come in." The room was much bigger than I expected, and full of people. Bonnie was seated on a low couch at the back.

"Please, come on in," she summoned. "What's your name?"

"Uh . . . Lo . . . is, Lois." I stuttered, paralyzed by the sudden realization of what a delusional sociopath I was to think I could enter the dressing room of a headliner and receive private mentoring before the second half of the concert began.

"Hi, Lois," she graciously replied. "I'm Bonnie. This is Mitch and Sarah, and that's Joanne. Meet Gwen and Miguel. There's Stefan. Jonah, meet Lois . . . " She introduced me to each person in the room by name, and there were no fewer than twenty. By name! I was dumbfounded. She concluded with the lighthearted imperative, "Come sit by me."

Everyone was on the floor, mostly at the perimeter, but still, I had to walk around some and over others to reach her. I didn't say what I'd rehearsed: "I was wondering if you might have time to talk to me about what it's like being a woman with a career in music. I play piano, but recently got back into the French horn and am leaning toward making it my life's work." Instead I squeaked out with: "I was wondering if I could take you out to dinner." Where'd that insanity come from? I didn't have money to take anybody to dinner.

She looked at me askance, mischievously, and asked, "Just me or the whole band?"

"Oh." I spluttered. "You . . . and . . . the . . . band."

Charitably, she switched topics. "Tell me," she said. "How did 'Been In Love Too Long' come across to you?"

My embarrassment evaporated since this was a line of inquiry I could govern. "Oh," I said. "If you're worried about those two heckler chicks, don't be. It's always the few unhappies who make all the noise. No, your message came across just fine. Really well, in fact."

"Good," she said, "I'm glad you liked it."

She took me in, and her drummer at the time, Dennis Whitted, befriended me. I never quite understood why, since I was across the room from the four girls hanging all over him. I stayed with the band the three or four days they were in Boulder. Remaining images are numerous: the Travelodge, a late-night blues club, my home-baked bread, a pancake-house breakfast, a session in a basement studio in the mountains, the piano player's dexterity and talk of his upcoming wedding. But no discussion about music as a career choice. I see Bonnie pouring over the charts. She was not satisfied with her standings. She wanted to make it big. I wondered about that. As the years went by, I was glad to see she got her wish. Dennis, I was told too late, moved to Santa Cruz about the same time I did, news I regretted because had he not already passed on to the next life, I would have looked him up.

More like Siddhartha

4. *Nixon resigns*

On Thursday evening, August 8, 1974, I noticed it was very quiet out as I moseyed from the University of Colorado campus through the neighborhoods of Boulder to retrieve a few things I'd stored at a friend's house. I seemed to be the only person outside. I could see one family's TV just inside their open screen door. Then, because of the singular sound, I noticed that everybody's television seemed to be on the same channel. It reminded me of the rainy November day in 1972 when I voted for the first time. It was the first presidential election after eighteen-year-olds earned the right, and, like this political first, it too felt special – rainy-day special.

I stopped at a house where the door was ajar and the TV was facing the front entrance. Our president was speaking. So this was the reason the streets were empty. Then I remembered that he – President Nixon – his deception unearthed, was scheduled to speak to us, a nation of people shaking their heads in halting disbelief.

We do this when our leaders disappoint us, as if we know either they or we will never learn, but we don't know which.

> It is a sad fate for a man to die too well known
> to everybody else, and still unknown to himself.
> – Francis Bacon, "Of Great Place"

8
Julie Andrews, a hermit, a realization, and a reality

The summer of 1972 was the first of three I spent camping at the base of Sugarloaf Mountain in the foothills outside Boulder. Arriving from my latest go-round in Kent, I looked at the majesty of the Rockies and wondered why everyone wasn't preparing to leave the four walls of their homes and head into the mountains. When it became apparent they weren't, I was befuddled, but not discouraged. I knew I had to be outside. With weather like this, I thought to myself, come Fourth of July, surely everybody will pack up and head for the hills – just like all the moms and kids did at the beginning of *The Seven Year Itch*, when they crowded onto the subway for their big annual exodus from New York City. Didn't that happen here, too? It must. Everyone's just late this year, I bet.

The site I chose near Sugarloaf was on U.S. National Forest land, a mile past the last house on the ungraded dirt road that led to the mountain. The exact spot was on a hill above Switzerland Trail, which was really more a fire road than a trail. I pitched my tent in a hollow away from the chill of the open ridge, low enough to be protected from rain and wind. The back of the tent faced Four Mile Canyon, and it was where I took my meals and watched the sunset. Sometimes I imagined my campsite to be a sailing ship anchored offshore. My bow was head to wind, facing north. Sugarloaf Mountain was ninety degrees to starboard, at a distance halfway between my campsite and the last house. What I called Bald Mountain was closer, just on the other side of Switzerland Trail. About eighty feet from my stern was the overgrown Jeep trail I turned onto to get to the campsite from the dirt road. If I walked in that direction and up onto the highest point of the ridge, the most fantastic 360-degree IMAX view came instantly into focus.

    Looking southeast, I could see Denver and the plains. To the southwest, the foothills came into solid view, with Twin Sisters Peaks up on Magnolia Star Route easily pinpointed. West, the Continental Divide and white-capped Fourteeners spread out across the horizon like the sweep of a magic wand in fairyland. Continuing around, my own Bald and Sugarloaf mountains came into view, obscuring the course I suspected would take me to Cheyenne and points north: Wyoming, Montana, and on to Saskatchewan. I was living atop a slice of paradise pie. It was Julie Andrews and "the hills are alive" every single day.

    It took two of those glorious days to set up camp. The tent was big enough to hold my Goodwill Army-issue goose-down mummy bag, borrowed blankets for cushioning and extra warmth, two pillows, and a ten-inch-diameter tree-trunk round on which I placed five candles affixed with their own wax. Two apple crates near the door flap acted as cabinets. One was for my clothes. The other served as a cupboard for food I sometimes shared with my chipmunk neighbors. I nailed bandanas across the open fronts for curtain doors. The tops of this makeshift dresser and pantry became bookshelf, desk and kitchen counter. Outside the tent, I fashioned a

Julie Andrews, a hermit, a realization, and a reality

lean-to for firewood, tools, and kitchen utensils. I made a fire pit and erected a tripod to hold my soup pot.

With the camp in order, summer could begin. An ordinary day went like this: Up with the sun, I had no reason to rush. The latrine was a walk in one direction, and washing was a walk in another. After two weeks of hauling water from town in canteens strung around my neck, I discovered a spring a short distance from the campsite. Spellbound by fresh water coming right out of a hummock green from the life-giving nourishment, I dug out a reservoir a foot wide and built a dam of rocks across the lower end. It worked like a charm. Later, I learned how to tap into the spring with a small hose, creating a continuous flow of water. I did not wash with soap, as I was afraid of contaminating the water. My bar of Ivory was saved for the showers I took two or three times a week in the dorms at the university. I didn't, however, worry about spitting out toothpaste, figuring there were a few things that Mother Nature would have to accept a compromise on.

After grooming came breakfast. My preference was Grape-Nuts in goat-milk yogurt with a dash of blue and white sky and a pinch of fluffy cloud. Then, still with no semblance of haste, I scoured the cereal bowl and spoon with dirt (the precursor to Ajax cleanser), rinsing each with water from the spring. Grooming didn't include getting dressed, which was good, because next on the agenda was sunbathing, and no one bathes with clothes on.

Before most people left for work, I was drenched with sun, the energy from it penetrating every pore of my skin. One day, when I raised my head to interject some movement into the hot listlessness of this daily sun sauna, my eyes met with a phenomenal sight. Little creatures, not alarmed by my presence, were out doing what little creatures evidently do when no human is tromping through. Quietly, I watched. There was a lizard on one rock and a garter snake on another, sunbathing as I was. Several more lizards scrambled about in their cockeyed two-legs-left-two-legs-right style of getting about. Chipmunks scampered, and several varieties of songbird bobbed, pecked, scratched, and flew about, chattering the news of the day to all who cared to listen. There were two plump bunny rabbits, cute as buttons, sitting nose to nose, sniffing at something. Music entered my head, either Grieg's "Morning Mood" from *Peer Gynt*, or the early part of Rossini's *William Tell Overture*, I wasn't sure which, but it didn't matter. I laughed and was happy.

Lying naked in the sun felt grand, and it was easy to do, but moving about naked through the day's chores took some getting used to. Working, bending down, and feeling thigh against torso – skin to skin – was, at the outset, startling, a novelty that left me embarrassed and giddy. Then a loss of ego drew me into the picture of this new existence. Making the bed, taking a whisk broom to the tent floor and a rake to the ground near the site, cleaning up the fire ring, chopping wood in preparation for dinner, gathering wood to add to the supply already in the lean-to, tidying up – all were soon done comfortably in my birthday suit. A layer of clothing no longer separated me from the animals. Mother Nature gently touched my shoulder, whispering a reminder, "It's OK. You've always been a part of us. You just forgot for a while."

I needed to go to town every day for one of my part-time jobs and also because I was playing in the university orchestra, so the next order of business was dressing and packing. Sometimes, before striking out for town, I'd scout around, scavenging old miners' debris or

Julie Andrews, a hermit, a realization, and a reality

developing a better mental map of the nearby topography. When time permitted, I'd hike up Bald Mountain or Sugarloaf or along Switzerland Trail, eager to see coyotes. Then I'd close up the tent, skedaddle the two miles to the road and put my thumb out.

◊

It was providence that got me into the orchestra. I hadn't played the French horn much since high school, and I missed it. As a student at the university in Boulder, I got permission to use the battered Holton I found buried in the back of the band room there. As I was walking out from practicing one morning, with the horn under my arm, the orchestra conductor saw me.

"Ah," he cried. "You're the very one we've been looking for. We're performing Beethoven's Seventh at the end of the month, and we need a fourth horn. Can you be at rehearsal today? You know the part?"

"Yes, sir, I do." *Do I know the part? Every horn player knows that part. It's the undercurrent that pushes the sea forward, the low rumbling in the Presto that is one of Beethoven's many porters transporting the sounds the audience came to hear.*

"Good. Four o'clock. Warmed up. Ready to play."

And so, Beethoven's *Symphony No. 7* became part of my ordinary day.

After rehearsal, I'd do my shopping, get my mail from the post office, and maybe visit a friend while waiting out the thunder and lightning from the squall that commonly came through in the late afternoon. Then, on Canyon Drive, I'd retrace my hitchhiking steps to my home in the hills.

The majority of rides dropped me off at the Sugarloaf Star Route turnoff, where I'd wait for somebody who lived up Sugarloaf Road to come by and pick me up.

THE CALL TO COME IN

Some time in mid-July, folks got to know me, suggesting times to be at the turnoff, or, in a few cases, when to meet at the Piggly Wiggly or the post office. After that, the wait wasn't so bad, but so many long minutes were spent in the company of the birds, wildflowers, grasses, bugs, pebbles, asphalt, and dirt at that niche of road that I gained a familiarity with it in the same way you might with the library or coffee shop, the locker room, the cubicle at work, or your desk at school. It's funny how we make friends with a place.

Once I arrived at the intersection below the foot of the mountain, I embarked on my second two-mile walk of the day. Half of the hike was an incline, open with expansive far-off views behind me. Then the road leveled off, and the quaking aspen, ponderosa pine, juniper, cactus, yellow and orange lichen, crumbly dirt, rock (lots of rock), Jeep trails, and blasting holes from gold-mining days were right at hand. As I lumbered along, I could hear chipmunks and birds carrying on as if they were up to the most important thing on the planet, and though it wasn't an hour since the rain stopped, the arid climate was again present everywhere.

I'd get back to the campsite in time to make dinner and watch the sun go down. Because of the cumulonimbus cherub-clouds left in the wake of the storm, sunsets were spectacular, and because the camp was situated in view of Four Mile Canyon, I looked out across a large open space ideal for witnessing this silent evidence of Earth's role in the clockwork of the solar system.

One evening, while reclining against my favorite boulder, waiting for some split peas to simmer into soup, a strong swishing sound filled the air above my head. A hawk – a nighthawk, it turned out – flew out into the canyon, soared high, came down some, flew farther out,

Julie Andrews, a hermit, a realization, and a reality

came back, shot up again, and then, zoom! He dove in a sharply vertical attitude, bringing a most remarkable noise straight down with him. He did this over and over again, positively riveting me. "By Jove," I declared. "We're having dinner together – he, his flying insects, and me, my green-pea porridge!"

It became a regular date. My next-door neighbor whistled past my head, closer and closer, on his way to grab a bite to eat. Maybe he considered us friends and wanted to snitch on what he eavesdropped from above. More likely, I was in his territory, and he was giving me fair warning. As I sat each evening upon day, awed by this avian's prominent display, I learned the noise was not coming from his throat, but from his wings braking out of the fast dive. Waiting for dusk to enfold me, it became an impressive encore to an already impressive performance. When it was too dark for either of us to see, I doused the fire and repaired to my cozy cluster of belongings. Lighting the candles, I wrote letters, and, last on the list of an ordinary day, snuggled in to read Edgar Rice Burroughs's *Tarzan of the Apes*.

◊

That year, I wintered in Ohio, working, taking classes, cementing friendships, but still with no direction in sight. Corrine gave me no plausible excuse to prolong the agony this time, for she was busy pursuing a career in drug running. Overcoming lost nerve, she was now hiding crystal meth in her bra. "New York to the Caribbean and back, 34A on departure to 38DD on the return," she gloated. "For Christ's sake, Cory, you're the one who's going to go down, not the guys you're working for," I chided her. "Yeah," she replied, foolishly unaffected by what she must have known was true, "but I get to jet set. They play a lot of backgammon down there. Did you know that? It's fun."

Come spring, wistful thoughts of Colorado brought me back to the turnoff at Sugarloaf Star Route. The second summer was much the same as the first, except that the book title changed from *Tarzan* to *The Sun Also Rises*, the orchestra performed Puccini's *Tosca* rather than Beethoven's Seventh, and the nighthawk showed up with a mate. The difference was three names added to the camp register: Hugh Davey, Dan J. Terrell, and Zebulon Pike, Jr.

Hugh picked me up on my first hitch up Canyon Drive. Small talk revealed small world. Coincidentally, Hugh was from Kent, and we had a lot of people in common. Instead of dropping me at his turnoff at Magnolia Star Route, he took me on up to mine. The next day, he took me to where the walking portion of my daily commute began. He pointed at Twin Sisters Peaks and told me his house was at the base of a mountain, too. Three days later, we bounced along in his International all the way to my campsite so he could meet the nighthawk and see how I lived. That night, we lay beside each other, formulating a plan for sending messages with smoke signals or flags. As the tips of our fingers played itsy-bitsy spider and the tips of our toes foraged for tickle spots, we were content in the message we were sending then and there: whenever we wanted, we could look out across to where the other lived and feel as good as we did at that moment.

Hugh liked that I was a musician. He'd make a point of arriving early to pick me up from rehearsals of *Tosca*, waiting in a front row seat where he could wave at me in the orchestra pit. When he came to pick me up from practicing piano, I'd wait until he knocked on the door of

Julie Andrews, a hermit, a realization, and a reality

the practice room. One time he came in, bent down for a hello kiss, and then silently sat tailor fashion next to the baby grand and closed his eyes and listened. I liked that he liked that I was a musician, too.

In the early part of August, country music from a radio somewhere invaded the privacy of my sunbathing ritual. "How very odd," said I to nobody, using the literary inflection I like when I'm feeling playful. "Who could this interloper be?" I dressed and warily followed the sound until I spied a school bus imitating an RV at a KOA Kampground. There was an oxidized aluminum table out front, a welcome mat at the door, and two surly-looking couples in a half-circle of folding lawn chairs. They were drinking coffee from truck-stop mugs, and they saw me coming.

"Hell-o," I said hesitantly, as I continued walking. "I could hear your radio."

"Could you, now? Followed the music, did you? Well, sit down and join us for breakfast," the jocular voice of the most grizzled of them boomed. He turned to the woman on his left. "Mary, get this gal a cup of joe." Turning back to me, he practically shouted, "Are we neighbors?"

"I guess we are, but I've never seen anybody up here before."

"What do you mean, 'up here'?"

"I'm camping over there," I said, weakly lifting a heavy arm in the direction of Camelot as it faded away.

"Then you're camping on my land, girlie. What's your name?"

"I am? But . . . "

Mary brought out the java, handed it to me half-heartedly and asked if anybody else was ready for a second round. She got a quorum of affirmatives.

THE CALL TO COME IN

"Now don't get riled. We're not gonna bite, and I ain't kickin' you off, but you need to know this is my claim. I got squatter's rights, and I'm takin' 'em. All the way to the bank." His friends snickered. "Now, what'd you say your name was?"

That's how I met Dan J. Terrell – Arkansas Dan the Man. We became the unlikeliest of friends, an elephant seal and a moth. He was a lascivious old coot, but after backing off the first time, I told him to knock it off. After that, we found a rapport that suited us well. My nudist colony days were over, but not because I was afraid my new neighbors would spy on me. It was because they wouldn't have understood. They were like nine-year-old boys learning where babies come from. They giggled at anything closely resembling sex, and even though Mary was *not* the wife and the other two were in some sort of card-playing, boozing, dirty joking, double dating collusion with her and Dan, their sins were all venial.

Since I aspired to owning property someday, Dan's assertion about claims and squatter's rights piqued my interest. Hugh drove me to Denver to investigate, and Dan was absolutely correct. Here we were, more than a hundred years after gold was discovered in Colorado, and you could still stake a claim. The stipulation was that you had to work it a certain amount every year. If you did, the land was yours. I lacked the tenacity to do that, but Dan didn't. The mold *he* was cast from broke shortly after he emerged from the womb. What I liked most about him was that his RV wasn't really an RV. It was a school bus.

Later on that August, Hugh left to study environmental law at Ohio's Case Western Reserve, and Zebulon Pike, Jr. came to live with me. Zeb was a yellow Labrador puppy. I have no recollection of how we met, but

Julie Andrews, a hermit, a realization, and a reality

after we did, we fell right in step with each other. He let me train him the way I wanted and idolized me for it. I, in return, let him steal my heart, and thus we became best of companions.

With the approach of summer's end, Dan told me he wanted to leave the school bus where it sat. He said it was "durn right *lewd*-icrous" to drive it to Little Rock, where it would remain parked until next June, when he would turn around and drive back to where it was parked now. "If there was somebody who might keep an eye on it, and maybe live in it and take care of it – somebody I could trust – why, I'd be obliged. It wouldn't even matter if there was a dog involved." Having descended into a winter of discontent before autumn so much as poked its head around the corner, the idea appealed to me. I wouldn't have to invest energy in moving back to Ohio. Instead, I could stay put until I figured out what to do with the rest of my life. No rent. No roommates. Just Zeb and me. I liked it. I said OK.

◊

There isn't a heck of a lot of room in a school bus. That was for certain. The driver's area was wasted as living space, although the door mechanism made up for that; I defied anyone within a thousand-mile radius to come up with a front door classier than mine. The rest of the bus was made into a mobile home by dismantling all but the first bench, which was kept for a passenger's seat. Behind it, a couch, end table, drop-leaf table and folding chairs fitted nicely. Beyond these was a kitchenette, and the rear of the bus was filled with four built-in berths, a dresser and a camper-style bathroom. Bulkheads fore and aft of the kitchen area gave the bus the feel of having three rooms.

THE CALL TO COME IN

The only viable space for yoga was in the center aisle of the main salon, and it was tight, almost a predicament, but not impossible. I don't recall how I became interested in yoga, just as I don't remember how I acquired Zeb. Under the auspices of Richard Hittleman, along with the photographs of the girl I assumed was his star pupil, his book, *Yoga 28-Day Exercise Plan*, became my Sherpa. Standing on my head for the first time was an inebriating feat, especially having learned how from an instruction manual. Zeb played the acrobat, nipping at the peculiarity of human hair spread out all over our very narrow living room floor as he desperately tried to get me to come out from under it.

By early September, the hermit's life with Zeb was no longer compatible with the loud music, dope, massive amounts of stuff, and perpetual motion of my friends in town. I was lonely for family, but hanging out with them – my surrogate family – was no longer appealing. Everybody, it seemed, needed to be doing something every second. Nobody could sit still for a minute! It was culture shock whenever I visited. In the end, I preferred not to expose myself to their diversions. I invited them up to visit me, but they were as uncomfortable with my lifestyle as I was with theirs. My time alone grew greater; my time with friends diminished. If girls have caves, mine was yellow and black and surrounded with windows.

When my real family – my parents – came to visit in September, I welcomed them with open arms. We'd reconciled, as families do, with many phone calls under our belts. Dad's preferred TV shows still took priority; Mom was faithful to the same shopping mall, yet neither of these facts of life bothered me anymore. I was just

Julie Andrews, a hermit, a realization, and a reality

glad we were getting along and glad they were coming to see me.

At my dad's suggestion, I rented a car and picked them up at Stapleton Airport. Mom's forty-eighth birthday was five days away, so we decided to spend the week on a celebratory tour of western Colorado, stopping at all the vista points to bask in the unfathomable textures of the Rocky Mountains.

At Black Canyon, in Gunnison National Park, my dad and I shared a daydream, something we hadn't done since I was a prepubescent child. We imagined ourselves living down in the canyon before the devices of modern man were invented to enslave us. We talked about how we'd hunt and fish, and take our time doing everything we did. We surveyed the view and decided on the spot where we'd build a cabin. Languishing in this fabrication, we walked back to the car, where Mom was waiting.

Wanting to do something special to remember the actual day of her birth, I made reservations at my favorite restaurant, the Gold Hill Inn, and surprised her with a flaming Baked Alaska. She still tells the story of that cake, the restaurant, and the ride there – how no guardrails lined the mountain roads, and how my driving made her wish she was Catholic so she could genuflect, make the sign of the cross, and pray the Rosary, all while trying not to pee her pants. The story always ends with her saying that treacherous ride was nothing compared to the next day: "And if that wasn't enough, the next day she took us to where she was *living*."

"Where she was living? You mean what she was living *in*," my dad would interject.

On the way to the airport, they tried to get me to come home. "No," I said. "But thanks for asking."

THE CALL TO COME IN

◊

In October 1973, Saudi Arabia, along with Libya and a few other Arab states, gave me the nudge I needed to get on with my life by audaciously instituting an oil embargo against the United States. We were, you see, friends with their enemy. It was an ingenious weapon. Using it resulted in a drastic increase in gas prices. The effect was immediate.

Rather than engaging in a show of histrionics, however, Americans hunkered down and showed the countries of the Middle East we couldn't be foiled that easily. All across the nation, steps were taken to conserve energy: speed limits were reduced, thermostats were turned down, and carpooling was encouraged. The Wrigley Building in Chicago turned off the outside structure lights that had been on for fifty years. Bank of America didn't erect the "tree of lights" at its headquarters in San Francisco; billboard lights were turned off in Seattle; and Rhode Island went to daylight savings time so there'd be more natural light in the evenings. Colorado did its part, too, and that's where OPEC nabbed me.

The amount of liquid propane in the cylinder strapped onto the back of the bus was getting low. When I called to get more, I was told that in an effort to conserve, no requests for new accounts were being accepted. Dan had filled the tank in Arkansas. "Maybe you can get it off by yourself and take it down to the gas station, miss. They might fill it for you." I got a friend to help. We wrangled that cylinder like we were steer-roping at the rodeo, but to no avail. I learned about reverse threads and got a whiff that my school-bus days were numbered.

What could I do but climb aboard the bandwagon of conservation? Refrigerated foods were placed outside,

Julie Andrews, a hermit, a realization, and a reality

where the air was cooler. Peanut butter and jelly sandwiches were slated for breakfast; celery, carrots, crackers and dip made for a cold but healthy supper. I put on an extra sweater and let Zeb sleep with me. Then the snow came.

The dismal outlook smoldering for weeks engulfed me. Two friends I'd met while taking classes in Boulder the year before invited me to join them for Thanksgiving dinner. Sweet potatoes with mini marshmallows melted on top were my contribution to the day's cornucopia of scrumptious edibles. But to the consternation of my friends, I didn't stay long enough to find out how they or anything else tasted. The unflappable progression of the external world had pushed my unstable internal world until the measure of irritability within me reached maximum proportions, turning me and Zebulon around, and driving us back to the comfort of our home in the bus. But once there, I realized I was so frustrated that I might go bonkers. I'd come to the edge of a parapet beginning to crumble. If I didn't do something soon, it would break apart, and I'd fall with it into the abyss where people surely fell who didn't make something of themselves.

I had to get back outside. "Come on there, Master Pike. Let's go. Snow or no snow, we're goin' up Sugarloaf. I need to get outta here." Jamming my knit cap onto my head as I stepped from the bus for the second time that day, I glanced back. I caught sight of the school's French horn I'd hung on the bulkhead between the bed and kitchen area, and, without my noticing, took a mental snapshot of it.

The dusting of snow at the top of Sugarloaf resembled the sweetener the mountain was named for. Zeb and I sat in absent-minded affection looking at it and the broader view. Sounds coming on the updraft from

THE CALL TO COME IN

houses far below diverted my attention. Dads were revving chain saws; children were squealing mercilessly in their wintertime play; mothers were calling for all of them – kids *and* dads – to come in.

Without transition, for epiphanies require no time or space, the key turned in the lock. In my mind's eye, I saw the horn hanging on the bulkhead. It was music. It had always been music. I never believed I was good enough – could be good enough, on either horn or piano – to make my vision of it a reality. I had tried to minimize its importance, to discount its meaning, because I thought that to include it in my daily life – to fulfill my vision – meant it had to be what I did for a living. The reality I struggled with was that the opportunity for this was long past. But now I understood that music was too much a part of me. Music could be – had to be – in my life, but it did not have to put the bread on the table. Something else could do that, and whatever it was wouldn't be all that important. So long had I mired in my private torment, believing that the vision I couldn't shake could never live as one with the reality I couldn't dismiss, that I'd almost buckled under. Suddenly, I saw they didn't have to live as one.

The next day, I called the Denver Symphony, got the names and numbers of the horn section, called one, started taking proper lessons, and took my life out of idle and put it into first gear. What to do for a living was no longer a painful concern. It would fall into place soon on its own, I had no doubt.

◊

At the beginning of December, the propane was, ominously, close to gone. Zeb and I were going to bed at 7 p.m. because it was too cold to stay out from under the

Julie Andrews, a hermit, a realization, and a reality

covers. Wearing long johns, a turtleneck, pajamas, scarf, gloves and a watch cap for bedtime garb, I read for as long as I could and then slept for as long as I could. The fellow who lived in the last house on Sugarloaf Mountain Road offered me a ride to and from Boulder, cutting my daily walk from four miles to two, just the knowledge of which made extricating myself from bed in the mornings less dreaded. Unfortunately, this reprieve was temporary because the ever deepening snow and increasingly frigid nights were making the 8 a.m. deadline difficult to meet. Hunkered down under blankets and sleeping bag, chewing on a cold grilled cheese sandwich from a diner in town, I thought about investing in a pair of cross-country skis to relieve the situation. The hardened grease-saturated bread, however, brought me to the present, and, with a look of disdain at my so-called meal, I surrendered to the moment: I lit the stove. Zeb and I shared a can of Dinty Moore and let the bus get nice and toasty. As the night wore on and the silently falling snow descended upon us, three witches waltzed round and round and round the cauldron of our cave and sealed our fate.

◊

Zeb was a trouper about staying behind at the bus when I left in the mornings, but the next day, he insisted on following me. Each time I looked back, there he was, on his haunches, regarding me expectantly, but each time, I'd yell at him, "Go home, Zeb. Go on, now!" Another twenty yards, another look back, and there he'd be. "Zeb, I said go on home!" After the fifth or sixth time, he obeyed.

When I returned that afternoon, however, he didn't come trotting out to greet me as usual. "Zeb! Zeb!

THE CALL TO COME IN

Zebulon Pike, Jr., where are you?" He was nowhere to be found. Stomping through the snow every which way, left and right, all the way back to my ride's house, I searched for him, kicking at the snow, and calling his name.

"Have you seen Zeb?" I asked when I got there.

"No," my rideshare answered with clear concern. "Why? Is he missing?"

"He wanted to come with me today, but I wouldn't let him. He's never done that before. I kept yelling at him, and now he's gone and I can't find him."

"That pack of wild dogs came through earlier today. Maybe he decided to join up with them."

"Maybe it was coyotes. I kept telling him to go back. I'm worried he followed me too far and lost his way."

My nearest neighbor looked at me in a way that let me know neither of us wanted to continue speculating. "No telling what happened, Lois. I'm sorry. I'll keep a lookout for him."

"Thank you. God, I'm worried. Oh, hey – I meant to tell you this morning that I stayed warmer a lot longer than usual walking here, and I was wondering if you thought it might be because I put the gas on and let the bus get warm. You think I stayed warmer because my body temperature was higher?"

"Are you running out of gas?"

"Well, after last night, I'm completely out. It *was* nice not having to wear gloves to bed, though." A queer look came over his face that told me something was wrong. I'd admitted too much.

"You can't go back there, Lois. You'll freeze."

"No, I won't."

"Yes. You will." He made serious eye contact until what he said sunk in. Zeb was gone, and it was time for me to go, too. "Stay here tonight," he said. "You can get

Julie Andrews, a hermit, a realization, and a reality

your stuff out of the bus tomorrow morning. I'll come with you and help look for Zeb while we're at it."

Sadness fell down around me. "All right." I felt defeated, but letting Zeb down was unforgivable. "May I use your phone?"

"It's in the kitchen – on the wall next to the fridge. I'll go get the spare bedroom ready for you." I dialed slowly.

"Daddy?"

"What is it?"

"I want to come home."

9 Gaffed

Nothing surprised my dad. That's why *I* was surprised at *his* surprise when he saw me coming in the back door as he was going out.
"What are you doing here?"
"Hi, Dad. I got a ride from the airport. I didn't want to bother you."
"Picking my daughter up at the airport is not bothering me."
"I know, but . . . Hey, Skippy! Hey, boy. How's the Skipper-dipper-do? He's getting fat, Dad."
"Yeah, well, that's your mother's department. You want some coffee? I was just going out to the garage to get a fresh can." I watched him shuffle past me in his slippers. Home sweet home.
"No, thanks. What else ya got?"
"How about some Tastykakes?"
"Did you buy me Tastykakes?"
"I did. Nothing but the best for the wanderer."
"Got any milk?"
"That's a dumb question to ask a milkman. Go on in, and I'll fix you right up." The TV was on, loud and obnoxious as usual.
"Where's Mom?" I called into the kitchen.

"The old battle ax? She went to New York for the weekend."

"New York? What'd she go there for?" I'd never known my mom to go to anywhere for a weekend, let alone New York City. This was interesting. I stepped into the kitchen to hear more.

"She went with her girlfriends. She'll be home tonight."

"Her girlfriends?" Not only did my mother not go anywhere on weekends, she certainly never went there with girlfriends. I guessed things had changed since I left home. "What's on for tonight?"

"Mannix."

"Can I watch?"

"The chair's in there waitin' for ya. Go sit down. I'll bring you your snack."

"Man, oh, man! Dad – Butterscotch Krimpets and Chocolate Cupcakes. What are you trying to do to me?"

"That one's got cream inside."

"I know. Believe me, I know. Oh, man, this is good. Hey, it's starting."

He slid into his place on the couch. My concession to Dad's addiction was rare; my willingness to partake of it even more so. I settled deeper into the recliner, feeling more like I just returned from an expedition to the Himalayas rather than from a few cold weeks in Colorado.

Halfway through vicariously experiencing the second Mannix car chase of the evening, we heard the sound of the storm door opening, and then the back door being unlocked and opened as my mom made her entry.

"We're in here!" Dad shouted.

"We? Is she here already? Where is she? There you are. How'd you get here so fast?"

"My magic carpet."

Gaffed

"Smarty pants." She was happy; her cheeks rosy. "Whew, I'm bushed. Help me carry these things to the bedroom."

With no compunction about leaving Mannix in the lurch, I picked up Mom's suitcase, and Skippy and I tagged along behind her.

"Look at that dog. Following you wherever you go," said Mom.

"He is not! He's following you! You can't still be jealous."

"Sometimes I think he dreams about you. You knew he was supposed to be my dog."

"I can't believe this, Mom. That dog is clearly all yours. It's not my fault the breeder delivered him while I was at home and you were at work."

"Well, I still think it was mean of you for bonding with Skippy before I laid eyes on him."

It wasn't worth responding to her old resentment so I changed the subject and the impending mood.

"How was your trip?" I asked.

As she unpacked and changed into more comfortable clothes, we talked. "Great. How was your flight? Skippy, get down," she said, kneeling to appease him with a scratch behind the ear.

"It was OK. What'd you do?"

"Oh, the usual. We went to the art museum and the top of the Empire State Building, and . . . we went to a Broadway play. Oh, it was wonderful," she said on the exhale. She then clutched the blouse she was holding next to her heart and exclaimed, "We had a wonderful time!" With that, she hopped onto the bed like a little girl getting the birthday invitation she'd hoped for. She said the word "we" like that same little girl who knew the sender of the invitation without having to look. I knew who sent it, too. I went to the bedroom door and closed it.

"You better be careful how you say 'we' in front of Dad."

"What do you mean?" Without raising her head, her eyes traveled up to meet mine. A thief tired of hiding, a fox on the run, she was ready to be found out.

"You know what I mean." With that, the flush drained out of her face and onto the floral design of the bedspread. I sat down beside her. "Would I like him?" She studied her hands, which were now palms up in her lap. I waited. She took too long to answer, and she knew it. It was too late. She had no alternative.

"He makes me happy. He reads. He does sweet things for me, and he enjoys taking me to the theater."

"What's his name?"

"I'm not telling you."

"Why not?"

"Because I don't want to."

"What about Dad?"

"Oh, I'm not leaving your father. He's a good man and provides for me the best he can, but sometimes I just can't stand that television and his cigarette smoking and his grunts and belching. He never takes me anywhere, and when he does, he embarrasses me to no end. He doesn't know how to act in public. It makes me want to scream."

"Is this guy married?"

"No. He never married. He lives with his mother. His dad died when he was a boy. She sent him to a private boys' school, which he thinks the world of – it's where he got his education and learned how to be a gentleman."

"Which Dad isn't, I guess," I said, anger encroaching.

"If you're going to start accusing me, I'll stop talking."

Gaffed

"Sorry."

"You don't know what it's like. All these years. Did I ever tell you about David?"

"You've mentioned him, but you've never really told me much. He was the guy before Dad, right?"

"I met him after your dad. Did I tell you he died in the war?"

"No."

"Well, he did."

"Tell me about it."

"He died in France. There's not much to tell."

"So, all these years, you've been thinking about him?"

"Yes. I know it sounds crazy. I can't say how things would have turned out with him, but I can't help wondering. He was kind. Like . . . "

"Like Mr. No Name. And that's why you're with him?"

"Yes, I suppose so."

"Dad's just gruff, Mom. I wouldn't say he's unkind."

"It amounts to the same thing."

We sat with our thoughts for a few minutes. She was the first to speak.

"When your dad came home from overseas, getting married was the right thing to do, but I think after he made a home for us and for you, he felt he'd met his obligation. It was enough for him, and he thought it should have been enough for me. But it wasn't."

"Maybe he just couldn't give anymore. Maybe he gave all he could fighting, came home, started a life here, and got his part of the American Dream. Then he was done. Heck, I don't know, Mom. Maybe he gave all he could give, got all he wanted, and now he's tired."

"But it's not enough. Maybe he gave all he was willing to give and thinks I should like it or lump it and play my part, too. But a woman is not a man, and a man can't decide for a woman what her part is. It wasn't enough for me to be the girl who waited faithfully at home and then become the obedient wife who . . . it's not your dad's fault, Lois." Then the words I abhorred: "You can't expect one man to do it all."

"Wait a minute. I thought you were faithful to Dad while he was overseas."

"When he left, we agreed we'd see how we felt when the war was over. We made no commitments. Then I met David, but after he was killed, the letters between your dad and me became more serious, and yes, I was faithful."

"Did he know about David?"

"No, that would have been cruel. What do you take me for?"

It was the words of John Knowles that helped me understand my father, but it was Dorothy Parker's pen that revealed my mother's moment in history in the poem, "Penelope":

> In the pathway of the sun,
>   In the footsteps of a breeze,
> Where the world and sky are one,
>   He shall ride the silver seas
>   He shall cut the glittering wave.
> I shall sit at home, and rock;
> Rise, to heed a neighbor's knock;
> Brew my tea, and snip my thread;
> Bleach the linen for my bed.
>   They will call him brave.

I spent that winter in Vineland working the night shift as the admitting clerk in the hospital emergency room. On my first day off, I took a bus to Giardinelli's

Gaffed

instrument store in New York and bought the 1950 Reynolds Contempora French horn I would play for the next thirty years. The music teacher I found in Vineland billed himself as a Jack-of-all-brass-instrument-trades, proving the adage when I discovered he was master of none. The experience of taking lessons with the fourth horn in the Denver Symphony taught me that if I really wanted music to be the important focus in my life, I needed to be living near a major symphony.

This realization allowed the question of career, which had been sitting in the dugout, to approach the plate. Tying a "where" to the unknown "what" was promising. At least I'd have a location from which to bat. Not yet sold on the advantages of completing a college education, I had to do something that did not require a bachelor's degree, yet wouldn't bore me to tears. The play calculated, I just needed a little skill on the swing. This had me behind in the count, but not yet out. Networking via friends and the ladies at the reference desk in the library got me some leads on vocational schools in cities with orchestras. On the mound, the wind-up in motion, the release – and a call from a friend in Kent that threw me a curve.

"Hell-o."

"Hey. It's Arlene." Arlene was an old friend from the food co-op days who was dear to me and with whom I kept in touch.

"Arlene. Hey, what's goin' on? How the halibut are you?"

"Has Theresa called you, yet?"

"No."

"Hugh's dead."

"What?"

THE CALL TO COME IN

"Hugh's dead. His obituary was in the paper today. I wanted to be the one to tell you, so you'd get it without the sugar and honey-dipped Theresa-coating."

Sinking fast, I asked, "What happened?"

"He had an aneurysm. He died in bed at his place in Cleveland. A friend of his found him when he went over to see why Hugh was late to meet him."

All I could get out was "Oh," followed by an anemic, "Thanks for telling me."

My newly revived emotional equilibrium went into a nosedive. Hugh and I had spent the summer going back and forth between my campsite near Sugarloaf and his home at the base of Twin Sisters. He'd come to orchestra rehearsals to watch me play and give me a ride up the mountain. When he left at the end of summer, we hadn't established anything definitive, but we stayed in contact, hoping to spend some time together in Ohio after Christmas. I thought about him as a man I could marry, which was saying a lot for the loner chick who didn't let anybody in.

I didn't sleep that night, for my head was filled with thoughts of Hugh. Replay after replay of the things we did together and the things I envisioned we'd do went round and round until, at about 3 a.m., I noticed how brief the time was that I actually grieved. The true moments of mourning had been different from all the other hours of the vigil. They were more like the center of meditation – a place you don't know you've gone until you return. All the others were selfish indulgence.

A few days later, when I must have been looking particularly doleful, my mom stopped me in the hallway that led to the back of the house and asked what was wrong. That was all it took. Sliding down the damask wallpaper, my plaid pajamas catching on its raised pattern, I burst into tears.

"I want a home. I don't mean to make you feel bad, but this one doesn't work for me anymore. I want my own."

"You're not making me feel bad. That's the way it's supposed to be. No, honey, you're not making me feel bad at all."

"I'm not?" I asked, as I wiped tear sniffles onto my pajama sleeve.

"No, you're not. You should want a home of your own."

"Oh, Mom, I'm twenty-four years old!"

"Be patient. Things don't happen overnight. If you want it, it'll happen. You'll see."

◊

I returned to Colorado late that spring, because I didn't know what else to do. Hugh's mom said his friends could go through his house and pick something out to remember him by. I chose a photograph of Central Park that he and I had talked about. It hung in his bathroom above the toilet, next to the tub. One day, while I was showering, he came in and sat down on the toilet.

"What are you doing?" I asked.

"What one usually does on this specially-made-for-the-purpose seat. Do you mind?"

"No. I guess not." I had never been in a bathroom with a man before. It felt strange and possibly not right, like it was something you're only supposed to do with your husband. At first, we didn't speak.

To break the awkward silence, I said, "Tell me something."

"OK."

THE CALL TO COME IN

"That wrinkled-up photograph – is that an old man or an old woman?"

"It's an old man."

"Where is he?"

"In Central Park, across from Belvedere Castle and Turtle Pond."

"Why do you have it?"

A pleasant and casual conversation ensued as we each tended to business. It was an intimacy I'd never known before, so while I was going through the house looking for something to remember him by, I knew that was the memento I wanted. Now, it hangs on the wall in my entryway, with two letters hidden behind the frame. One is from Hugh's closest friend at the time; one is from his mom. Both are telling me of his death. It sounds crazy; I can't say how things would have turned out with him, but I can't help wondering. He was kind, and I missed him, sometimes, over all the years that followed.

◊

Camping wasn't making it for me this time around. Nothing much was. I was working as a line girl at Furr's Cafeteria in Boulder, handing out red and orange sugar water. I wasn't practicing horn nor was I playing piano, but I was socializing. Generally, I was a flounder. Burying myself in the sand with my eyes peering out one side of my head, I hoped nobody gaffed me as I scooted along. In mid-summer, I received a letter from my mom, typed on bright yellow stationery.

July 28, 1974

Dear Lois,

I'm waiting for Walt to pick me up. As always, he's late. Dad's golfing team is having their annual

Gaffed

picnic, and I'm to meet him at Centerton with Walt. Dad invited Walt and his family as his guests.

I spent three days preparing for it. Baked a cake, made potato salad, made eggplant; made hamburgers, hot dogs and all that goes with it. The team is providing the corn, soda and beer.

Guess what? Walt's here. Will continue when I get back.

Well, we're back. It was hot. Didn't eat half the food. I brought the mustard you made, and everyone couldn't get over how good it was.

Johnny (Walt's boy) said, "How did she make it?" I gave Louise a small jar of it. Hope you don't mind.

Trish (at work) is pregnant. I had a long talk with her, and she wants to continue working. I told her she would have to put in at least twenty hours a week. She thinks she can manage that. If it doesn't work out, I'll have to go through training someone.

Helen (at work) is breaking up with her husband. I should say he walked out on her. She is in a bad way, but she has been asking for it. She hasn't been what you would call a stay-at-home devoted one, either. They were married last September. Trish and I kid around with her, saying she should celebrate her first wedding anniversary by having an annulment(not really funny).

I have another week-and-three-days' vacation left for this year. Dad suggested I spend three at the shore, and then he can get a week in September or November, and maybe we can do something together.

Lois, I don't think I ever told you how much I do love your father. You know how he waits on me and does so many things to please me. I speak and he makes things for me. Sometimes I get angry because he doesn't educate his mind more by reading or taking a course somewhere in something, but his good points outweigh his weak ones. I suppose I do things that he doesn't like, either. But it has been a good marriage. Almost twenty-nine years.

THE CALL TO COME IN

Went to visit Grandpop. He was asking about you and wanted to know if you're still making cheese. He can't understand why you have to go away all the time. He is slowing down a bit. Getting up at eight, not six. He only farms a few things now, like potatoes, peas and corn. He was eighty-seven last birthday. Oh yes, you were here.

I wish we could hear you on the horn. You must be improving. The ribbon on this typewriter should be turning about now, but it looks like I have to help it. There, I did.

Boy, I'm writing a lot. You know how much I don't like to. But I guess it's because I have you on my mind all the time and miss you very much, and pray you're taking care of yourself. I hope everything that's good for you works out. It's difficult to know what is good, but often just a little faith will bring it to pass, and all is well.

I'm getting tired. It's been a long day. Take care, and we love you very, very, very much. Remember, "I love you so much, I don't know how much."(Quote from little Lois.)

       Mother

It took until October for me to respond. Then I did the one thing that may have compelled me, finally, to grow up. For her birthday, I sent my mom a copy of the book *Ragtime* by E.L. Doctorow with this inscription:

> I have seen you as a child.
> I have seen you as a woman.
> You are my mother, my sister,
> and my friend.
> I love you.

I signed it, "Anelle," which is a play on Lena spelled backwards, and the name she once told me she wanted to christen me but didn't.

Part Three

The Lament

We all were sea-swallow'd, though some cast againe,
(And by that destiny) to performe an act
Whereof, what's past is Prologue, what to come,
In yours, and my discharge.
                    Antonio in *The Tempest* (II.i)

10 A home of my own

"Mommy, Mommy! Come quick. Polly Esther's in trouble!"

"Seanie. Sweetie. What's the matter?"

"Look, Mommy. Look!"

"Oh, my gosh. Jeez Louise! Honey, go get your dad. Hurry! Run! Tell him the lambing has started. Patrick!"

It was March 1988, fourteen years after I cried to my mom over not having a home of my own. Now I had not only a home, I had a home*stead*. On that day, it looked like we were going to get yet another lesson in animal husbandry, right there in our own paddock, in dirt wet with rain from the previous night. I shooed the other ewes away, dragged a bale of straw out of the barn, popped it open, and scattered it in a wide, thick semicircle around and under Polly Esther, the whole time watching her and waiting for my partner, in wedlock as well as in business and homesteading, to come down from the house. We weren't ready, but in less than a minute and a half, he came through the gate, swiping redwood sawdust from his jeans. Together we played the midwife for Polly in the birthing of her twin babies. Over the course of the next few days, we did the same for Dorothea and Nanette. With the full complement of springtime's Easter-bonnet finery for a backdrop to our toil, we soon had a barn

THE LAMENT

full of bleating lambs newly inducted into the already burgeoning community of animals living on God's Little Acre, the name Patrick and I gave our piece of the planet.

This appellation did not manifest itself overnight. Ten years earlier, in the fall of 1977, our measure of real estate was nothing more than a hill of decomposed granite, its clumped and yellow grains overgrown with Scotch broom and poison oak. At its crest, the cellar and sub-floor of a house sat poised and ready for the wall-raising that would be our official first date.

Our unofficial first date was blind. It was arranged by mutual friends, Kay and Neal. Kay was a friend of mine from the veterinary clinic in Santa Cruz where I was working as a technician. Pat worked with Neal as a machinist for the Lick Observatory machine shop based on the campus of the university in Santa Cruz. Kay and Neal would often report to each other the stories of woe told by the two lovelorn puppies at their respective workplaces. Kay decided to do something about it by giving a dinner party and inviting both Pat and me. To make them happy afterward, Pat and I exchanged numbers. That's how we put it; but secretly, we were attracted to each other. I liked Pat's button-up, hand-sewn moccasins. He liked my smile. When he asked me to come to his wall-raising, I viewed the event more as my chance to learn how to build the house my old co-op cohorts and I often spoke of, rather than an afternoon with a potential boyfriend. Irrespective of that, or maybe because of it, he let me come back whenever I wanted. Whenever I wanted became every day. Soon we were rewarding ourselves for a hard day's work with walks in the woods or dinners at the local Italian restaurant. Within seven

A home of my own

months, Patrick and I, with the help of his best friend Ed, turned that initial wall into a genuine abode.

"Well," he concluded one Saturday while he was filling finish-nail holes in the bathroom window trim and I was installing driftwood cabinet handles we'd combed from the beach, "you've spent all this time helping me build the house, shouldn't you move in and live in it with me, too?" This was sound reasoning.

We married in May 1978, honeymooning in Pat's Econoline van, or, as he called it, the Great White Rhinoceros. We brought along Windigo, our malamute-wolf, and weaved along the California coast until we got to Crater Lake, Oregon, all the while discussing the terrific things we'd do with our first twenty-five years. When we returned home, we continued the train of thought by planting a garden and preparing the ground at the bottom of our property for an orchard. We staked a fence around the perimeter, and with all the perspiration required, erected retaining walls and tiers with sets of stairs so we could easily go between the house and barn, the garden and orchard. We then returned to the top of the acre and put an addition onto the house.

It went on like this for nine years. For nine years we had the perfect marriage. Somewhere in that ninth year, though, something went wrong. Even though the Scotch broom and poison oak were replaced with ivy; the garden thrived in rich, black loam where the decomposed granite used to be; a barnyard was brimming with farm animals; a supportive family of friends and relatives surrounded us; and the orchard was planted with a certain Valentine bouquet of bare-root fruit trees, something was amiss.

We knew we had come to a place on the matrimonial time line marked with a toothpick tag, but we didn't know what it signified. As far as we knew, we'd done everything we were supposed to do. We had weekly date nights. They were usually on Saturdays and, just as usually, we went to dinner at one of our two or three favorite restaurants. We also worked on projects together. One December, our friends Jack and Carol taught us how to work with stained glass. It was a lot of fun, and needless to say, everybody got a stained glass window hanging for Christmas that year. From time to time we walked Fall Creek or the local water company's watershed property, both adjacent to our house. We did this so we could check in on how we were feeling about us. We didn't do this as often after the boys were born, but at that point, we made sure to have family time. Bicycling Henry Cowell State Park was often the choice for that part of our perfect marriage.

 We did all the right things, yet our life together reminded me of the paint-by-number kits I loved doing every summer in the backyard studio at my Aunt Margaret's. Even though I fastidiously filled in all the colors, the separation between them was too distinct, too noticeable. Finally, holding a finished piece at arm's length, I saw that my work had no life to it because I'd been tracing a template made by somebody else.

 This wasn't completely true when it came to the work Pat and I had put into our marriage. Our best guess was that our emptiness had some Freudian thing to do with our parents. We decided to get counseling, and what we learned was this: We were each a product of a stale marriage between a couple proficient at ignoring the elephant in the room. Realizing we were experiencing our own ramifications of connubial lethargy, we didn't want to follow suit, but the imprint of our role models was impossible to eradicate. After nine years, date nights

A home of my own

were not really dates because they weren't romantic. Fun projects stopped. Walks continued, including lots of talk – about everything but us. Family time was a superficial activity, not a time of bonding.

Striving to shake the detachment we felt became an exasperating tug o' war. Injecting even a modicum of vitality into our own marriage proved arduous and uncomfortable. It was easier to look outside ourselves for a remedy. Pat looked at *Penthouse Magazine* ("I was curious about the pictures of Madonna they've been talking about on the news."), and I made googly eyes at Ian ("It's just a crush."). Why we desperately defended individuality while trying to maintain a marital bond beats me, but that's what we did. The counselor asked about something that arrested my thoughts. I had an idea of it, but except for transitory moments, wasn't sure I'd ever felt it. It was something I knew had to be within me as well as within my relationship to Pat. What she asked us about was joy. When was the last time we felt joyful?

◊

At a session that took place early in the autumn prior to Polly Esther's big day, in that part of the season that speaks of its arrival in scents and sighs and susurrations, we agreed that our marriage, by then ten years long, was worth working on for one more year before throwing in the towel. To allow the lifestyle we created with unflagging industry to disintegrate would have made all the effort of constructing it futile. Yet, we didn't have what we needed to keep it intact. We'd had the tools necessary for building a solid home and an enviable way of living, but we were missing the nuts and bolts required to make it last.

THE LAMENT

"The two of you have created a perfect world. You really have," the counselor said. "What you need to work on now is you, the two of you – the thing that makes you a couple. The thing that goes on between the two of you, not between you and the world you've made. Do you think you could do that? Is that worth a year?"

Like two remorseful fifth graders in front of the assistant principal after a schoolyard scuffle, we responded in unison, "Yes." And then, "We'll try."

"Good. Let's see, then." Swiveling around to her desk, our therapist retrieved her schedule book. We watched her leaf through the pages of what would be our last year together as if they were a flip book of cartoon figures rashly racing toward the edge of the flat world they didn't ask to be living on. "Next August twenty-seventh. Saturday. Exactly a year. How's that sound?"

"OK," the duly reprimanded playground pair replied, and with the date that would dangle in front of us like a hairy monster spider for the next 366 days (for 1988 was a leap year), we staggered out.

Three months into the experiment, I began a new journal. It contained a heading that gave it the look of a term paper – or maybe a gravestone. The cynical, self-deprecating tone of the opening paragraph made it plain that it was the diary of a divorce.

> November 23rd 1987
> Lois Wayne T_____
> Age: 37
> Married 10 years
> Two children 3 & 5
>   What a title page. Statistically, clinically, it tells it all. Classic example. But let's ask the heart. That's

A home of my own

where the story lies. "Thank you for staying home and trying to keep the family together," he said. "A lesser person would have left me by now, and I know you are trying." What a guy. But how about me? Trying baloney. I'm fantasizing a whole other world, waiting for something to happen beyond my control in this one. Fat chance. But I've still got some diplomatic immunity left. And I intend to use it all up. And what the hell does that mean? It means the control was mine all along.

I went in the water today. It's always the same – incredible. I catch some waves, but mostly I have a love affair with the ocean. It talks to me. It says something different each time. But always something that leaves me exhilarated. The kind of happiness I experience riding no hands, cruise speed on my bike. Only better. Is freedom selfish? I almost lost that girl. Lord, it was close. Scary close. I never knew I'd be able to get near that close. So I didn't pay attention and . . .

I see myself in four different rooms. 1) I've signed the papers. The place is mine. It is dusk and I go in. There in the empty room, I sit down and say, "Well, you got what you wanted." I cry a little. 2) The same room, only the kids are with me, and we are unpacking. There is some sadness in looking back, but mostly we're looking forward, and I am relieved. 3) At home. Resigned to unanswered questions and unhappiness. 4) Happy family. In the TV room. All four. Goofing around. Happier than before because of what we'd learned.

Now eight months into that pivotal year, it wasn't just Polly Esther who was in trouble. Pat and I were spinning round and round in a Disneyland teacup, captives of centrifugal force, wondering if the barricade we were up against would suddenly shatter, throwing us into outer space. Lambing was a distraction from the lunacy of it all, bringing some relief from the decision we knew we'd have to make by summer's end. It was nice to be doing something that made us feel close.

Other than Polly Esther, Dorothea, and Nanette, we had an imposing ram, a pig named Bacon, a horse, a cocky rooster, and what he perceived as his harem of ten Rhode Island Reds, a Banty, and three Cornish Cross. We also had the barn, a stable, and a coop to house them in, which we, of course, built. The menagerie was made complete with a turkey, rabbits, a pony, two dogs, two cats, and two little boys. The animals' ages varied between newborn and fully mature. Their care, feeding, and expected outcome were denotative; that is, we could get a pretty clear-cut definition on our pork and mutton. The two little boys were four and six. Their care, feeding, and expected outcome were embodied in another literary term: ambiguity. Raising animals was what writing a newspaper article might be like for a veteran journalist well schooled in the five W's – straightforward. Raising Austin and Sean was like writing an editorial – opinionated.

An editorial on raising children would predictably be answered with a barrage of letters from parents, if the parents had the time, but no young parent has time to read the op-ed page, let alone write a response. I felt like Susy Lansing, the au pair in Edith Wharton's novel, *The Glimpses of the Moon*, whose job reflected the haggard life of parents:

> . . . every moment of her waking hours was packed with things to do at once, and other things to remember to do later. There were only five Fulmers; but at times they were like an army with banners, and their power of self-multiplication was equalled only by the manner in which they could dwindle, vanish, grow mute, and become as it were a single tumbled brown

A home of my own

head bent over a book in some corner of the house in which nobody would ever have thought of hunting for them.

On the evening of the last day that "the baby sheepies came out," Sean, Austin, and I were "tumbled brown head bent over a book." Because kids have a pythonic way of showing their affection, we sat scrunched on our couch like little fluffed wrens huddled along a winter's branch. Tonight's classic was Dr. Seuss's *The Butter Battle Book*. Just as we were turning the page to get our hundred thousandth look at the triple-sling jigger that Chief Yookeroo had ordered the Boys in the Back Room to design, Austin stopped and commanded:

"Tell us a Mommy-Daddy story."

"Yeah. Tell us a Mommy-Daddy story," Sean chimed in.

"Oh, you don't want to hear a dumb old Mommy-Daddy story."

"Yes, we do."

"We do."

"We do!"

"Tell us, Mommy, tell us."

"Tell us about you and Daddy and Windy, and how you made Cody come out."

"Daddy-Mommy. Daddy-Mommy. Windy! Daddy-Mommy. Windy! Daddy-Mommy-Windy!"

"Daddy-Mommy-Windy!"

My cherubs had a knack for expressing themselves regardless of others' desires to do likewise. The resulting din entered my brain from all sides. But the goading of want was a wise thing. It knew to never make its case without the pinches, pulls, giggles, and love punches that made a mom melt.

"Oh, OK. You wouldn't rather hear about how you two came into this world?"

"Yeah, that one!" the ever-accommodating Sean joyfully sang out.

"Yeah, that one, too," Austin eagerly concurred. "But this one first, Mommy. Ple-e-e-ase."

"Well, I don't know." I paused for effect – for moms like to have fun, too. "One night . . . "

"Yay!"

"Yay!"

"One night," I continued, as I tilted my head down and rubbed noses with each of my offspring, "when your dad, Windigo, and I were driving home from Tu-tu's with all our Christmas presents in the back of the Rhino . . . "

"I forget what the Rhino was, Mommy."

"You stupid. It was Dad's van."

"Don't talk to your brother like that, Austy. Be nice and listen. When Daddy and I were coming home with our Christmas presents that night, we went around a curve on that nasty-wasty, curvy-wurvy Route 9 . . ."

"Daddy was driving too fast, Mommy," Austin said in his factual-attention-to-detail way.

"Yes. But we leave that part to the imagination. Now as I was saying . . . while we were going around that super tight curve, the side door of the Rhino burst open, and out flew all of our brand new toys and things. Maybe not all of them, but a bunch of them. We could tell because we heard them. We realized we mustn't have closed the door properly back at Tu-tu and Pa-pa's."

"Grown-ups don't play with toys," Sean rebuked. I could see he was starting to sketch illustrations in the picture book of his mind.

"Believe me, they were toys. Now, are you guys going to let me tell the story, or not?" Silence was the

A home of my own

affirmation. "All right, then. Move over, Rover. You're squishing me." Wriggles and jiggles dying away, I continued uninterrupted . . .

We wanted to pull over, but that road is so narrow, we had to go a ways before we found a place. It was very dark. Daddy got the flashlight from the glovie, and we hopped out to go and see what we could see. There was a steep drop-off down to the river where our presents spilled out, but with some scrambling to keep ourselves upright, and some rummaging in the wet, yucky, dead leaves, we found everything. When we got back to the van, I noticed that Windigo was gone. So I said to Daddy,

"Hey, where's Windy?"

"I don't know," he said, "She must've gotten out when we did."

And I said, "Oh, no! What should we do?"

"Start calling, I guess," Daddy told me.

So we did, like this: "Windy! Windy! Windigo. Here, girl. Here Windy, Windy, Windy."

I looked down at my sugar-pies. "Come on, you guys. Help out."

"Windy! Windy! Windy, Windy, Windy!" Sean and Austin both hallooed, never taking their minds off the telling of the tale. I smiled.

Then Daddy said, "This isn't doing any good. Let me think." We sat in the van for a while and looked at each other. I could tell your dad was worried. He really loved that dog, you know. Then he said, "Hold it! What's that?"

I looked out the window. "It's Windy! Oh, Windy, you good girl, you. There you are! You scared us. What were you doing? Helping us look for the presents? Did you find an old bone instead? Come on. Into the Rhino with you. There ya go." Daddy drove off and that was that.

THE LAMENT

When we got home, we unloaded everything and had supper – scrambled eggs with sliced-up hot dogs mixed in. Daddy said he'd better go up and feed Cody because it was getting late, and he was probably hungry. Cody was a dog, a malamute-wolf like Windy. He belonged to our friends up the road who always went away for Christmas, so while they were gone, we fed Cody. I like doing stuff like that, so I asked your dad if I could come with him. "OK," he said. "But let's leave Windy home. One heart attack a night is enough."

Our friends lived up along Empire Grade, where there aren't very many houses, and it's rocky and sandy and flat some and hilly some, and dry with lots of pine trees, and there are coyotes and great horned owls. When we got there, I went to the garden hose to get water while Daddy went and got the bag of dog food. Cody lived outside in a big wire pen, where he was also kept tied to a leash whenever the family was away because malamute-wolves have this ancestral call of the wild in them. That means they are always wanting to run free and go hunting.

Cody had a nice doghouse, with a rug and a food bowl and water, and bones from the butcher, so he was OK, but when Daddy reached the pen, he made a terrible discovery. Cody wasn't there! Daddy ran to me, yelling, "Lois, Lois! Cody's gone!" We couldn't believe it. We must have forgotten to put his leash on last time, and a wire fence is no obstacle for a wolf. We felt really bad because we knew that and we were supposed to be taking care of him.

We looked all over – through the brush and hedges, and into the trees – but he was nowhere to be found. It was late by now – 10 o'clock. The moon was up, and I can remember the white, sandy dirt and rocks reflecting its light as we searched. We called and called, like we'd done with Windy. Somehow, we knew we wouldn't be as lucky this time and that getting Cody back wouldn't be as easy, but we called with all our might, anyway. "Cody! Cody! Cody-ohh-dy!" Nothing. What else could we do? Not one sound was coming back at us!

I stopped and waited, to give my boys the time they needed to break from their separate story-dreams so that they could speak their lines from our most cherished of Mommy-Daddy narratives.

"Co – dy," Austin tremulously summoned into the dark night of our story. "Co – dy."

"Oh, Co – dy. Co-ohhh-dy. Where are you, Cody?" Sean called with anxious concern. They knew what was coming, and they couldn't wait. I increased the tension.

I asked Daddy. "What are we going to do?"

"We're going to do what I was going to do back there on Route 9 when I thought I'd lost Windy. Come on, let's go."

"We can't go, Pat. We have to find Cody."

"We're going to go! Come on, get in the van."

"But . . . "

"We have to go get Windy!"

"Huh?"

There was no time to waste answering questions from your goofy mom. Daddy had some thinking to do. We went down the hill and got Windy and brought her back to Cody's pen.

Now it so happened that Cody and Windy were brother and sister. Both were from the same litter of malamute-wolf puppies, and wolves live in packs, but sometimes they divide up – to go on patrol and important stuff like that – and then they aren't sure where the rest of the pack is so they call out to each other – kind of like I do when I want you to come in for dinner. You know it's me because of my special, "Time to come in!" whistle. Wolves have a special way of calling each other, too. They howl. Your dad figured Cody thought of his human family as the pack, and when they left, he'd naturally want to go find them. Daddy remembered about wolves howling and hoped he could get Windy to call Cody to come home.

There we were: Daddy, Windy, and me. Your dad was the first to go. He knelt down low next to Windy and wrapped his arm around her thick, plush fur as she sat on her haunches, and, quietly at first, he called "Ah-oooo. Ah-oooo. Ooo, ooo, ooooo!" Then he tried again, higher and louder and longer, "Ah-ooooooooooo." Windy started getting agitated. She moved back and forth from one front paw to the other. You see, once a wolf hears a howl, she can't resist joining in. In fact, she can't help herself. I was next. I cupped my hands around my mouth, lifted my head and howled my best howl, "Ah-oooo. Ah-ooooooooo." Then Daddy and I howled. Windy was really antsy, now. She tried to forget she was a wolf, but that call of the wild was too strong. She raised her head and stretched her long neck high to the moon and let loose: "Ah-ooooooooo. Oooooooooo." Nothing!

Sean and Austin once again took the cue, and a better climax to a bedtime story there never was. The three of us howled and howled, until my mother instincts told me even the best climax must capitulate to the denouement.

"Shhh!" I suddenly said, quieting my two wolf cubs. "Listen!" Having reverted back to my own childhood, I felt like Princess Summerfall Winterspring whispering something to Buffalo Bob while the kids in the peanut gallery leaned out of their seats to hear what it was. "It's

A home of my own

Cody! Can you hear him? It's like Windy and Mommy and Daddy did that night. The howling worked, you guys. It worked! From way off in the distance, we could hear it. Then it got closer and closer, and we knew it was Cody calling back. Daddy and I stopped and let Windy and Cody carry on their own conversation. When Cody got close enough that we could hear running and twigs breaking, Daddy let Windy go, and before we knew it, two dogs came crashing in at our feet, and we were all jumping for joy. There was petting and roughhousing and "Whoop-de-doos" like you wouldn't believe, and you know . . . dogs and little boys are a lot alike. They always want to play longer, even when they know it's time to come in. But Windy and Cody were so tuckered out that night that Windy went right to the van, and Cody didn't have to be coaxed into his pen. When he was inside, Daddy secured him on his leash. He made sure of that! We filled his food and water bowls full to the top and gave him three big Milkbones. We gave three to Windy, too. Then we said "Good-night," climbed into the good old White Rhino, headed for home and went to bed. . . . Just like you two are going to do right now."

The many time tendrils of marriage continued to steal their way into our intimacies. Wharton's story of the Fulmer family continued to speak to me:

> . . . there was little time or space for the indulgence of private sorrows. From morning till night there was always some immediate practical demand on one's attention; and Susy was beginning to see how, in contracted households, children may play a part less romantic but not less useful than that assigned to them in fiction, through the mere fact of giving

their parents no leisure to dwell on irremediable grievances.

Adding an acre crowded with farm animals to Wharton's postulate guaranteed its accuracy.

"You just coming up from the barn?" I asked.

"Yeah."

"How's everybody doin' down there?"

"They're fine. How was it up here tonight?"

"Oh, we got through it without them hitting each other, so that was good. They weaseled the story of Windy and Cody out of me."

"I heard you. It's a winner. You want some ice cream?"

"Yes, please. It's *All Creatures* night. You going to watch it with me?"

"Yep." He went to the kitchen, while I, as Pat would say, "fired up" the TV. He returned with our two favorite stone-ground pottery bowls heaped with mint chocolate chip ice cream that looked like mountains under glossy laminates of hot fudge. Setting mine down in front of me, he expelled a deep breath.

"What a week this has been."

"Tell me about it. But it's over, and we did the lambing all by ourselves."

"We can think that, if you want. Your mom called today. She said something about coming out in June, as usual."

"Pat! Why didn't you tell me she called?"

"I just did."

"Did she say exactly when they'll be here?"

"Yeah, but I forget. She wants you to call her."

"Well, it's too late, now. I'll have to do it tomorrow."

"She said something about your old friend, Cory, too."

A home of my own

"Oh, phooey. I forgot. Cory tried to reach me at their house. She lost our phone number, I guess. I need to get back to her. She and her husband are breaking up."

"Huh. Must be contagious."

"Don't say that. We haven't broken up, yet. Gee whiz, we're supposed to be trying. I thought today was good. Didn't you?"

"Yes. It was." He looked at me through eyes the grated iron doors of a coal furnace. The fire behind them flickered. Lately, good days were not helping put that angry fire out as we thought they would; instead, they seemed to fan the flames of the bad memories and contempt that lay in the recesses of Patrick's heart. The conversational tone we maintained as the fire burned was part of the pathology of our disease.

"What did Cory do for *her* mid-life crisis?"

"What? Pat, I did *not* have an affair with Ian." For almost a year, that name had not been spoken. Taboo in our household, *it* was the elephant in *our* room. The barest allusion to it in eye contact or body language had not been dared, and with each avoidance, the elephant grew ever larger. Unfair, but there it was. I said it. "How many times do I have to tell you that it was just that once. And it wasn't a mid-life crisis."

"Sure."

I tried to take back the hurtful slap, blaming its caustic poignancy on our long day. "Oh, come on. We've had such a nice few days."

"You know what? I'm beat. I don't need to watch *All Creatures* tonight. I'm going to bed."

Shoveling chunks of coal into my own kiln of rancor, I thought, *Be that way!* But I said, "All right. I'll come up in a while."

"OK." As if by habit or because of a soft spot given to fonder memories, he conceded to our sense of decency. "See you in the morning," he said.

I stared at his half-empty ice cream bowl. Rather than make a seething comment about it, I reduced my favorite reaction to Pat's irritating ways to a glower and simply stated "Good-night."

I was wiped out, too, but stayed up to lose myself in the week's episode of a happier couple's life and to wait until my husband was safely asleep on his side of the bed.

> In my own very self, I am part of my family.
> – D. H. Lawrence, *Apocalypse*

11 Family ties

Luciano Pavarotti spent his life bestowing gifts of song. His voice was like a red carpet spread for others to receive respite from the cracked and gravel-strewn pavement beneath their feet. I believe this to be true, but for me, it is only hearsay, for I have never heard a Pavarotti aria from beginning to end.

I received a different type of gift from the opera star, a present I had the pleasure of unwrapping at the start of every one of the six summers my parents came to California to stay with Patrick and me and the boys. The gift Pavarotti gave to me was the image he painted in the opening sentences of his first autobiography; an image that, like the melodious gift of voice he gave to thousands, touched me in a way that had special meaning.

In the passage, he describes his childhood in Modena, Italy, where he lived with adoring aunts and cousins and a loving grandmother who took care of him while his parents worked. There were wide-open spaces for the young ones to play, and though the family didn't have much, they always felt they had enough.

I loved this idea of three generations living in a three-story stone villa on the edge of a Tre Venese vineyard, everybody looking after everybody else right down the line, the way it should be. Jocund children wearing happy spaghetti-smeared faces. Hot-blooded parents and grandparents, content in their years, still in love; trust and security the family tie.

Such active minds we humans have! When I pulled Pavarotti's book down from the shelf to verify that what he'd written was what I recalled, I discovered, to my chagrin, that it was not. Yes, there was a lot of family and a doting grandmother, but there were also a philandering grandfather, an aunt who died an untimely death, and sixteen other families, not all of the Pavarotti clan, living in a large apartment building. Like the party game "Gossip," I heard something very different from what was originally stated. From the full sentences the famous singer wrote, I extrapolated only the words and phrases needed to create a nostalgic painting of the Old World I preferred to visualize.

My grandfather, who emigrated from Stella Cilento, Italy, in 1913 with his wife and four children, who farmed for a living and pressed the grape for relaxation, and with whom I was close, died in 1980. I read Pavarotti's book, *My Own Story*, in 1981 while I was pregnant with Austin and still thinking about my grandpa. It must have been in this heightened condition of hormonal influence that I became quarry to imagery inspired by the notorious maternal feelings that accompany pregnancy. Proving useful the first June I drew upon it, the portrait I painted, which I titled "My Own Image," returned a week or two prior to my folks' arrival each summer. By June of 1988, it was a well-established truth that catapulted me directly into a reality maintained with the cooperation of my parents and children. Pat cooperated, too – at first. After that, I'm not so sure.

Falling in behind Signora Pavarotti, our Italian grandmother – my mom – helped out at home, too, making

Family ties

everything look easy. And for her, it *was* easy because it was an excuse to be with us. Cooking and cleaning were not chores, they were opportunities to spend time with grandchildren. Dusting and vacuuming were synchronized with morning cartoons. Especially important was wiping away the however imaginary overnight build-up of soot that settled under the couch where Austin and Sean sat preoccupied with *The Care Bears*. When *I* was a kid preoccupied with *The Mickey Mouse Club*, I was convinced she performed this same menial task in front of me for the sole purpose of wrecking my day. Forcing me to lift my feet and pushing aside my cereal spoon hand with jabs of the vacuum brush were not viewed as love taps. Her grandsons did not see it this way.

After the day's quota of cartoons, they, at their grandmother's behest, got to share in her convivial take on housework. Shelling peas and mopping floors made for friendly recreation; picking vegetables and collecting eggs were games of hide and seek; doing the dishes was a water sport. The rambunctious interplay between her and my boys, – "Gra'ma, you're silly!" – made me realize that all she was trying to do was make life fun and that, where I irately ignored her for the Mouseketeers, her loving efforts were meeting with success in her grandsons.

Beside helping out around the house, the presence of our matriarch assuaged the stress of hiring a sitter. Not only did it permit me the freedom to manage our business, but it gave me the chance to pursue my creative outlet in the orchestra pit of the local summer stage. Unimpeded by the worry of having a string of mother's helpers on hand while I juggled rehearsal, performance, and work hours was worth its weight in gold. Unlike the average babysitter, a grandmother wouldn't neglect her charges. Breathing over the phone to boyfriend while airbrushing toenails, flipping through *Cosmo* and popping Pepperidge Farm Goldfish would not eclipse the clamor ("What's that *noise?*") of boys boxing in the next room if Grams was holding down the fort. I could come home late, confident I'd not see my sons in a catatonic state in front of the TV or find out they'd been served Pop Tarts and chicken nuggets for supper. I could relax because the house was clean and I knew my boys were taken care of properly. The only advantage the outside babysitter could possibly have over Grandma was that I had no family history with the teenager from down the street.

◊

"So, Mom, what's going on with Cory?" We were standing next to each other at the kitchen counter preparing the gala repast we'd come up with for that afternoon's diversion.

"Oh, honey, haven't you called her yet? It's been four months since she called."

"No, I keep meaning to, but the rehearsal schedule's a bear and the three-hour time difference always gets me. Hand me that paring knife so I can slice up these apples, would you? Plus, the last time I talked to her, she warned me not to be frightened of her prematurely aged face when we visit. It creeped me out. She said the doctor told her it was from all the drugs she did."

"Well, take a minute today and call. I'm sure she'd appreciate it. Here, that knife might need sharpening."

"Yes, Mother. What else shall we put in this orchard picnic of ours?"

"Did you get the chips?"

Family ties

"Oh, right. Thanks. Do you mind finishing up here while I make the burgers and get the grill going? Those are really cute paper plates. Where'd you find them?"

"No, I don't mind. Sean picked them out yesterday when we took our walk into Felton. He's a little doll, that one."

"My cucumber cutie – and here he is! Hi, sweetheart. Where's your brother?"

"Mommy, Sue's here. Can they come to our picnic?'

"I don't see why not."

Running out almost before he ran in, our breathless courier hollered back, "He's the daddy! I'm the puppy!"

"What? What are you guys doing?"

"Knock. Knock."

"Hey, Sue, Come on in. You and the girls are welcome to join us. We've got plenty." Sue Johnson was our neighbor at the bottom of the hill on the other side of the fence from the fruit trees.

"Thank you. We'd love to. It's the perfect day for a picnic. I brought up that rabbit recipe you were asking for." She put an index card down on the chopping block where I was working. "Hi, Mrs. Van Buren. Nice to see you."

"Nice to see you, too, Sue," my mom replied as she poured cold water onto the hot potatoes. "I'm glad you can come to our picnic."

"Let me see that recipe." Setting the apple appetizer aside, I wiped my hands and picked up the card. It was decorated with a border of marjoram and lavender, from which a polka-dotted lilac ribbon loosely traversed the perimeter until it became a bow tied around the artistic display of herbs. The words "Here's What's Cookin'" were printed on it, followed by Sue's handwritten "Lapin Gibellote."

"Classy card," I said. "Oo-la-la. French. Lapin . . . " I flung my arm flamboyantly, "Jib-a, Gee-bel, Geb-a . . . " I gave up. "How do you pronounce this?"

"I don't know. It's rabbit stew. How can I help with the fixins'?"

"Rabid Sue?" I joshed. "You don't look rabid."

"Aren't you the comedian," my mother remarked dryly. She turned to Sue, "You can mince this celery for the potato salad."

"Where are the kids?" I asked. "It's too quiet."

"They're all right. My girls conned your boys into playing house."

"Oh, I get it now," my mother said. "The daddy and the puppy. How'd Austin get talked into that?"

"So he can demand payback in a few years when *he* wants to play house," I sniggered.

"I think it's 'doctor' the boys'll be wanting to play," Sue put in.

"Oh, yeah, right. Dear Lord. I don't want to think about it. Hey, Sue, now that my hands are deep in this hamburger, could you get the onion flakes for me? They're in that cabinet there next to the oven." She put her knife down and got them. Opening the bottle, she held it upside down over the bowl, shaking some of its contents into the mess of hamburger meat. I felt like a potter in need of a wheel.

"You want more?"

"No, that's good. Thanks."

On her way back to the celery, Sue stopped at the teak-framed five-by-seven photograph I'd placed on the windowsill the day before because it looked good against the sunlight streaming through the madrone and bay trees outside. "That's a great shot of you two. I never noticed it before."

Family ties

"I brought it out this trip," my mom informed her. "I have a copy at home. Isn't it lovely? It was taken at the restaurant in the hotel where we were staying in Portland. We took a girls' trip up there while Pat and Big Austin stayed down here and watched the store."

"I don't remember you doing that."

"I was three months pregnant with Little Austin. There he is in my belly. See?" We laughed at what we couldn't really see.

"It looks like the two of us," my mom said. "But it's really our first photograph of three generations."

Sue picked up the photo in order to study it more closely. "The lighting, and your eyelet lace collar, and the way Lois is standing behind you with her hand on the chair back make it look like a vintage Civil War tintype. It's very nice."

"We like it," my mom said.

It *was* a nice photograph and I *did* like it, but there was something else going on in that picture that couldn't be seen. I had came down to the lobby about fifteen minutes after my mom and several minutes before the camera's shutter snapped. I saw her drop something into the outgoing mail basket at the hotel desk in a manner that was oddly aloof and desultory, making me suspicious. Why would she send Dad a postcard from Oregon to California during what amounted to a long weekend trip? I hung back so she wouldn't see me, and then went over and casually took a look. It was a glossy picture postcard commonly found in hotels and pharmacies. This one featured the cityscape with Mt. Hood in the background. Afraid of getting caught, I turned it over and read quickly:

> Having a great time in Portland. Went to a hat shop that reminded me of the old days. Miss you and

THE LAMENT

wish you were here. Hope everything's going well at work. Will call when I get home.

Love, Me

I slid my gaze to the right-hand side of the card. It was addressed to a guy named Ron something. I remember thinking, "Jesus!" And like the match that burns twice, the card fell back in with the rest of the outgoing mail. I tried to keep my composure as I walked to the table where she was already seated, and where the photographer was waiting. Just as my belly wasn't showing my pregnancy, my face didn't show that, at the instant we were advised to say, "Cheese!" I was thinking, "Well, well. I finally know his name."

Sue put the photograph back on the windowsill. The three of us stared at it a minute longer. Then the sound of kids running up the steps in a balled-up jumble of bodies interrupted our thoughts.

"Uh-oh. The troops are coming in from the front lines," I said.

"Hungry, guys and gals?" Sue accentuated the "hun" of hungry in the rhetorical question, sounding like Harold Hill launching into a sales pitch for trombones in *The Music Man*.

"Help us lug this stuff down the hill," my mother told Sean and Austin. "We have just enough time to set up before your mom comes down with the hamburgers."

"Rachael and Sara, give them a hand," Sue instructed her daughters.

Photo forgotten, the day continued, but that evening, the memory returned to haunt me. Reminded of what I

Family ties

learned in Portland, troubled thoughts pressed down on the afternoon's light-hearted mood. At the time, I filed the information away. Maybe I was too busy with the pregnancy. Maybe I didn't want to rock the boat. I forgot about it, and life went on. But now the picture was a part of our home's decor, and the moments leading up to the click of the camera rose in my consciousness, roosting there like the chickens in our hen house. I wished we hadn't talked about it, scrutinized it, analyzed it, stared at it. Was it the act of Mom making a copy and presenting it as a gift that was getting to me? I started doing the math, reckoning how many years ago the photo was taken. *Let's see. I was three months pregnant with Austin. He's now six. Seven years ago! When did she and I have our tell-all chat?* I took my thinking farther back. *It was the winter Hugh died. I was living at home for the last time.*

I started using my fingers to count out the years: *I was in Minnesota for the Bicentennial. I'd already been there almost a year so it was in 1974 she made her big confession. Seven years again! Fourteen years she's been seeing this guy. No wait. Jeeeez! That's right. She's been seeing him since I was in high school. Holy cow! That's one helluva long-term liaison. Here I am thinking about divorce, trying to figure out how to make it work with Pat, and she's... Could she be? Still?... Nah. That's not possible, but methinks it's time to talk to her again.* "Heck," I said aloud to myself, "maybe I should take on a permanent lover."

I thought about it for a few days – whether to talk to her or not. Repeatedly glancing at the five-by-seven caused me to remember more than the scene behind the picture postcard. A torrent of images from the half-dozen years before I married surfaced, speeding by like the many seasons of changing fashions in the window

THE LAMENT

dressings that rushed by George in the 1960 film of H.G. Wells's *The Time Machine*.

There were Mom and Dad on their way to Venezuela. What an unorthodox thing that was for them to do. I saw Mom visiting me for a week when I lived in Minneapolis, and Dad's week-long trip to Los Gatos, where I took a job shortly after moving to California, and from where we drove a loop – Los Gatos, Morgan Hill, Gilroy, Carmel Valley, Carmel, Monterey, Santa Cruz, and back to Los Gatos – so I could get to know the lay of the land. There was the crash outside Kansas City which totaled the car I was driving, and there were Mom's tears as the stewardess pushed me in a wheelchair into the waiting area at the Philadelphia Airport afterward. I saw the house I rented in Maine for a few months burning down and the call I made to Dad about it. I was drunk as a skunk, but he didn't care. I saw myself reading the newspaper article Mom sent featuring her as the "unsung hero" of volunteers at the hospital, and I heard Dad's voice over the phone as he told me stories of teaching her how to play golf.

My memory was so jostled by that one photograph that I began to philosophize about all photographs. My need to live in an organized universe contented itself with assigning photographs to just two categories: Emblems of Promise and Souvenirs of Secrets. I decided that for my mom, the photo of us taken in Oregon was a promise *and* a secret. To her, it represented love and the hope of generations. My experience of the photograph left me with only a souvenir of a secret. It reminded me that my mom was someone I didn't really know.

I wanted to replace the bad picture with a good picture. Maybe the snapshot from my wedding album of their waltz, her skirt sweeping through May's fragrant

Family ties

air, her smile greeting the sky above Dad's shoulder as they twirled forever in the midst of the dance. But I couldn't exchange my souvenir for her emblem by a mere switch of snapshots. I had to take the photo out of the Souvenirs of Secrets column and put it in the Emblems of Promise column. When I did, I realized, as I had many times before, that each person's experience of history is personal. Pondering a photograph is just another look in the mirror. I decided to let the whole thing ride. Now wasn't the time to talk to her.

Orchard picnics were routine for our fun-in-the-sun choice of summer entertainment with Gra'ma. So were driving to Ben Lomond Park to play in the San Lorenzo River, hiking along Fall Creek, taking swimming lessons, or just swinging on the swings at home and riding bikes up and down the private road we lived on. Grandma was always on duty, the boys' detailed reports a testimonial to it: "Mommy, look. We baked cookies, and Gra'ma let us put icing squiggles on them. I did that one. You want it?" "Mommy, Gra'ma let me pull the wagon with Sean in the back all the way to Roaring Camp. We rode the train and bought candy sticks. I got root-beer flavor." "Mommy, we went to story time at the library today." "Then Gra'ma took us for ice cream!" I was remiss in appreciating my mother as Mom, but I certainly appreciated her as "Gra'ma."

What the boys looked forward to most throughout the week was stopping off to see the staff sergeant, better known as Grandpop, on duty at the store. Flush from their latest beach or boardwalk adventure, my mom and the kids would come in, she would plop down with a "Whew," and they'd be cut loose. Austin headed directly for the cash register to check the dates on all the nickels. Sean ran up into the storage loft to spy on all the customers. My dad always gave them a few minutes to fluff their feathers before he put them to work. Then Sean became stock boy, making good use of the pricing gun, and Austin became clerk, waiting on customers and counting out change. Seeing my dad with them like that reminded me of my grandfather and how he let me attach folded cardboard price tags to baskets of potatoes and green beans and make change from the dented metal box he used for a cash register in his roadside vegetable stand.

The store was our bait and tackle shop on the Santa Cruz Municipal Wharf. It was established in 1946 by Pat's dad, Ed, who registered it with the county clerk as Santa Cruz Boat Rentals, making that its fictitious business name, the merchant's equivalent to a birth certificate. Overfishing of sardines in Monterey Bay was already showing signs of that industry's demise, but the catches for halibut, salmon, kingfish, sea bass, and cod were still plentiful and profitable. Slippery, slimy, wet, and bulging gunnysacks were not an unusual sight. Ed towed the rented skiffs in a wandering line behind his single motor – "like ducklings," he'd say – drop them off at the numerous fishing holes within several miles of the wharf, and return in five or six hours to pick them up. By 1979, he had twenty-five boats, each with an engine of its own, and many with stories of the one that got away. He'd made his money (enough to buy five or six commercial properties) and a name for himself (in service to the Coast Guard, the Wharf Tenants Association, and the California Department of Fish and Game). But Ed was tired. It was time for his son to take over.

Patrick and I debated for some weeks about whether or not to buy the business. He was still working as a

Family ties

machinist for Lick Observatory. I had quit the veterinary clinic and was majoring in music at the community college. If we bought the Boat Rentals, we'd have to change course completely. Pat would become a boat builder/outboard repairman; I would become a bookkeeper/store manager. Our lives would be subject to the seasons, the sunrises, the tides, the swells, the fog, and storms. Not completely satisfied with our current prospects, we realized that this new life would be the perfect match to God's Little Acre. We bought the business.

Increasing the fleet of bright yellow skiffs to thirty and adding thirteen six-horsepower Evinrudes, (holding eight out for spares), we followed Ed's lead, naming each engine after a friend or relative and dismantling reverse gear to reduce the chances of injury – to the pier and to our boats. Ed once said, "I used to tow folks out to fishing holes and drop their anchor, but you've got to have holes in your head to rent boats to people to go fishing in the ocean all on their own." After several years as proprietors, Pat and I were quoted as saying that other than life preservers, every skiff was issued a guardian angel who sat on the bow to protect our patrons from the hazards of the ocean and from themselves. Mostly themselves.

Santa Cruz Boat Rentals was the kind of place with pictures of the employees on the wall and a bulletin board filled to capacity with cartoons and newspaper clippings. We gave away coffee, joked with our workers, and when it was hot, sent them out for milkshakes "on the house." And it's a good thing the filmmaker for *The Time Machine* didn't use my display window to make his point on how fast time whizzed by in front of George as he was catapulted into the future, because I only changed our window dressing once in the seventeen years I was there.

THE LAMENT

Joking around got us through the day. It was our habit to answer the phone with a bawdy, "Boat Rentals!" One Saturday, during the lag before the boats started coming in, it was Pat's turn to pick up.

"Boat Rentals!" he barked in our customary way. Then he paused. If he was Scooby-Doo, his ears would have stood straight up, alert in comical canine attention. "Just a minute, please," he said in a very professional manner. "I'll ask." Loosely holding his hand over the receiver, he winked at us, smiling, and hollered, "Is Burt Reynolds here?" We stared at him.

Manager Nat, the only black manager on the wharf, was ever on his toes and ready to play. He called back, "The Bandit? He's not here. We sent him and Smokey out for pizza."

Pat turned back to the phone and politely stated, "I'm afraid he stepped out, ma'am. May I help you?" From then on, answering the phone "Burt Reynolds!" was a standing SCBR greeting.

Occasionally, our tomfoolery went too far. On another Saturday, Pat, Nat, and I happened to be leaning, all in a row, against the bait freezer, when a florid-faced pier fisherman tramped into the shop wanting the Angler's Top Three Most Burning Questions answered, and wanted them answered now.

Looking squarely at Pat, he thundered, "What's biting? Where are they? What's the best bait?"

This, the approximately gazillionth time that day we'd been afflicted with the banal list of queries directed at the only discernible Aryan male among us, was the last straw. Our need for sarcastic relief got the better of us, and in the space of a quick-witted minute, we acted very badly, making one wonder if fished-out oceans, theme parks, video arcades, food and wine festivals, health and

Family ties

fitness events, and America's evolving family structure weren't the only causes to effect the deterioration of fishing boat rentals on the Monterey Bay.

Pat, with the best disinterested eye he could muster, set the hook. "Don't ask me. I don't know a thing." The poor fellow, not yet wriggling but caught in his own paradigm, looked from the white guy to the black guy.

"Don't look at me," Nat said, reeling him in with the impassively glazed focus that goes right through a person.

In gaping disbelief, but with only one door left to open, he turned to me. Raising my hands, palms up, I shrugged my shoulders, put my head at a forty-five degree angle, twisted my face in an I-don't-know-either attitude, and said, "What do I know? I'm just a girl."

I wish I could say I landed him, but the line broke and he got away. As he walked out, he turned, and justifiably incensed, snorted back at us, "You three stooges can go to hell!" We felt scolded, but only until our lost revenue was out of sight.

"I wanna be Curly."

"I call dibs on Mo."

"You can't be Curly. Your hair is straight as a board. I should be Curly."

"But wasn't Larry the really, really, dumb one?"

"Yeah, so?"

◊

When we bought the business, fishing was still good – maybe not what it was in 1946, but respectable. On the Sunday evening before our very first Monday morning bank deposit, Pat and I cranked up the volume to the Pink Floyd song, *Money*. We then sat in the middle of the living-room rug and played 52 Card Pickup with the weekend's take. Neither of us had ever *seen* so much cash!

It's too bad we didn't know we were in the twilight hours of the business's boom years. If we had known, we might have tried to make more money than we did. But probably not. The fact of the matter was that we were wretched entrepreneurs. Salesmen used to accuse us of being in business to make friends, not money. We plainly and simply didn't take the idea of the business model very seriously. It was too easy not to. The municipal wharf was part of a tourist town. Our nearest competitor was six miles down the coast; the next closest, more than three hours away in Morro Bay. Besides, advertising to fishermen was really not necessary. When the fish were in, we were sold out. It was as simple as that. To say fishing is more an obsession than a sport is an understatement.

For many the immigrant, fishing was more than that. It was a way of life. Broken English was a commonly heard language in our store, and I learned to differentiate between the names, faces, and statures of Koreans, Chinese, Japanese, Vietnamese, Filipinos, and Samoans. It was these dedicated fishermen who kept us solvent for as long as we were. During those early years, we couldn't even keep them out of our leaky boats.

"Believe me, we're out of boats. You don't want that one. It leaks."

"No care. Want go fishing."

"But . . ."

"You rent boat me."

"Look, you're going to come back knee deep in saltwater. You don't want that, do you?"

"Wet shoe no problem. We pay. Get boat. Go fish."

Family ties

"OK, then. Here, you might need this." Deploying a bailing bucket to the determined piscator, we'd add, "No extra cost."

Seeing these men across the counter at six in the morning and again at three in the afternoon week after week after week, taught me to respect the individuality of their cultures. I came to praise, rather than scoff, the haul of what we considered scrap fish taken back to San Jose to feed the neighborhood, and to commend, rather than ridicule, the guy whose fishing pole was a Coke can wrapped with string and who didn't care about wet shoes because he wasn't wearing any. I learned what lumpia is and why first birthdays are a hugely festive occasion for Filipinos. I also learned how difficult it was for older Asian men to be told what to do by a woman young enough to be their daughter.

The rental agreement specified that the boats were for fishing only, but a small percentage of our clientele had more pressing plans that, by virtue of their prodigious nature, nullified the contract. One can fake a suicide, conduct an illicit love affair, transport contraband, joy ride, or picnic on a hidden beach inaccessible from shore, secure in the knowledge nobody's going to intrude on the invitation-only fête. What we never openly admitted was that these shenanigans made for far better stories than those of the fisher-people who reported, however enthusiastically, on the one that got away.

It was two of our more gregarious customers, taking it upon themselves to entertain Santa Cruz with our rental skiffs, who were responsible for the most infamous tale of how far a $100 deposit can go. The story made the front page of *The Sentinel*, our local newspaper, and for years, the article, insouciantly torn out by surfers, meticulously cut out by old-timers, could be read in its entirety by pushing aside the refrigerator magnets partially covering the words recounting the day the fishermen went surfing.

The original account was buried too deep in the archives to dig out, but a more readily accessible tribute written on the fiftieth anniversary of the Boat Rentals recalled the event:

> It happened during a big swell at Lighthouse Point in April 1993 when a fellow from East Palo Alto apparently tried to surf a big wave and didn't make it. Surfers who were watching as he and his son took off on the wave said they appeared to floor the motor on their rental skiff as they proceeded down the mountain of water. The boat caught the wave crest and made it about halfway down before the bow dug in and sent the boat's two occupants flying. The rental boat was ruined.

Not to mention the motor. Criminy. I watched the whole thing through binoculars, incredulous at the sight of the son perched out on the bow like he was attempting to hang ten. I exploded with the "Jesus!" I reserve for such occasions, and without another word, my employees watched as I turned to the cash drawer, retrieved the $100 deposit and deposited it into my back pocket.

◊

My dad fit right in at the wharf. He loved every aspect of life at the Boat Rentals, not in an affectionate way, certainly, but more like the love someone feels when he says, "I love comedies!"

Dad's consensus about the folks who came into the store, about people in general, actually, was the same as it was about his favorite sitcoms: they were moronic

Family ties

but thoroughly amusing. His version of a show about the Boat Rentals might have been called something like *Hook, Line and Sink 'Em*. It would have been a game show, and Dad would have been master of ceremonies. His physique and personality were better suited to be Archie Bunker or Ralph Kramden, but for this show, he would make the perfect Groucho Marx.

In reality, my dad did make the Boat Rentals a sort of game show. The play of the game was, as on *You Bet Your Life*, secondary to the interplay between the host and the contestants. Travelers wandered in from all over the world, often in family groups, to buy miscellaneous sundries: soda, candy, t-shirts, visor caps, sunglasses, and the like. Dad started the game by asking where they were from. This broke the ice, striking up an exchange of questions that soon put him in the position of answering more than he was asking. A suave game-show host with a sense of humor and the soothing ability of a psychiatrist, he capitalized on the burning desire tourists have for asking the obvious that locals tire of hearing. That's where the game got interesting.

Implying he was a native Santa Cruzan, Dad brought the "contestants" under his wing, assuring them no question was stupid. They soon felt comfortable, and, hungry for the answers in this vacationers' version of Trivial Pursuit, hung onto every one of my dad's words, believing them all. With the completion of the sale, the game was over. Each contestant, once again a customer, and, like little elephant Babar who was "well satisfied with his purchases," left the shop in a flurry of friendly gestures of departure to my dad, who was also satisfied, having verified his general consensus about people, and thus winning the game.

THE LAMENT

Which guide book, I wondered, or taxi driver, airline steward, fellow passenger, or well-traveled friend informed the returned globetrotters that the "bridge" they had been on didn't really go to Monterey or the island out past it wasn't really Hawaii, that the 1906 earthquake didn't swallow anybody up, and the Empire State Building wasn't really inspired by the height of the California redwoods? "But the nice man in the store said that when the architect was visiting Santa Cruz, he saw one and all of a sudden knew that if a tree could get that tall, why not a building?"

Dad's most deliberate ruse was reserved for our boat renters. Much of the amusement they supplied was augmented with indisputably proven Intelligent Design – my dad's. Based on Big Austin's extensive experience out on the water, they . . . but wait. My dad never stepped foot in one of our boats!

"You get that catch out at Three Trees?" As if he knew where Three Trees was.

"Well, we don't know. We got them about a mile out trolling just beyond the kelp."

"Oh, yeah? Show me on this map." Hunching over our hand-drawn chart, Dad took mental note of everything reported on and every spot fingers pointed to. "Looks like you were fishing Pink House to me," he proposed with scholarly observation. Still labeled as pink on the diagram, the house on West Cliff Drive used for sighting one of the better fishing holes had been painted some indistinguishable color years ago. Everybody knew that. Almost everybody.

"It's fading, but pink's hard to miss. Let me look at that again." The old man of the sea turned the map toward him and then studiously remarked, "Wasn't there anything on land that stood out?"

Family ties

"There was a church with a big cross on it."

"Oh. Why didn't you say so? Now I gotcha. You fellas found one of my old standbys – doesn't always answer your prayers, but man, when it does . . . Here, let's go out back on the deck behind the store so you can show me." Once "out back," he'd have them indicate the location where they made their haul.

In this manner, Dad systematically plied the pertinent data from anyone who came back with his limit. He'd log the valuable communication with choice bits he'd already stored away from past cross-examinations and then dispense it to renters who needed expert advice. Vainglorious in his plagiaries, he made them seem all the more his own, bequeathing even the least of our renters a star to steer by. Many a fish was caught in this invisible net, and many an SCBR boat renter deemed my dad some sort of demigod when the benign hoax sent them home victorious.

Mom with the boys. Dad at the store. Never in those six consecutive summers did Pavarotti's gift disappoint. Not even in the last, especially not in the last, for the summer of 1988 was the happiest of them all. Where, though, were Pat and I? Our year was coming to a close, and we hadn't worked on our marriage. At the last minute, we asked my dad to stay on an extra week so we could have some get-away time. In the plaintive way people have when being taken for granted is a privilege and saying, "You didn't have to ask," is an honor, he went to find his grandsons.

12 A year and a day

We decided to go up the coast after work, have dinner at Gazos Creek Restaurant, and then continue on past San Francisco to Point Reyes National Seashore where we'd spend three days hiking. We hadn't had much time alone over the summer, but I remember feeling like we were on the mend. You're never more aware of a situation than when you're in the middle of denying it, I suppose, but nobody knows that until it's all over.

We got to the restaurant at Gazos Creek at about 6 p.m. It was a lonely place, miles from anywhere, with gas pumps out front that had been out of service for years. The pallid cornflower blue siding was thin and blistered, and there were no trees or landscaping to help keep the pallor away. The restaurant's dusty outward appearance was seen by the poetic as the torn and faded book jacket of a library volume shared by devout readers. The prosaic saw it as the hidden entrance to a speakeasy where one need only know the password to get into the party that was going on inside. Most of the time, the old building was overlooked as cars drove past on the scenic route to San Francisco, their passengers viewing it as a deserted Western outpost where only the curious and the passionate might find value in its forgotten history. Sometimes, when a drive along the coast was a weekend evening's lazy thought, the restaurant became a destination; often, as the prosaic correctly surmised, there was a party going on inside what was later called Gazos Creek Grill.

The night Patrick and I went in, there were a couple of jolly fellows at the bar comparing chain saws. As the maître d' led us to a table in the dining room, the more demonstrative of the two revved his up, proving nothing about the chain saw but everything about the establishment's ambiance. In sociable accord, all heads but ours turned smiling toward the bar. Every party has a pooper. This party had two.

After we ordered, we sat there. And we sat there. And we sat there. For the first time in eleven years, I did not make conversation.

I never noticed it before – that what I did in our relationship was make conversation. I also never noticed that Pat didn't. This night, I was tired. Finally, finally, tired. Tired of making all the effort, tired of taking the lead. So for once, I didn't. I just . . . didn't. And we sat there.

I willed myself to not talk, and so, through the entire meal, we didn't.

A profound sadness came over me. *This is impossible. It takes two people to make a marriage work. Pat knows that.* But he had given up and left it to me. The burden was mine. I was the one who was going to have to save us.

An hour-and-a-half went by without a word. Not one word. Not "How's your steak?" or "Hope he doesn't cut a slab out of the bar with that thing," or "I hope my mom got home all right." Not a word.

All that talk. All of those years. Did any of it ever need to happen? It didn't. In that hour-and-a-half, I learned that it didn't. I never needed to talk, and Pat would have been fine with that, with my not trying so

A year and a day

hard. Maybe if there hadn't been so much talk, there would have been room to speak.

Where I tried too hard, though, Pat could have tried harder. He could have said something. Now, there was only one thing left to say, and it was up to me to say it. It was my penalty. We paid for dinner and left.

Once in the car, Pat suggested we pull off at the Pigeon Point Lighthouse. It was only three miles more up Highway 1, but we'd never been there. We parked, got out, and walked to the ice plant on the hill just north of the light. We sat down, resigning to small talk, the tone of it putting us in mind of our old familiar selves – a comfortable place, but a place that had become the hollow sound of a wishing well. I reluctantly brought us back to the task my heart knew was at hand.

"I'm really afraid of saying what I want to say."

"What do you want to say?" he asked softly, patiently, evocatively, trying not to cajole or act anxious, sensing the moment had arrived.

"I . . . I think . . . I . . . Oh, God. This is so difficult." He waited for the words to reach the lip of the decanter, their meniscal bulge forming at its edge, growing fuller and fuller, until – "I think I want a divorce" splashed out.

He leaned back – just like that – and relaxed into the ice plant with a sigh of relief that I watched as well as heard and will never, ever forget.

"Why were you afraid to say that? Did you think it'd make me mad?" he asked.

"I don't know. Yes. You've gotten mad about so much since this all started."

"But why were you afraid of saying that? Why did you think *that* would make me mad?"

"Maybe it's the thing I wanted you to be mad about."

THE LAMENT

With the girls-sure-don't-know-much look that men can't seem to hide, he said, "I'm not upset that you want to leave me. I was upset that you – you really don't get it, do you? It doesn't matter that it was only one time, or that you knew right after that it was a mistake. Knowing afterward doesn't mean anything. An employee? Come on, Lois. You really should have known before, not after."

That was it. That was all. The marriage was over. I had said the most incredibly painful thing I ever said, only to find it was what Patrick was waiting for – waiting, for a year and a day, for the words that would set us free.

◊

Two years before I spoke those most difficult words, I had an emotional outburst that may have been what started me down the path to the ice plant at Pigeon Point. The boys and I had gone to Vineland for Thanksgiving. While we were there, my parents thought it would be fun for Austin and Sean to see the house their mom was brought up in. So, after the big meal, we piled into Grandma's Mercedes 190E (sequel to the long-gone days of the Thunderbird) and took off for 810 Broadway, a blue-gray, postwar, Cape Cod style bungalow on a street lined with postwar middle-class houses just like it.

A large field, plowed and planted for more years than I'd been alive, separated Broadway from the next street over. As I pointed to the three trees along the edge of it where we neighborhood kids used to play Hobo Camping, Peter Pan, and Pirate Ship (the trees, masts; the field, ocean), I caught sight of the English-style lantern at the end of the driveway that Dad and I strung Christmas lights from every December between 1953 and 1961. *Wow*, I thought. Then I saw that the swing set in the backyard was the same, too. *Whoa*, I added. A woman

A year and a day

was closing the garage door as we went by. Mom, excitedly shaking Dad's right shoulder, called out, "Stop, Austin. Back up. Look! Grace is home." I inwardly spurted out another expletive, *Gosh!* Then it really hit me. *The Messinas bought this place when I was twelve and have yet to replace that old pole lamp!* Dad put the Benz in park long enough to tell Mrs. Messina that we were just driving by to show the grandkids the old family dwelling, when she invited us in for a closer look. Dad took no time in turning off the ignition. The boys and I took no time in getting out.

Stepping inside the front door, Mom, Dad, and I gasped. The living room wallpaper and knick-knack shelves were the same as when we left! The three of us fell silent, woozy from blurry flashbacks. This was no entry to the old family dwelling. It was a turnstile to the past. The boys, sensing something phantasmal was afoot, became like awestruck tourists grouped around a Sistine Chapel docent. *Astonishing!* I gulped. We followed Mrs. Messina farther into the room, scanning the scene before us as if we really were in the Sistine Chapel. Then my dad, almost reverently, said, "I want to see my workshop." Without delay, our tour guide took us to the basement.

While Dad walked back to his old workbench, I stared at the still unfinished wall at the bottom of the stairs. In between the studs, written in chalk, were the words "Club Members Only Past This Point." The club rules that Suzanne, Charlotte and I had written – 1, 2, 3, and 4 – and signed, twenty-four years earlier, were listed below it. In *chalk*. My twelve-year-old handwriting. In chalk! Cardboard lapel pins sashayed across my mind – we had made them in the shape of megaphones covered with construction paper across which we wrote our club's name, *Calling All Boys*. I began to teeter.

Mrs. Messina, or "Oh, Grace," as my mom kept repeating, was starting to remind me of Mrs. Whatsit from *A Wrinkle in Time* as she beamed like she'd been waiting several hundred years for us to drop by. Dad came around the corner from his old workshop, looking like a moviegoer exiting a midnight showing of *On The Beach* or maybe the remake of *The Manchurian Candidate*. Weak-kneed, I said, "There's something I want to see."

"Come on upstairs, then," Mrs. Messina said. The response startled me. How'd she know what I wanted was upstairs?

Feet moving at snail's pace, giving spirit the energy it needed to speed further back through time, I led everybody from 1961 to 1957. We stopped in the tiny cul-de-sac kitchen my mom always said couldn't possibly have too many cooks in it. The stove was at the end of the cul-de-sac. To the right of the stove was a counter that extended to that portion of the tiny room that held the refrigerator. Under the part of the counter between the stove and the refrigerator were three drawers, but under the part that abutted the stove, there was a dead space. I asked if I might remove the three drawers. Mrs. Whatsit smiled, "No, I don't mind, dear." My family, too dumbstruck to be embarrassed by my impudence, watched as I confidently pulled each drawer from its frame, carefully stacking them on the floor in front of the refrigerator. Mom was even too nonplussed to exclaim "Lois!"

When all three were out, I instructed Little Austin to crawl in through the space left by the larger bottom drawer. I then put all the drawers back in. Austin soon discovered what any child or member of the *Calling All Boys* club would discover: the dead space under

A year and a day

the counter beyond the drawers was big enough to allow him – or her – to turn and fit comfortably into it. A flashlight supplied by accommodating friends soon revealed a secret place no adult would ever find. A cave boy could have fun playing Dragon, demanding food from the people and threatening them with fire breath if they didn't comply. A cave girl could bring in her Mr. Potato Head or a *Nancy* comic book and have fun sticking a silly mustache on a real potato or snuggling in for a good read until her fellow club members informed her that her time was up – it was their turn.

As I was explaining this, Austin called out, "Mommy, this is cool. Can I stay in here awhile? Hey, I found something!"

"You found something?"

"Come on, Austin, let's get you out of there," my dad said, as he reopened the entrance to the cavern. Little Austin climbed out into the light of day.

Sean leaned in. "What is it, Austy? Let me see."

"No, it's mine," Austin snarled, closing his fist and holding the prize tightly to his chest.

"No, I think it must belong to your mother," his grandfather sternly stated. "Let's take a look."

Austin opened his hand to reveal a round, metal, yellow and black can that I recognized as a typewriter ribbon tin. Handing it to me, he said, "What do you think is in there, Mommy?"

"I don't know, honey. Let's open it and see. Come on, Seanie. Come look." I pried open the tin. It was full of buttons. "My buttons!" I cried.

"Oh, my goodness," Mom burst out. "Those are the buttons I let you pick from my button box! You used to spend hours and hours looking through it until one day

I gave you that tin and told you to pick some out to keep for your own."

Shuddering, I turned to Mrs. Messina-Whatsit, "They're yours, Mrs. Messina. They were in the house when you bought it."

"No, dear, they're yours."

"But this one is bone and must be a hundred years old."

"Don't you worry. They're yours."

It was time to go. Light-headed from time travel, we put ourselves back together, headed down the driveway, got in the car, and said our good-byes.

I was showing the boys the buttons when Mom started complaining about Dad's driving.

"Do you have to drive so close?"

"I'm not driving close. We're going twenty-five miles an hour, for God's sake."

"I don't care how slow the car in front is making us go. If something ran out in front of him, he'd have to slam on his brakes and you'd hit him. You know we can't afford that."

In singsong voice, Daddy imitated, "You know we can't afford that." Then in an exasperated statement-of-masculine-fact voice, he declared, "This thing's a tank, Lena. Nothing will hurt it at twenty-five miles an hour!"

The boys and I stopped what we were doing. This was unbelievable. As my parents continued their age-old fight, I felt my legs shrinking, getting shorter and shorter.

"But *we* might hurt *him*. You're making me nervous. Would it kill you to back off? The kids are in the car."

My legs were now too short for my knees to bend over the edge of the seat. They were like Seanie's, sticking straight out.

"Why don't *you* back off, Lena?"

A year and a day

"Here we go again."

"Go pound sand!"

"Why do you have to talk to me like that?" Her voice was becoming subdued. I could see my Sunday School patent-leather buckle shoes and my socks with the frill around the edges. I watched my feet clink together, back and forth and back and forth, waiting for my mommy and daddy to stop fighting.

"Because you make me!"

"I don't make you."

"Shut up!" I screamed. "How can you two still be fighting over the same damn stuff after all these years?" Dead silence.

No one dared utter another word until we got inside the house.

We were all kind of bumping into each other, trying to get our coats off so we could get to our respective corners, when Mom grabbed Dad, and then she grabbed me.

"She needs us right now. Please," my mother murmured. "What happened at the Messina's today was more than any of us could take." Hair, ears, cheeks, necks, lips were all brushing up against each other, and suddenly we were in a group hug, an awkward embrace. We had never experienced such a moment. The tension gave way when Dad held us tighter, but it wasn't until my sons joined in that I tearfully pleaded, "How can two people be married for so long and not have figured out how to be happy?"

◊

For months – two years! – I struggled with that plea and all the subsequent thoughts and feelings it stirred up. Soliciting my mom and closest girlfriends to join in, I embarked on an odyssey characterized by the oscillations of difficult questions. What would happen to the Boat Rentals? What about the house? How about our family and friends? Didn't I owe them something? Commitment. What does it mean? Are you committed if you live together separately? What about the boys? Did I want them growing up in the shadow of an unhappy marriage? Wasn't it my responsibility to make it happy? How could I do that by myself?

Sifting through the storehouse of untapped metaphors for a way to express the suffering this quandary caused, one would think I'd have chosen something Dantesque, and indeed, there were times when I thought I was in Purgatory. No, when I dug down for the quality of this dangerous undertaking, I saw myself on a path in a yellow wood – Robert Frost's yellow wood. I had read so many of his poems that I could have been trundling up the rocky path in "Two Look at Two" or the snow-packed murky Vermont trail in "The Wood-Pile" or the evening's trail alluded to in "Come In." I was traveling along on all of them in a conceit I couldn't throw off, yet one that didn't make sense. How could such an excruciating experience put me in mind of a walking tour through bucolic settings? Then I saw the Walkman bobbing up and down in my belt loop and heard Mahler's Fourth coming through on the earphones plugged into my head. What's this? Why would I compare the travails of a beleaguered woman in the throes of a life decision not only to a stroll in the woods, but one filled with symphonic surround sound as well?

Frost's poetry radiated an unhurried, circumspect pace, while the fully scored instrumentation of Gustav Mahler's symphony, which requires all the sections of the orchestra to pay strict attention, kept the music driving onward. I thought about how both artists express a

A year and a day

hope that survives the despair and a pain that knows the rhythm and magnificence of the natural world. Then it made sense, and the unraveling began.

I would not divorce unless I could stay on at the wharf, not because it was lucrative or a great career path, but because it provided the flexibility I needed to tend to my sons. I'd waive any right I had to staying on in the house. After all, it was originally Pat's project, his dream. It didn't matter that much to me because my nomadic tendencies would not interpret the upheaval of a move as disruptive, but just the next thing to do. The extent of my actions on my friends and family, I was, alas, not sage enough to foresee. I did know that the resilience and faith of those who love us, though it may waver, rarely topples over, so that was a worry I could check off the list. On the perplexities of commitment, additional questions presented themselves. Doesn't commitment mean staying together forever because you said you would? Aren't you supposed to accept changes in your partner as the years go by? Isn't that what makes you a better person? A virtuous human being? Rationalizing this away took up the bulk of those two years and is the one that, to this day, is not settled for me.

My biggest concerns were Austin and Sean. I did not want the same bad role models for marriage that were ingrained in me to be passed down to them. I did not want them living with two miserable people trapped in a miserable predicament. I'd had a recurrent fantasy about my parents getting divorced. I did not want my sons having the same.

As each question fell to the wayside, the wayfarer methodically proceeded forward. Sitting down next to her husband in the ice plant at Pigeon Point lighthouse that Sunday night in late August, it was apparent he'd

THE LAMENT

been out for a long walk, too. All that remained was the verdict that I'd so fearfully pronounced.

13

Why is it that a lie will let us keep going along the same as always, but the truth insists on changing everything?

Pat remarried the following year, in June 1989. I had purchased a condominium in January, a half mile from the wharf. My parents came out for the first two weeks to help the boys and me with the move and the adjustment. One evening, while waiting for Mom to finish cooking dinner, Dad said he and I should, as he put it, "take a before-supper constitutional."

While Mom concentrated on stuffing green peppers, we abducted a loaf of garlic bread from the refrigerator and skedaddled out on burglar's tiptoe to feed the ducks in the nearby lagoon. The winter's night air was cold, crisp, and clear; the sky a black scrim in front of stars that looked like tiny Christmas lights sprinkled across the universe.

We talked about everything that had happened over the past year or so. Normally this would have been an improbable conversation between my father and me, but as the various pleats of the mantle of my marriage had unfolded and the thread of their sewing unraveled, I found that this was the talk that older, retired people wanted to have. They were not meddlers or busybodies, but gentlefolk seasoned by their years who did not want

THE LAMENT

to see me so all alone in my story. So they told theirs, letting me in on an unfortunate reality of the adult world they could no longer protect me from: Fairy-tale weddings there may be, but there is no such thing as a fairy-tale marriage. I was stunned to find out how many of the couples I thought to be long-lived husband and wife teams were actually second, sometimes third marriages, and their kids a compilation of stepchildren. Now my dad wanted to tell his story.

"You know, honey, I've always felt bad about what I did to your mother."

"What'd you do? Are you talking about way back when?"

"Way back when," he reverberated from far down the canyon of time.

"Why?"

"I got carried away with the ski club."

"Is that why you quit?"

"Yes."

"I always thought it was because of your knee."

"That's what we wanted you to think."

"What happened, Daddy? Tell me. I've never really known."

"Oh, I guess I was having too much fun. Scared of getting old, when I look back on it."

This was a conversation like the almost finished Sunday *Times* crossword puzzle. Only a few missing letters are needed to complete it. Reading the clues out loud is worth a try. "How long did it last?"

"A year."

A year? I was floored. *Did I hear him say a year?* A year meant a relationship. It meant there had been a name. A name that for that amount of time began many a conversation, ended many a thought. A name called out,

The truth insists on changing everything

whispered. A sound his ears recognized and the taste his tongue knew. A name he was not free to speak but may have loved. *A year,* I heard him say.

The wood ducks had gone home for the night, but we remained beneath the lamp post of a boardwalk bridge, throwing out pieces of bread, watching their ever-widening circles as they floated away.

"Didn't you ever stop to think about it?" he wondered.

"No. I guess not. That night came and went, and then everything was back to normal. Besides, it wasn't my place to ask."

"Well, it's time for me to tell. Your mother knew there was something going on. It was all coming to a head. Somebody told her something, and we had a fight. She was sick of the lies and of putting up with me. She'd taken all she could. I couldn't blame her. I was sick of it, too. Tired of pussy-footin' around. Something had to give."

"I don't remember you guys fighting that night."

"You were out somewhere. I left before you got home. I wanted to see *her* and didn't think your mom would follow me. I didn't care. I was only planning on going out for a couple of hours, but then I just didn't feel like going home. Maybe I knew it was over. Maybe I wasn't sure."

"So when I got home, Mom and I went looking for you."

"That's right."

"You know, I remember being in the front entry, seeing Mom by the fireplace and her turning around. I must have just come through the front door. She probably told me to keep my coat on because we were going out. I definitely remember her being upset and that whatever it was, it was important enough not to argue, but to just go."

"Your mom knew where I might be and who I might be with. But by then, I didn't give a damn. I needed to spend a whole night with *her*. I needed to find out."

"But you were at the doughnut shop having a cup of coffee."

"That's right."

Our walk in the night unconsciously timed to the pace of our conversation, we started back. The movement gave me the time I needed to understand.

"Oh, no, Dad, wait. Are you telling me it was the doughnut shop girl?"

"I am."

"Wow, Dad. Wow. What happened after we went looking for you?"

"I had to make a decision."

"What do you mean?"

"Your mom gave me an ultimatum."

"She did? What was it?"

"She said that if I didn't come home and stay home, she'd make it so I couldn't see you."

This made for an uncomfortable break in the conversation. But I had to keep going. Seventeen across – five more letters – and I could fill in the rest for myself. I took a stab at it.

"Could she have done that? I don't see Mom doing that."

"Back then, yeah, she could have done that, but you're right, she wouldn't have. It was a scare tactic."

"So why did you fall for it?"

"Because it worked. The thought hit me like a ton of bricks. It brought me to my senses."

"It was all so long ago."

"And there isn't a day goes by that I don't feel guilty."

The truth insists on changing everything

◊

They left for New Jersey a few days later in a tangle of kisses, well-wishes, embraces and reminders. "Don't forget to be good for your mommy." "Take that car in before it stops running altogether." "Remember to send your new address out. Everybody's always asking about that daughter of mine who went to California." "We love you!"

After they were gone and I had time to digest the events of their visit, I got to thinking: *If Dad had known about Mom in the same way she knew about him, "way back when," what would have happened? If she had disclosed her secret, would they, too, have sought a divorce?*

It wasn't right that Dad was found out when Mom wasn't. He'd been repenting all these years while she'd been carrying on. How could she do that to him? How could she let him continue to feel guilty day after day? Did she know? Her affair should have ended when Daddy came back. Why didn't it?

And with that, I began chewing on yet another of the apples I seemed to enjoy picking from the Tree of Knowledge of Good and Evil. This session ended with me telling me: *The problem for me wasn't the difference between right and wrong, but the contemplation of it. And there's the rub!* Brought full-circle to the question at hand, I concluded, *Well, Mother, the gig is up. You've been too long at the fair, and I'm comin' to take you home.* But how?

I waited for summer, when I knew they'd return to help out with the boys and the store. Then I watched for my chance. Memorial Day weekend passed, and the busy season kicked in. Arriving the third week of June, Dad worked the counter as usual and Sean, Austin, and Grandma came and went as they pleased. Now that I had a place close to the wharf, Dad and I were greeted by the rising sun every morning at 5:30 as we walked to work. Its pink and flamingo orange regale only those whose long labors merit such an introduction to the day.

The opportunity to take my mother to task came in late July.

◊

Ever since I was a girl, my mom took me out on a regular basis to buy new clothes. We used to go twice a year, winter and summer, to accommodate New Jersey's four distinct seasons and my changing body size, but Central California's moderate climate and my full-grown size 8 scaled it back to an annual outing. As much as she hated – as *we* hated – shopping, we were disinclined to abolish the tradition because it gave us girl time that couldn't be simulated in very many other ways. We'd chit-chat in the freestyle manner people have when walking alongside each other. We'd window shop, compare style options, go in, try on assorted trappings, settle on purchases and then treat ourselves to lunch. 1989's mother-daughter spending spree showed no signs of being different. After recruiting Grandpa to babysit and Patrick to fill in at the Boat Rentals, we chose a warm and windless weekday to take the train into San Francisco and have our ladies' holiday.

"Neiman Marcus is fun to go into at Christmas, Mom, but all that department store hustle and bustle is overwhelming any other time of the year. Let's go over to Sutter and look for a boutique."

"The word boutique makes my pocketbook skittish, but let's go if you want. Then we'll have lunch. What do you feel like?"

The truth insists on changing everything

"Hurry. Here, let's cut through Union Square. Oh, look at the bagpipes. I love bagpipes. Do you remember the time we had those messy ice cream sundaes for lunch? I want to do that again."

"We'll get fat!"

"We're already fat!"

"Then it doesn't matter, does it? We can start the diet tomorrow."

We found a dress shop and an ice cream parlor. While we waited for our decadent midday feast to be served, I, by way of conversation, commented on the recent risings of the sun. "The fog has taken a couple of days off, and the early morning sky has been, uh – I don't know, glorious. Yes, that's it: glorious. You don't know what you're missing."

"My sleep. Why do people out here call it 'fog'? It's not fog, it's overcast."

"I know. I've never been comfortable calling it 'fog' either. Remember the time we were going to that church conference? It was so thick that the lights on the car in front of us looked like those little red hot cinnamon candies."

"Carl from church was with us," Mom recalled.

"Oh, yeah. He'd just come out of that terrible car accident. He was wearing some kind of protective headgear or neck brace or something, remember?"

"All I remember," she added," is thinking about what he must have been going through in the back seat while I was trying to keep us on the road, praying the driver in front of me knew where he was going."

"People out here don't know what fog is. Maybe the ones inland do. They have what's called tule fog. I think it might be the real thing."

THE LAMENT

The aromas of warm strawberries and caramel syrup soon got our attention. Knuckling under, we yielded to their promise of epicurean delight, surrendering to the euphoria only such a confection can convey. I realized she was right where I wanted her.

"So, Mother."

"What now?"

"How's Ron?"

"What?" My question put an end to everything – motion, time, Earth's rotation, the moon's phases – the entire solar system! Everything.

"I said, 'How's Ron?'" The cessation of all persisted. She was thinking into her dessert dish, inspecting what was left of the sundae, wishing she hadn't heard me, wanting, but not wanting, to turn the page, round the corner, find out what happens if you let yourself keep falling and see, once and for all, if you die and if death hurts.

It was cruel of me to leave her there like that so I said, "I found out his name when we were in Portland. I saw you drop a postcard in the mail bin at the hotel. I snuck over and read it."

She looked up. Not ready to hit the ground, she soberly responded, "I never could pull anything over on you."

"So how is he?" I prodded.

Her gaze remained fixed. "He's fine."

As straight-faced as a person can be who is inwardly screaming, "Jesus! They're still together!?" I replied, "Glad to hear it. Say 'Hi' for me, won't you?"

"I can do that," she flatly rejoined. We finished eating our ice cream. Her saying hello to Ron for me became a part of who we were to become.

The truth insists on changing everything

◊

At the end of Act I of *Camelot*, when the curtain falls on an emotionally exhausted King Arthur, he is alone on stage. No one – not the audience, the actors, the ushers, the crew, the conductor, the orchestra, nor King Arthur himself – no one stirs, for all have just witnessed the unremitting struggle between the mind, body, and heart of a man, and in empathy or in awe, they recognize his pain. Lancelot has been knighted; Guenevere has repaired to her chambers; the Court has filed out. The two have sinned against their king; the many await his decision. Only Excalibur abides.

A year after my father spoke of his guilt and my mother admitted hers to me again, I recognized that pain. As an orchestra member in a summer production of the famous musical, I was a witness, and though I, too, was silenced by the king's soliloquy, my eyes were not open to its message until the tenth or twelfth time I heard it. Then suddenly I understood: The male ego is strong; the civilized man, ever-vigilant, grows weary. The woman who knows this has wisdom; the woman who does not, does not.

Would that Cabrillo Stage had chosen to produce *Camelot* in 1987, when Pat and I had just begun counseling, rather than in 1990, after we divorced.

Would that the wisdom of the mother had been that of the daughter.

14
One shoe off and one shoe on

In April of 1990, *USA Today* ran an article on the twentieth commemoration of the shootings at Kent State. My mom sent me a copy. I knew, of course, that May 4th was approaching, because I always knew when May 4th was near, but I didn't realize that it had been twenty years. My friend Scott, who had been shot, was listed in the section entitled "Where wounded are now." I realized I was probably the only person in the Monterey Bay area who had been there, and because of that, I had a responsibility to the community to give an account of what happened that day.

I gathered my courage, and on the morning of the anniversary, valiantly pulled open the door to the *Santa Cruz Sentinel*'s offices. The newspaper's receptionist looked up at me as if I appeared from out of nowhere, which was exactly how I felt. Aware of her job description, she, as amiably as she could, asked, "May I help you?"

"I was at Kent State," was all I was able to get out. We froze in position: she registering her first impressions of this ghost of a woman, me stupidly standing there like a dimwit in front of a tree while a lumberjack was yelling, "Tim*ber!*" Then, suddenly, with a "Hold on, don't move a muscle, stay right there," gesture, she rose and ran up the stairs. When she returned, there was a gentleman with her who introduced himself and asked if I'd like to have a seat at his desk.

I should have known. I was in Berkeley the last time this happened, on the first anniversary of the shootings, and I drew quite a crowd. I'd spent the night with friends in San Francisco, and I wanted to get a look at the neighboring city made famous for its political spunk. As I wandered about Telegraph Avenue, I remembered I was in need of a pair of good walking shoes, so I stopped in a shoe store. The radio was playing. The news came on, headlining the anniversary. While the salesman was lethargically preparing to help me try on a pair of Hush Puppies, I mentioned that I had been at Kent State. He froze – my foot in mid-air, his grasp an inch from my right heel, disbelief changing his expression from that of a bored store clerk, to that of a lottery winner. He straightened, said "You're kidding!" and before I could draw a breath, he went running out the door the same way the receptionist ran up the stairs nineteen years later. One shoe off and one shoe on, I leaned forward, peering after him as he waved his shoe horn and hollered up and down the street, "Hey, there's a girl in here who was at Kent State. Over here, everybody! Over here!" Within two minutes, an avalanche of free-speech advocates rushed into the store, and there was no way I was getting out of there until I told all.

Telling all to a single journalist on the twentieth anniversary wasn't as overwhelming, but it was just as unnerving. Entering the house afterward, drained from the experience, I heard the phone ringing. It was the local TV station. *Guess those guys talk to each other,* I thought. After

One shoe off and one shoe on

we hung up, two other stations called, but the first fellow was already at the door with his cameraman. I still have the tape of it. I've shown it and the newspaper article to a few of my freshman English classes, but mostly, I don't.

Part Four

Out for Stars

I have had three honest-to-God epiphanies in my life. The first was on Sugarloaf Mountain when I figured out that music was intrinsic to my well being. The last began on a beach north of Santa Cruz in December 1999 and ended six months later in the High Sierra back country. The second took place near Monument Valley, Utah, in 1996.

15 Something cut loose inside

Even though Pat was now married to someone else, he and I remained business partners. Within a year of the divorce, he'd begun boarding horses and making redwood garden furniture, turning God's Little Acre into Pat's Little Stay-At-Home Basement Business. This suited him, and I didn't mind when I eventually became sole proprietor of the Boat Rentals because I didn't really know what else to do. Despite the fact that selling squid, anchovies, blood worms, and a few fishy gift items had long ago lost its appeal, and the dream of doing well enough to get out of minding the store on a daily basis had long ago faded, the freedom to arrange my schedule to fit Sean and Austin's was something I wasn't going to give up. Nevertheless I probed the want ads for alternative careers that would give me the same flexibility. Figuring that someone with seventeen years of experience at running a business would be viewed as a valuable asset to any organization's top management, I tried for several executive directorships. To my dismay, I learned that having a bachelor's degree was the first criterion that search teams looked for, especially when more than 100 applicants were competing for the same position.

Maybe I could have run the Boat Rentals while going to school or working my way into another career, but as it was for Pat, the writing was on the wall for me. My tour of duty at Santa Cruz Boat Rentals was soon to come to a close. I didn't know it yet, but I felt it. Taking a drive could ease the pressure and bring some perspective to the situation.

◊

Monument Valley was nature in a different mood. It was Utah's Big Rock Candy Mountain, its Oz, or maybe its Narnia. Until, that is, we stopped and got out. Then it was more like entering MoMA, the d'Orsay, or El Prado, all of which my latest boyfriend Christopher and I were able to compare to the famous sandstone buttes. But first, we had to stop and get out.

Christopher's email message from the school he was attending in Chicago read like it came through a telegraph office: "you get you to midway airport. i get you home." I never did know how one of his dad's farm trucks got to Chicago with no driver to bring it back, but nothing aggravated Chris more than the ennui of minutiae, so I just went along for the return trip to California and didn't ask questions.

Too much in love to let on how exasperating his behavior could be, I waited, while trying to hide my impatience, as Chris fiddled with a last-minute, self-mandated chore before we drove the pickup out of the cold, damp subterranean public parking garage.

"What, pray tell, are you doing?"

"Speaker wires." Perhaps Samuel Morse invented the telegraph to give men a legitimate reason for saying as little as possible.

"Just what exciting radio stations do you expect to find driving across Kansas?"

Something cut loose inside

"We'll tell each other stories in Kansas. I thought you brought Mozart or somebody like that with you."

"Oh, you're right. I also brought an old music textbook I had lying around. I thought maybe I could give you some background on what you'll be hearing. What d'ya say instead of telling stories, we teach each other something we know a lot about? I could tell you about music history while we're listening to Mozart or 'somebody like that.' I'll bet you've never heard of Leoš Janáček."

"Yanacheck? Wow. Great name. OK I'll teach you about the futures market."

"The what?"

"Perfect. Classes start . . . " He looked at his wristwatch, " . . . in approximately 196 miles. Shall we get outta here?"

◊

We drove and talked and talked and drove, Illinois to Missouri, Kansas to Colorado. I learned how convoluted guessing games with your money can be. He learned the differences between the Classical and the Romantic periods. On spring break from Northwestern's Kellogg School of Management, Chris was enthusiastic about sharing his recently acquired knowledge. It's still mind boggling how an idea as systematic as estimating what soybeans will be worth in seven or eight months is so darned arousing to some folks, but it speaks of our proclivity to put emotion into everything, even mathematics. My lectures were not as mentally onerous, but more akin to an easy-listening radio station. All Chris had to do was sit back and enjoy. Note-taking was not a requirement, and the syllabus made no mention of a final exam.

Home schooling, or, more accurately, truck schooling, in this two-teacher, two-student, two-subject academy rolled along at as dandy a clip as its classroom on wheels did. By the time we reached Vail, daily concerns, behind or before us, were obliterated by our lively discussions. All that was left was the present.

"All right, Chris. The German Requiem, *Ein deutsches Requiem*, was written for his mother, but she wasn't the only older woman Brahms had affection for. Check this out. When he was twenty years old, he started hanging out with Robert and Clara Schumann. They became great friends, but Mr. Schumann (I'll play you some of his stuff later. Talk about Romanticism!) went nutty and ended up in an insane asylum. Clara and Johannes, fourteen years her junior – she was thirty-four – became devoted to each other. Here it says he composed a piece, 'a trial flight in a form that Brahms was to infuse with new meaning, and it is dedicated to Clara.'

"Clara, Christopher, Clara. It's called "Short Variations on a Theme by Him. Dedicated to Her." That's not obvious or anything. Let's see. After Schumann died, they went away together. ' . . . with only her maid to chaperon them.' Ha! And people talked. People gossiped. See, Chris. *See?* She was fourteen years older than he was, and it didn't matter. I'm only nine years older than you. They stayed friends for the rest of their lives. We could. Don't you think?"

"I have no doubt."

We were tacit as the remainder of Brahms's Serenade No. 1 carried us off to lands unknown, when I suddenly said, "I know what I'm going to do."

"Oh, yeah? What?"

"I'm going to sell the business, go back to school, and become a teacher."

"You're joking. A music teacher?"

Something cut loose inside

"No, I'm not joking. I wish I could be a music teacher, but no, I need to be marketable. I'm going to become an English teacher. High school."

"Really. You know all this? Why not a math teacher? Why not elementary school?"

"Because ever since I turned eight years old, I've always had a book next to my bed. No, wait. I've always had *two* books, sometimes more, next to my bed, and I was one of those kids in second grade who couldn't wait to dissect sentences. And I want to teach high school because that's the age my sons are, and I'm comfortable with it. Little kids are too loud."

"I see."

"I'll need to learn Spanish and get my master's. More money, you know. And. And. *A-a-a-nd* . . . " Excitement mounting, I sped up. "I'll get retirement and medical and dental benefits! Why didn't I think of this sooner? I'll get summers *off!*"

"How do you know all this?"

"My mother-in-law and both of my sisters-in-law were teachers."

"I meant, how do you know you're going to do all this?"

"I don't know. It just came to me."

"When?"

◊

The absence of a thing is what often reveals it. I once heard Ken Kesey say that you don't believe in auras until you see a body without one. An accomplished drummer gives you the rhythm by leaving out some of the beat; artists and architects provide only the illusion of contour. "My silence is my answer," Chris once said to me. Absence of sound, absence of lines, absence of words, absence of feeling. When we fill in the spaces, we penetrate the meaning. Notes are easier to play than rests.

Five years into the future, I would, as a matter of course, introduce the concept of absence to my students through a passage in Richard Connell's "The Most Dangerous Game," a short story included in many a ninth-grade curriculum throughout the United States. General Zaroff extends his malevolent amusement of the hunt by momentarily allowing Rainsford, the hunted, to get away. But Connell doesn't explain this. Instead, he describes the scene.

"So what just happened?" I ask. "Anybody? No? Come on, you guys. You know how to do this. I see you out there in the halls. Eduardo, wasn't that you I saw aiming a big ol' smile at Bianca Mendez this morning? And you thought you were hiding it under your coat collar."

Stifled laughter.

"OK, let's read it again. No, wait. Meghan, read it to us. The rest of you, watch me."

As she reads, I act out the passage.

"It was General Zaroff," Meghan begins. "He made his way along with his eyes fixed in utmost concentration on the ground before him."

I begin a slow, contemplative stride across the front of the room. Meghan continues.

"He paused, almost beneath the tree, dropped to his knees and studied the ground."

I do the same. The kids in the back push up out of their seats so they can see.

"Rainsford's impulse was to hurl himself down like a panther, but he saw that the general's right hand held something metallic – a small automatic pistol. The hunter shook his head several times . . ."

I shake mine.

Something cut loose inside

"... as if he were puzzled. Then he straightened up and took from his case one of his black cigarettes; its pungent incenselike smoke floated up to Rainsford's nostrils."

All eyes but Meghan's are on me as I slowly stand up and take an imaginary black cigarette from its imaginary case. She continues.

"Rainsford held his breath. The general's eyes had left the ground and were traveling inch by inch up the tree." So do mine.

We're all having fun, now. The kids are totally entranced to see their teacher smoking a black cigarette. They can't wait for what happens next. With an impeccably calculated pause, Meghan reads on. "Rainsford froze there, every muscle tensed for a spring. But the sharp eyes of the hunter stopped before they reached the limb where Rainsford lay; a smile spread over his brown face."

I had their rapt attention. They were psyched, but it was the next part I had to do just right.

"Very deliberately he blew a smoke ring into the air; then he turned his back on the tree and walked carelessly away, back along the trail he had come."

I casually walk back across the room, imaginary smoke ring hanging in the air. At the last footfall, when I know they got it, I stop, face them, and pull a Groucho Marx, tapping an imaginary cigar and flexing my eyebrows.

They laugh. Meghan looks up. I ask again, "OK, so what happened?" Before the question is out of my mouth, a student, usually one of my more unruly boys, belts out, "Zaroff knows Rainsford's there. He's just messin' with him."

"Yes! You got it! Cool, huh?" Teachers live for the group Ah-ha!

My students don't forget the lesson. They bring it with them to *To Kill a Mockingbird*, so that by the time we reach the end of Chapter 7, where Jem cries, they don't need me to act it out. Their own minds' eyes have learned to take pleasure in seeing a picture in words that aren't all there.

This is what Monument Valley was like. It was the spaces that made me never want to leave, that never left me. There wasn't much color, nor was there much detail. Nothing rococo, but what there was went on forever. The language of sandstone and sky, clouds and towers, the dry and the brittle, was like that of old friends: not afraid. I couldn't stay away. Something cut loose inside, and somewhere during the interlude between Monument Valley and Zion National Park on the western side of Utah, my life changed.

◊

"What do you mean *when*, Chris? It all came to me just now. All at once. But listen: I should be able to get enough for the Boat Rentals to live for a couple of years while I'm getting my credential. I'll have to finish getting my bachelor's first, but that's no biggy. I'll sell the condo and keep that money liquid, just in case. The boys and I can live in a rental. There should be enough in the bank when I start teaching to buy again. A house. Not a condominium. Homeowners' associations are oligarchies. Have you ever lived in one? Jesus Lord."

"No, and I don't want to, and who cares? Are you serious about what you're talking about?"

"Yep. I'll be a good teacher. I'm totally comfortable in front of a bunch of kids. I teach private horn lessons; I taught Sunday School; I was a parent helper for both Austin and Sean; I was a docent for the County

Something cut loose inside

Symphony and the Cultural Council, and I was camp counselor for the music camp. I'll get to write my own lesson plans, and I'll still be my own boss – inside the classroom, anyway. I'll have to get into UCSC. I'll apply to San Jose State and Monterey Bay as back-up, but the plan won't work as well unless I get into the university at Santa Cruz."

"You've got it all figured out, don't you? You know, you'll have to apply for your bachelor's and again for graduate school. Institutions of higher learning don't generally let you stay on in the same school for your master's."

"We'll see about that."

"Aren't you a little old?"

"Nope. The field of education is one of the few that values experience. Chris, I'll be fifty years old when I start teaching. Fifty. Wow! Christopher!"

"Lois!"

"Do you think I'm crazy?"

"Well, not many people put everything on the line, but no, I don't think you're crazy. I think you have an admirable sense of adventure. I'm envious."

"Oh."

"What do *you* think?"

"I think I hope you're right."

16 A thousand-piece puzzle

There were no distractions. Every single thing I wanted to happen happened – more than happened. There was no waiting. I stood in no lines. I was never placed on hold and there were no phone menus. Somebody always answered.

Austin had hoped to own the Boat Rentals someday. I felt bad about it, but when I apologized for pulling that rug right out from under him, his cheerful "That's OK, Mom" contained, but for a word, the same love as my "That's OK, honey" I often spoke in similar circumstances. My parents, in turn, took the news of my new life plan in the Eeyorishly lugubrious "What's she doing now?" sort of way they had whenever I acquainted them with my latest venture.

"Hi, Dad."

"Lena! It's your daughter." Scrape, crackle, static noise, clunk.

"I got it! You can hang up now! — Lois?"

"I'm here."

"How was your road trip?"

"It went well. How are you doing?"

"I'm fine. I woke up with a headache today, but I'm fine."

"Well, hopefully it's nothing. How's Dad?"

"He's good."

"How about Ron? Have you seen him lately?"

"Oh, yes. Last week. What's going on?" She knew there was a crux to this matter.

"I'm selling the Boat Rentals and going back to school to become a teacher."

"Austin! Pick up the phone!"

"What now?" I could hear him say as another shuffle superimposed itself over a pause while he grumbled his way to the infamous kitchen phone.

"I'm selling the Boat Rentals and going back to school to become a teacher."

"Go on," they echoed Eeyore.

◊

A ploy, a finger prick I used to push my students into getting good grades was to tell them the story of how the admissions gal at the university in Santa Cruz actually went all the way back to my high-school transcript to seek out courses that fulfilled requirements for the literature program I was applying for. "See, you guys? You never know what the future holds."

It was too late to start school that fall, so while waiting for winter quarter to begin, I picked up a few units at the community college. I also went to Paris with Chris. While there, I had my waist-length hair cut *very* short and sold the Boat Rentals in a few overseas phone calls for $20,000 over the asking price. I then rode on the back of Chris's Harley Road King through fields of red poppies toward Barcelona, where he was studying for a semester. Our mirth, displayed in a coquettish sidelong look and a flickering wave of good-bye – *"Adiós amigo. Farewell!"* – kept me company as I boarded the train for

A thousand-piece puzzle

visits to Malaga, Madrid, and Salamanca to investigate language schools to attend the following summer.

Upon my arrival back in California, there was a fellow knocking on my door wondering if I might be interested in selling the condo. "Come right in," said I. "It's your lucky day."

◊

Lit 101("Theory and Interpretation: Marxist Theory"), Brit Lit ("Reading the Traditional Canon"), and "Literature and Empire." I was warned about taking a full load "after so many years."

A girl who's been crooning the lyrics to "Young at Heart" almost since Sinatra made them famous back in 1953 ignores such social precepts. Slipping into the role of student as easily as I might have slipped on a banana slug in the surrounding redwood forest, I had no difficulty settling into phase one of New Life Plan. The younger generation accepted me; my profs praised my work; and there were times when I thought so hard, I swore smoke and steam vented through my ears. Yet I never once looked back. My sons thought they had a pretty cool mom. Austin noted that he and I would be graduating together at the beginning of the next century.

◊

As gracefully and silently as a swan touching down on still water, certain chunks of time, however brief, convey memorable departures from day-to-day life. Salamanca, Spain, where I chose to study Spanish the following summer, was like that for me. I immersed myself not only in the language, but in the time out of everyday time it levied upon me. Waiting beneath the town clock in the *plaza mayor* – the *plaza mayor* and its old men – to meet up with classmates for some *café con leche,* or, in the commotion of *buenas tardes,* to meet them later for tapas, was a welcome exercise in tranquility. Jogging to the river to see the Art Nouveau and Art Deco Museum was a revitalizing interval after a long day of conjugating Spanish verbs. Wandering through the open air market became a weekly event I happily anticipated, and coming out of a performance of Bizet's *Carmen* at midnight to be cast into a throng of families out strolling, they too having just left the theatre or some similar social function, was a lesson in culture I found refreshing. Each day of the six weeks I was there, the town clock seemed to wind down, its hands moving ever more slowly with every turn of the hour, every passing day, until time had no relevance at all.

◊

My Spanish teacher back in the States recommended I not leave *España* without taking the opportunity to go to *Monte Perdido* in the Pyrenees. Showing me a map, she described the area in that animated way people have when reviving cherished travel discoveries. Influenced by the excitement in her voice and the energy in her movements, I listened carefully so I'd have a place to take my parents on the sightseeing tour I promised them when they came to meet me at the end of my last class in Salamanca.

Parque Nacional de Ordesa is now on *my* list of cherished travel discoveries. The parador in Bielsa, where we stayed, is tucked into a hill at the dead end of a long, mountainous climb that twists and turns through the alpine serenity of the Pyrenees. The Spanish paradors are hotels set up by the government in refurbished historic

A thousand-piece puzzle

buildings (old castles, monasteries, fortresses) to enhance tourism. Ours was situated on the edge of the national park, above a river across from a canyon wall streaked with at least a dozen waterfalls.

As I stood on the deck of the hotel's restaurant, I felt as if I were looking through a wide-angle lens or a huge bay window onto the world. The narrow waterfalls, each the width of the stream feeding it, fell hundreds of feet to the river below. This Hobbit Land, this Country of the Gnomes, was irresistible. I had to get closer.

"Mom. Dad. Do you mind?"

"No, of course not. We'll have a nice lunch and be here when you get back. You go and have a good time."

"Be careful," my dad admonished. "It looks like there's snow up there."

He was right. There was snow up there. And ice. But the ice wasn't solid. It was the kind that forms thin, rippled, dirt-and grass-speckled sheets. Were a black beetle to cross my path, I might proclaim dominance. and squash it flat. Hiking up as high as I dared along one of the falls, maybe 300 feet, I wanted to do just that to the ice covering the gurgling, happy, rivulet. Raising my boot, I exclaimed, "Excuse me. I can't help this. It won't hurt, but I must." Splash! It was exquisite. I chortled, calling out "You and I both knew that would happen!" as the water continued her fall down the mountain.

Upon returning, I could tell things weren't right between my parents. While I was outside getting my heart rate up and filling my blood vessels with fresh oxygen, they were breathing the toxic air of an argument. The ice that formed around *them* was solid, neither to be broken through, nor spoken of.

As we drove to Madrid to catch their flight early the next morning, the outside temperature warmed as we came down in elevation, but the chill inside remained. The fight was a bad one. With no television for him to watch and no bedroom for her to escape to, they had only their child, acting as trip adviser, to relieve the tension. My over-enthusiastic attempts made matters worse rather than better, the worst being when we got to Madrid.

I'd had so much fun in the Metro stations in France that I thought a ride on the Madrid subway might lighten the mood. I forgot that it was the beginning of August, when Europeans go on holiday. This day, it seemed, they were going en masse. The antiquated, yet vivid, images of stuffing a phone booth and "packing 'em in like sardines" are too loose an analogy for the onrush of human madness we sustained. Fill a subway car with telephone booths. Stuff each telephone booth with people. Jam wriggling sardines into any space that might be left. Put a Gary Larson *Far Side* caption beneath this cartoon, and you've got the picture. There was literally no room to move. Perspiring profusely, Dad underscored the scene with his own concise caption, "If I had a heart attack right now, I wouldn't be able to fall over. My *God*, I'd have to die standing up!"

I don't know what the fight was about, but the many hours separating it from our arrival at the airport were not enough to diffuse its strength. It would be two more hours until the plane took off, and still they did not consent to be near each other. I went back and forth between them – now Mom, now Dad – the same corner man tending to both boxers. We became a celluloid transparency of three solitary figures overlaid onto a student's exercise in stop-motion filmmaking entitled *An Afternoon in the Waiting Area of the Madrid Barajas International Airport*.

Married for more than forty years, they knew everything about the other's existence – all the parts of life's

A thousand-piece puzzle

experiences, together and before. This fight, each fight – *all* their fights – came down to the effect this knowledge could extract. Crestfallen, the slump of their shoulders cried out for pity that busy travelers couldn't stop for. Tired from the stubbornness, from the constriction of holding feelings in and the momentary relief of releasing them, they turned disconsolately for help to the only other person who knew them as well as they knew themselves. I was surprised by my father's depth of insight into his wife's personality; I was disappointed by my mother's continued rigidity on the whole question of her happiness. The only words I remember were my own, spoken after I listened to Mom's complaints and after I'd already gone over to Dad's side of the boxing ring to hear his.

"Did you know that I used to wish you and Dad would get divorced? All through growing up, I wished it. Did you know that? For Christ's sake, Mom, you're turning seventy soon, and I'm still wishing it!"

She glared at me. I'm sure she was thinking, "Don't take the Lord's name in vain."

"Look at me, Mom." Her face was like a rock. "You still have time. Please. Will you, please?" She didn't budge. "Mom, listen to me: You have two choices: Get out or Get happy. Choose one, please."

The boarding call sounded the bell for this championship match. I watched as they walked down the ramp toward the plane.

◊

The next time I visited New Jersey, I noticed a thousand-piece puzzle, glued and mounted like a signed print.

"Is that one of yours, Dad?"

"Yeah. Do you like it?"

"Sure."

"Don't you recognize it?" my mom asked, walking in from the kitchen, her hands in a dishtowel.

"I guess not."

"Those mountains are the Pyrenees."

"Oh, I see."

"We put it up to remind us of the vacation we had with our daughter in Spain. We were so impressed. We talk about it a lot. Your dad likes to tell the story of the subway ride."

17 Lois Lane

I received my bachelor's in literature from UC Santa Cruz in June of 1998. Forty out of more than 120 applicants were accepted into the Master's in Education program to begin there that October. I was one of them.

But it was summer, and the boys were out of school. I was ready to party. Sean was deep into ska, and Austin needed to practice his driving skills. We came up with a plan: Fly east to New York. Rent car. Go to Manhattan for a few days to check out Moon Ska Records and explore the Big Apple. Drive down to Vineland to visit grandparents for a week. Leave Sean in Vineland while Austin and Mom, but mostly Austin, drive rental car back to California. Meet up with Sean in Santa Cruz.

"May I bring Kevin?" Austin asked.

"What?"

"Can Kevin Thorpe go with us?"

"Your friend from the teen center? That's a good idea. Why don't you give him a call? Hey, Seanie! Come here. Guess what?"

"What, Mama?"

"Looks like we're goin'."

"We are? Yippee!"

Sean was fourteen. Austin, two years his senior. A shopping list of names and phrases, the fullness of the experience each evoked, was the fullness of life itself. C.S. Lewis, J.D. Salinger, the Beatles, Spin Doctors, Metallica, and NOFX, my boys assessed the opinions of other men. They took piano lessons and drum lessons. They played softball, basketball, and golf; ran cross-country, skied, and skateboarded. Austin collected baseball cards; Sean collected Legos. There were Zelda and Mario Brothers, the pine car derby, lots of sleepovers, and lots of bicycle-tire screeching on neighborhood pavement. Sean took me to the mother-son dance; Austin bought me three small juice glasses he found at the flea market that I used for decades. Sean entered his junk collection in the county fair; Austin invented the Pencil Passer for Invent America. The junk wasn't 100 percent junk. It was broken objects Sean took apart to see how they worked. The Pencil Passer was a fat souvenir pencil we sliced the eraser from and bored a hole into so a note could be put inside before replacing the eraser and passing the innocuous-looking device to that cute girl two rows over.

 I held before me the nostalgia of a Norman Rockwell print, some image from my childhood of how the world should be – a truth that took place long before I was born. I hoped that my sons, too, could learn of truths that came to be long before they were born. The indulgences of a happy boy's life were the lucky springboard for my boys, my sons, who were becoming men.

 Except for once, I was a good mom through it all – an extraordinary mom, actually. But by the time Austin was advancing to Big Man On Campus in high school and Sean was toughing it out in middle school, I was losing any strong sense of self I'd acquired during *my* formative years. Where was the girl who explored avenues of adventure? That girl of tenacious determination? The girl who could legitimately answer the pick-up line "Got a match?" with "Not since Superman died."

The one exception, however, gave rise to a story that made it clear that that girl's sense of self was merely dormant. All it needed was a proper lull at a dinner party, maybe at the end of the meal when everybody is still chuckling over the first story told; or maybe as the group reconvenes from stretching, some having cleared the table, some, with an eye for dessert, striking up small talk with the host as they follow him into the kitchen; and some, with thoughts of Bacchus numbing, showing interest in the choice of port set out on the table.

"Austin and Sean were about eleven and thirteen when it happened," I begin. "I started sailing a few years earlier and drinking soon after that, the two, of course, historically forever entwined – 'Yo-ho-ho and a bottle' and all that. It wasn't long before I became friends with the captain from Yacht Octavia."

If the room assumes a round-the-campfire feel, I know I've been given the go-ahead to continue . . .

The general routine was to go from a back-slapping beer at the dock — "Did you see their faces when we blew by 'em at the windward mark?" — to a cocktail at the yacht club — "Great sail!" — to shots at the nearby, shall we say, establishment — "Gorgeous day! Damn, if the right side of the course wasn't favored again!"

Single malts for our crowd still a year away, the captain and I were, on this evening, sharing a Jack Daniels. The bar was L-shaped. We were seated in the center of the vertical side of the L, watching the jukebox, the pool table, the pinball machine, and all the people as they moved about in the mirror in front of us and behind the bartender. We could feel the room, and it felt good.

Somehow, we got on the subject of names: how we got ours, what we suffered because of them, nicknames we endured – that sort of thing. I mentioned I'd always wanted to get hold of the street sign Lois Lane from the east side of town. The captain commented he always wanted an Octavia Street sign from San Francisco.

"Why don't you get it for me?" he suggested.

"Why don't you get me Lois Lane, Mr. Octavia?" I quipped. Then, for fun, I made him an offer. "I'll get you Octavia Street if you get me Lois Lane."

"You get me the Octavia sign first," he said. "And I don't want one of those new kind. I want one of the old metal ones – black letters raised on white enamel. From the thirties. You know the ones I mean."

"Yeah, I know the ones you mean," I told him.

That was it, until a couple of months later when I and my attorney friend, Phil, went on our annual date to San Francisco to hear the symphony at Davies Hall. As we were leaving the performance, heading up Hayes toward Highway 101, I happened to look out the passenger's window and saw that we were driving past Octavia Street.

"Hey, Phil," I said. "Turn right and go back a block. I want to see something."

He complied, good friend that he was, and as we drove around I asked, "What would you have to do to get a street sign down?"

"Commit larceny."

"No, I mean, what tools would you need to do it?"

He peered out the windshield at the sign in question. "A pair of sheet metal shears."

And a ladder, I thought. Out loud, I asked him to turn right again and tour the area. He obliged while I craned to get a fix on the perfect sign. After a few minutes, I told him we could go, and that was that.

About a week later, I went to the local hardware store and bought a three-step wooden step stool. The week after that, when one of the wharf crew came into the bait shop for his daily candy bar, I asked if the City of Santa Cruz owned a pair of sheet-metal cutters. "Oh, sure," he said. "Do you want to borrow them?"

Now it was time to do some serious thinking. I'd scoped out a quiet, residential part of Octavia Street and obtained a ladder and shears – a good start. But when should this heist take place? Two in the morning sounded good. That would give time enough to get there and back before I had to wake my boys and get them off to school. Then I remembered this caper was to take place in the bustling City by the Bay, not the all-but-sleepy fishing village of Santa Cruz, so I asked myself, "How about four?"

"No," I answered me. "Four is getting too close to deliveries time and when commuters start waking up. How about 3:30?"

"Yes, 3:30. Do the deed, which should take about ten minutes, and then get the hell out of there and get home."

"OK, now what day?" I inquired of the Lois Lane within me.

"Not a weekend, certainly. When else would there be fewer people out? Uh . . . bad weather. But not pouring rain. That would make the job more difficult. A drizzle."

"Yes, a drizzle would be perfect. A little fog, too."

I threw the tools of the trade, as I now thought of them, into the back of the truck I used for hauling gas and boats, and started watching the weather.

Another couple of weeks went by. I all but forgot about the drunken wager until one misty evening, when it struck me that this was the night. I don't know how I knew that. I just knew it.

At any rate, I got out my black turtleneck and jeans, and set the alarm for 1:30. The boys would be sound asleep by then. I couldn't believe I was leaving my sons alone in the night, with nobody watching them and nobody knowing where I'd be; but a bargain was a bargain, and Lois Lane was a woman of her word, so what else could I do?

There was a light rain, just as I'd counted on. I drove the hour-and-a-half it took to reach Davies Hall and get my bearings. Do you have any idea how many people are still awake at 3:30 a.m. on a Tuesday in a foggy mist on a side street in San Francisco? It's unbelievable. I parked a block away from the designated sign, burrowed into my seat, and waited fifteen minutes. Things seemed to quiet down, so I drove another block, within sight of the target, and parked again. In less than ten minutes, a delivery truck pulled up to the curb two doors down. A garage door opened. I withdrew from sight again, but could hear three or four guys yakkin' it up. This was supposed to be a residential part of Octavia Street! What was up with these guys? It sounded like some type of soup-kitchen delivery or something. I waited, my side hurting from being folded in half in the front seat of the truck. Finally, it was quiet again, and I knew it was now or never.

I moved closer to the sign, parking at the edge of a driveway. The nearest streetlight was on the opposite side of the street, so I felt safe on that score. Besides, it was pretty foggy by now. I quietly opened the tailgate, took out the ladder and set it up. Then I got the shears and climbed. What's this? No snip, snip as I expected. I cut and cut, sweat mixing in with the drizzle on my face.

It took both hands, and it took forever, but I got it, and there was nobody anywhere.

That was the first strap. There were two. Getting nervous as hell, my arms hurt from the overhead work. I needed a break.

Leaving the ladder by the pole, I retreated to the truck for a breather and to calm down. Knowing what to expect this time, I took a few deep breaths, got my nerve back and went for it. The second strap was problematic because I had to hold the weight of the sign while I cut. Little by little, I wrenched the metal until it snapped – just ahead of my nerves. Then . . . I got it. Down it came. I slid the sign, ladder, and cutters into the back of the truck, shut the gate, hurried to the driver's seat, started her up, and took off. My right foot was shaking so badly from the adrenalin rush, I could barely drive. I kept seeing my old boyfriend Hugh's gas-pedal foot going like Thumper's up to his house on Magnolia Star Route that warm and sunny Colorado day in 1974 as we careened around those graded dirt road curves in his big ol' convertible Caddy. He had to pee so badly his shorts were in danger of getting baptized by his own holy water.

How can anybody be a crook more than once? The excitement was much scarier than it was exhilarating.

Anyway, soon I was bouncing up and down in my seat yelping joyously, "Woo-hoo. I did it!"

Ninety minutes later, I rolled into Santa Cruz in time to wake Sean and Austin, make breakfast, prepare their Super Mom lunches, and take them to school in Felton, six miles away. We always took the scenic redwood-lined and winding route, making the round trip about forty minutes long. Add another fifteen for some grocery shopping and I'd be home within the hour to start vacuuming.

OUT FOR STARS

When I got there, I spied a business card wedged between the metal frame and the screen of the door. It belonged to a Santa Cruz police officer. On the back was written, "Sgt. Fewer from the San Francisco Police Department would like to speak with you. 415-553-. . ." *Oh, shit.*

Shaking again, but not from excitement this time, I called a friend who worked with juveniles, to see what she might know about the consequences of my crime. At least I wasn't kidding myself about what type of crime I'd committed. Then I called another friend who'd gotten in trouble with the law before. After they were each through laughing, they told me what they knew. They agreed that the last thing I should do was call the SFPD. "Call a lawyer," they both advised.

Phil's a contractual attorney and a friend, so he couldn't represent me, but he recommended the fellow who did. When *he* got over laughing, he said he'd make a few calls. About an hour later, I was informed to bring $250 (the lawyer's fee, not the City of San Francisco's) and the sign, wrapped, to his office for him to mail back to its rightful owner. I was to wear gloves while I packed it to keep any hint of finger prints off (I never understood why), and I was to have it there by the next afternoon.

That meant I'd have it in my possession for almost a whole day. I called the captain. We met that evening, along with a few of our yo-ho-ho friends, for a photo shoot – me with the sign under my chin, like a mug shot. We didn't need to mention that the deal on Lois Lane was off.

The next day, I took a sheepish walk through the attorney's lobby with the wrapped sign under my arm like a large cartoon salmon. The secretaries were all side glances and sniggles as I went into the counselor's office to drop it off and where the whole affair ended pretty simply. "Since you're forty-five years old with no priors," he said, "Sgt. Fewer instructed me to tell you that if you give the City of San Francisco its property back, they'll forget about it. No questions asked. Although frankly, Miss Lane, I think they have a few."

◊

Years later, I moved into a third-floor downtown apartment with a tall picture window facing the street. Placing the rocking chair I rock-a-bye-babied Sean in in front of it, I'd sit and watch the world go by through the deciduous changes of the sycamore trees that lined the sidewalk. Surveying all below me, I'd observe balding heads and assess parallel parking techniques and wonder about people who eat pizza while they walk. Sometimes I'd think of that person who may also have felt the superiority of a god on Mt. Olympus, placidly watching from the warmth of his third-floor apartment, thoroughly entertained, waiting for the error, for the moment he could pick up the phone.

I shouldn't have closed the tailgate.

> So priketh hem Nature in hir corages –
> Thanne longen folk to goon on pilgrimages.
> – Geoffrey Chaucer, Prologue to *The Canterbury Tales*

18 How past and present meet

On the plane ride to New York, Austin and I configured our cross-country daydream with the penciled sketch of a plot summary. Austin wanted to eat a steak at Dan's in Luray, Virginia, go to the Pro Football Hall of Fame in Canton, Ohio, and buy lots of fireworks everywhere in Tennessee. I wanted to show him the Smithsonian, Kent, the Rockies, and the Grand Canyon. We soon learned that these stops, as well as Austin's original desire to practice driving and my need to let my hair down after two years of schoolwork, weren't the real reasons for making this trip. The underlying purpose for our journey – the intention generally not spoken of, but which is often the reality of a thing – didn't become apparent until we entered the children's room of the New York Public Library on 53rd near Fifth.

I wanted to go in because that's what I do. I go into libraries. Austin and his friend Kevin followed close behind as I looked for what I call the bower, the leafy shelter – every library has one – where books become the closest thing to being in nature without being in a forest.

My search for this hideaway in the Donnell Library Center was cut short when Austin and I chanced upon – practically bumped into – icons of trust we thought we'd left behind years ago in a story book.

OUT FOR STARS

Bump, bump, bump, we were on a hunt for a hefalump, or so it seemed, when, stepping out of the elevator onto the second floor, we suddenly stopped, frozen in time. There, before us, sat Pooh, Piglet, Eeyore, Kanga, and Tigger in a glass case, waiting. We stared, and all in a shimmering instant, we understood why we were going on this excursion. Austin was beginning his flight from the nest; I was retracing the first steps I'd taken from mine. He was spreading his wings; I was making a pilgrimage. Knowing we were safe in the love borne of a happy childhood, it was time for us to put away childish things. We took a picture.

I didn't know where Sean was while all this was going on, probably browsing the library's CD collection, just as I didn't know where Austin and Kevin were when I escorted Sean into Moon Ska Records. The famous ska music label's storefront, a crowded, below-street-level hole in the wall in the East Village, was not far from where we were staying. As soon as we entered, its physical presence turned us into two friends hypnotized. This was the Big Apple we'd wanted to experience, a part of town that didn't belong to tourists. But tourists we were, caught in the stupid daze of our kind. We bought a shirt, patches, CDs, and an album before stepping back out into the sunlight. We were not released from our hypnotic state, however, until a sweaty, smelly, loud bunch of very big guys behind a chain-link fence regaled us with a city park basketball game. We watched through the ornament of summer trees growing in and out along the fence, giving us a sense of sway, leaving us "well satisfied with our purchases."

To say I escorted Sean into Moon Ska Records isn't quite correct. Sean was coming out of his youth, edging toward the rim of the nest. It was critical to his

How past and present meet

developing adolescence that *he* take *me* into the record shop and for me to let him. Besides, he was doing me a favor by staying at my folk's house while his brother and I were on the road. We'd learned a few weeks earlier that my dad was sick. He had been diagnosed with liver cancer in June. Unfortunately, this was after we made arrangements for the trip. I didn't know what his symptoms were or how the problem was identified. He wasn't in pain(it would be more than two years before he was) but I felt guilty that I would be with him for only a few days before traipsing off on a 3,000-mile junket just after receiving such inauspicious news. Sean's remaining behind gave me comfort. He was our emissary, watching over his grandparents while they watched over him, allowing Austin and me to perform freely our rite of passage.

◊

The rental car and its four occupants did well on the trial run between New York City and Vineland. I thought of visiting Cory on the way down, but alas, the ease of email never got a chance to replace the effort of handwritten letters for us, and phone calls had long since died away. With the advantage of hometown connections, though, Robin and I were not deprived the click of the touch pad, and our meeting was greeted with pleasurable anticipation. He'd become athletic director at the high school and wanted to show me his office. We sat and talked, and I was glad to be in contact with him again.

For the most part, the time in Vineland was yet another whirlwind tour of my place of origin: a day at the shore, authentic Italian ravioli, fireflies in the backyard, and a stroll around Parvin State Park. Unlike in years past, the focus of this visit was not customary activities and expected obligations, but preparing for the long drive west. Surviving the claustrophobic trap brought on by needling interviews from relatives and old friends still unconvinced of what goes on in California assured Austin, Kevin, and me that we'd do well withstanding the austerities that three weeks together in the space of 110 cubic feet required.

We left on a Wednesday, charting a course for the National Air and Space Museum and Luray, Virginia, for melt-in-your-mouth prime rib at Dan's. Three days later, we were in Kent. Twenty-five years before, it was my island; now, nothing looked the same. Soon, though, my eyes adjusted, and some of the old places came into focus. Jerry's Diner, where I worked the graveyard shift, was there. Hahn's Bakery and Kline's, the market where I could exchange food stamps for cash, were not. The Brady Street house was there and no different. Memories were jogged. I saw Theresa, Arlene, and myself, arm in arm, happy as could be, looking like three Soviet workers from a propaganda poster of the 1930s, coming out of a Russian factory, but instead of wearing kerchiefs, we were sporting calico bandanas and were coming out of a pizza place down by the railroad tracks. I heard Guffer's gentle reproof of my bad habit of cursing as he took both my hands up into his at the intersection of Water and Main. "It doesn't become you," he said. Other street names came back to me within a few hours. I knew we were on the right track for finding the Johnson Road house because crossing the Cuyahoga River felt as familiar as going home.

I showed Austin all of these places, spoke to him of all these things, but the long and infrequent waves of nostalgia can be but briefly paired with the short and

How past and present meet

sprightly energies of two teenage boys. As politely as the ants in their pants allowed, Austin and Kevin bowed out of further sentimental journeys, preferring to go off on foot while I drove up to campus, Taylor Hall, and the parking lot.

Having to reorient myself, I began to consider how past and present meet only in our minds. I had been a part of what happened on May 4, 1970, yet I felt a stranger to its memorial. Uncertain of the way, I walked tentatively along the path leading to the plaza where I paused to view the daffodils and granite pillars presented by the designers of this place – the granite a tribute to the dead here in Ohio and the thousands of flowers planted in remembrance of those lost in Vietnam, one for each of the fallen. As unyielding as the rock, as alive as the blossoms each spring, these symbols inextricably linked the soldier and the student in the ideals of their youth.

I caught sight of some brochures with a written description of the events of 1970. I took one. Reading it over casually, curiously, I saw that the past and present do not just meet in the mind. They also meet in artifacts. Are not a bone, a chip of clay, and an arrowhead markers of the past? Studying the pamphlet's map of the site, I continued the thought: A human appendix. It's there, but it doesn't do anything except make us ask why. What's it for? How did it come to be? When did it have meaning? This printed paper was an artifact, like when I ran into – who was it? – at that funeral. We got to talking about something or other we did together in the old days and discovered our memories were a match, a precise fit. It was so exciting.

Here, I felt as if I knew the three men who authored the brochure. They shocked me with a recounting of events so close to my own recollection that I felt they consulted me on its writing. Why hadn't this sort of connection ever occurred with my Kent friends – Norm or Holly or Mark, Arlene or Theresa? They must have been there. Yet, I don't remember so much as a reference being made. It was as if we were Navajos, reluctant to speak the names of the dead.

Suddenly, I wasn't alone. Could it be true? Is the verified accuracy of memory confirmation we are not alone? Or is it a heart-shaped balloon, cut loose, drifting, floating, lifting higher and higher into the atmosphere? Someone sees it. She points. The day goes on.

By this time in my contemplations, I'd arrived back at Taylor Hall and the spot where I stood when the shooting stopped. I looked at the map's thirteen circled letters, A through M, denoting the locations where the nine wounded and four dead had fallen. How close I had been!

I got into the car to go meet Austin and Kevin for our appointment with the Pro Football Hall of Fame. I heaved a sigh, culminating the day's solemnity with a final summation: How soon my tale of black squirrels and innocence became the story of 58,175 daffodils on a hill.

19 "He was the parts manager"

As planned, Sean was waiting at his dad's when we got back home to Santa Cruz. Just about the time school was due to start for all three of us, our landlord raised the rent. He'd sworn he wouldn't do that, and like so many promises, it was as disappointingly hollow as the hollow chocolate Easter bunny thought to be solid. Trusting we were still in the bubble of good fortune that had begun with my epiphany, I gave notice. In less than a week, we found a place within a mile of campus that had a two-year lease perfectly timed to run out at the end of my graduate studies. A whitewashed, low-ceilinged farmhouse, it sat by a creek with blackberry bushes and wildflowers, and had French windows that opened out, letting in a spidery world pursued by dozens of spider eaters. In addition, the house came with a couch on the back porch, a hammock, two beach chairs by the creek, and two great horned owls for company in the night.

Also at about this time, I told my mom that I wanted her to open the lines of communication between Ron and me. He had become such a regular item on our telephone conversation agenda that I felt as if I knew him. Surely, he knew all about me. After all, he'd been in earshot of my life since I was in junior high school. Now

I was forty-eight, and it seemed fitting that we break through the social restraints and get to know each other.

◊

"Hi Mom. It's me."

"Hi, Lois." Her voice always had an out-of-breath quality to it when she answered the phone. It wasn't the dragged-myself-up-the-stairs stereotype of someone her age, but the let-me-put-my-things-down-I-was-just-coming-in cheerfulness of someone always on the go and happy about it. "How are you? Are you settled in, yet?"

"We're getting there. I ran over two bushes trying to back the truck in close enough to the porch to unload the piano. The neighbor wasn't too pleased."

"Weren't the boys there to help you?"

"Oh, yes. Sean and three of his pals."

"That poor piano. It's moved an awful lot."

"Austin and Sean would agree with you on that. How's Dad?"

"Oh, he's doing good. The cancer doesn't seem to bother him that much."

"Hmm. I don't get it. I guess it's too soon, but I'm glad he's not suffering."

"No, he won't put up with that. When he starts to hurt, he won't be with us much longer."

"I agree with you there. How about Ron? How's he doing? He was under the weather the last time we talked."

"He's all right. He went to the doctor and got some pills. We're not seeing much of each other. I'm afraid to stay away from the house for too long. Ron and I talk, but that's about all. Your father needs me right now."

"Well, that's good of you, Mom. When are you going to give me his phone number?"

"He was the parts manager"

"Whose?"

"Ron's."

"What? Never."

"How about if something happened to you? He wouldn't know about it. You don't want him finding out you're dead from reading it in the paper, do you?"

"Oh, Lois."

"No. Come on, Mom. I'm serious. Ever since Dad got sick, I've been thinking. Isn't it time Ron and I made contact?"

"No."

"How come?"

"He's not ready, and neither am I. That's how come."

"Gee whiz, Mom. Aren't I ever going to get to meet him?"

"You already have."

"What? When?"

"When you worked with me that summer at the dealership. Don't you remember? He was the parts manager."

"You're kidding. Ma-a-a-m," I said, drawing out the vowel in Mom like a schoolgirl balking at the news that she has to do her chores before she'll be allowed to go to the dance. "You never told me that!" There went my, "debonair chap, refined, graying at the temples," theory. The guy I remembered as parts manager looked more like Ichabod Crane.

"Yes, I did tell you that."

"I don't think so, but you know, I do remember him. He used to come through the office and drop off invoices or files, some kind of paperwork like that, on your desk, or maybe – what was her name? The head secretary – Jean's desk."

"That was him."

"If we already know each other, there's no reason for us not to connect."

"No."

"How about giving him my number?"

"He won't call you."

"Well, give him my info anyway, will you?"

"He's already got it." That shut me up.

"Oh, I see. Hmm. Well. So, how are you? The bell choir keeping you on your toes?"

> When he sat in the grass and listened
> to the purling stream, the barriers set up in his mind
> by the stern day went down to ruin.
> – John Steinbeck, *The Red Pony*

20 Walking away

Depression creeps up on you. At least it did on me, but I couldn't get it to add up. My life was on track. Graduate school was going well, and the whitewashed farmhouse, though it'd been over a year since the boys and I moved in, was still the ideal place for us to live. In short, everything was great, and I'd be lying to say I wasn't happy. In fact, one of the items on my list of "Top-Ten Happiest Moments" comes from this period.

Our street came to a dead end along the southeastern boundary of the university property, so in dry weather, I biked to class and in wet, I walked. The "Happiest Moments" memory of how I got to school makes little distinction between the two types of days:

> Aware from the start that these two years will never come again, I inhale deeply their unique fragrance. This is easy to do on the campus of the University of California at Santa Cruz, for it is among the most beautiful in the United States. The weather sunny and dry, I pedal up the loop road, cycle around green fields, past groves of eucalyptus and redwood, close by grasses and wildflowers, beneath birds rapt in song, and always just ahead of the stunning view of ocean and town. Switching to overcast and wet weather, I step over a fence in full rain gear regalia, detouring around curious bovines as I walk across

the open expanse of pasture to reach my first class of the day. A fog comes in so thick I lose the way, and I have to employ my internal GPS to get back on course, all the while singing a nursery rhyme the boys and I know well. "One misty, moisty morning when cloudy was the weather, I chanced upon an old man who was all dressed in leather. He began to compliment and I began to grin. Saying, 'How do you do?' and 'How do you do?' and 'How do you do?' again."

Paradoxically, a memory from my list of "Top-Ten Darkest Hours" also comes from this period:

Deep into the night, I abruptly sit up, sharply awakened by, I assume, a bad dream. But I know it's more than that. Wrapped in a swirl of blankets, sheets, and pillows, I curl down in the center of the bed, hugging my shoulders in an attempt to protect myself from whatever it is. Any image I may ever have had of Julie Andrews spinning round, arms outstretched for that extremely long camera shot, has disappeared forever, replaced by an ever tightening eddy, a whirling vortex, twisting inward, faster and faster. I scream. If it is midnight, I call my friend Rupert. If it is 4:30, I call my mom in New Jersey.

Overall, the way I began to figure it was this: If a girl is ninety percent happy and ten percent not happy, she can make it through the rest of her life just fine. If she's eighty percent happy and twenty percent not happy, she'd better start paying attention to the thorn. If it gets to sixty/forty, guess what? She's not happy. By October of 1999, my percentages were not looking good.

To reverse the trend, I took to telling myself a bedtime story on those nights my demons were most industrious. Suicide was the obvious story line, but it was out of the question. Austin and Sean meant too much to

Walking away

me to approach that scenario, even in the form of a daydream. So I chose a never-ending yarn of exile, anguish, sorrow, contrition, self-pity, and forgiveness. I'd be like Philip Nolan in *The Man Without a Country*, but rather than living out my unpardonable existence on the open sea, passed from ship to ship, I'd be on land, walking, forever walking, horizon to horizon, far, far from home.

The story got more elaborate with each telling. I'd step off the front porch and head in the direction of the Central Valley. I don't know why. It had something to do with the rural, sparsely used, two-lane roads there. Was it a spin on my fantasy trek through the highlands of Scotland? If so, this newer version had me moving along sadly, somberly observing the scenery and the sense of walking. Each chapter had me fanning out, farther and farther, for days on end, to Alaska, to Argentina. One night, I somehow made it all the way to New Zealand, where the funeral dirge of this morbid travel log got mixed up with the whistling tune of an adventure. The grim lullaby now too outlandish, my pragmatic nature felt the need to suggest a stratagem – some planning – in the hope of expanding the concept of this long walk. "I'll take a day pack and a sleeping bag, and before I leave, I'll put all the money from the Boat Rentals and the condo onto a credit card and use it to buy the essentials, and I'll write a letter to the boys explaining everything." I didn't die. I didn't live. I did invariably fall asleep when the pitiful drama reached the point of no return.

Because there's truth to the premise that some people are born happy, dreary moods did not bring me down for more than twenty-four hours at a time, even at their worst. This made it more difficult to diagnose them as depression and easier to blame the cheerless days on stress, probably related to schoolwork deadlines. When the twenty-four hour periods became more frequent, alarm bells rang, and though convinced I was above what I considered maladies of weakness, I remained on alert, listening for the meaning behind the signals. It wasn't long before I found it.

◊

Every circle of friends has a core of individuals who enjoy entertaining. This is a boon and a benefit to the rest of us, who rely on these extroverted folks to keep the social calendar from becoming a flashback to the ugly side of high school – the side that saw kids out in the hall on Monday mornings with the word "Loser" stamped across their foreheads, as they stood by while other kids jabbered on about who did what and what happened where over the weekend.

Now, I could count on friends like Shirley to have the annual Easter Egg Hunt and Potluck Champagne Brunch; Susan and David to put on the Super Bowl Sunday Party; and Mark and Holly to throw the Visit from Santa Tequila Shots Christmas Bash.

During Sheryl's 1999 Thanksgiving Friday Leftovers Feast, somebody decided we needed to repeat the "What are you thankful for?" exercise everyone had more than likely tolerated the day before.

"Oh, please."

"Come on, it'll be fun. I'll start. I'm thankful to have you guys in my life."

"Then I must be thankful for sappy chicks."

"I'm thankful for all this great food."

"Me, too."

"Me, three. Sappy chicks??"

"All right, I'm in. I'm thankful I have a job I don't hate."

Walking away

"I'm just glad I have a job."
"I'm grateful for my health."
"Thank God my kids are healthy."
"Thank God my kids aren't in jail!"
"Thank God for Prozac!" Everybody laughed.
"I'd have never gotten through my divorce without it."
"I know somebody whose *dog* is on Prozac."
"What's Prozac?" I asked.

This comment drew immediate silence, during which it was clear that everyone was thinking, *you've got to be kidding*. Sheryl, courteously picking up the ball for the whole group, replied, "It's an antidepressant."

"Oh," I said. "Well, then, I thank the Lord I didn't know what Prozac was."

Later, after the party wound down and we'd said our good-byes, Allen and I, both lifers in this crowd, sat in his car going over the gossip and news of the evening. He and I had recently taken to going out, but whether we were dating or not was up for debate. He may have thought we were. I knew we weren't. On this night, though, I was hard pressed to argue the point. It felt good to lean up against him. Our conversation was the truest of any we'd had, and that felt good, too.

"I can't believe you never heard of Prozac."
"A person can't know everything."
"Have you heard about the world being round?"
"Ha. Ha."
"I was on Prozac."
"You were?" I said.
"Yep."
"What for?"
"I let my serotonin levels get too low and was pushing clinical depression."
"All right, so the world's round. What's serotonin?"

"Touchy, are we? I knew you didn't know. It was just a lead-in. It's what's called a neurotransmitter, a hormone. It's in your brain, and it sends messages between nerves. They think it helps give you a sense of well being. If you don't have enough of it, you can get tired, down, and eventually, you can end up clinically depressed."

"*They?* Now you need to explain clinically depressed."

"That's when you're so damned depressed, nothing matters. It's when you pretend you've got the flu and don't go to work. It's a vicious cycle, I can tell you. You're depressed, so you don't eat right, you don't sleep, you don't feel like exercising, and so you're more bummed out than when you started. Then your serotonin levels drop to an all-time low because you're not doing the good stuff that keeps them where they should be, and then you're up Shit Creek without a paddle."

"Unless you have Prozac, I take it."

"Yeah. A paddle in a pill."

"What's it feel like?"

"Depression?"

"No, silly. Prozac."

"How do you think it makes you feel? You feel better. Even keeled. You don't really *feel* anything. Elevated maybe, but not a high like on weed or speed, but normal. Kind of. You don't cry."

"You don't cry?"

"Not so much."

"I don't think I'd like that. How'd you know you were depressed? You seem OK to me."

"I *am* OK. What did you think? I don't know. I was on a downer for too long, so I went to a shrink."

"I see."

Prying further would have been impolite and broken the pleasantness of the moment, but not only that. There

Walking away

was something about this conversation. It wasn't about Allen. He didn't say it, but he didn't have to.

◊

A few days later, I happened to tune into a radio program about clinical depression. I'd probably heard others on the subject, but on this occasion, I listened. The girl interviewed was articulate and spoke with an intelligence that gave credibility to her personal experience and explanation of this delicate topic. Her voice was fluid, confident, and lacked the emotionalism of the overwrought so many radio interviewers capitalize on. This made her someone I was willing to pay attention to, and what she said hit home. I was tempting fate, and if I didn't watch it, I too, would have a story to tell of losing control to this invasive disorder.

Two things frightened me. First, a prescription for antidepressants was, for me, not a sign of getting help but a lapse in strength of character. Second, a year or two or five of it, and depression would become part of who I was, or someday, who I had been. Tending a garden *that* overgrown would be a waste of life's precious time. Just how long could a never-ending walk last? Not forever, if my belief in the power of introspection had anything to do with it. And it did. That the worst nights of my bad days, those on which I woke up screaming, didn't occur when Sean and Austin were with me was the tip-off that I was still undeniably in control.

◊

The next event on the social calendar was Nancy's Winter Solstice Party. Feathers and beads and stones and bones, chants and closed eyes and a witch that moaned.

Every year got more and more pagan, and I didn't believe in any of it. Yet, even the most vehement of nonbelievers might have been compelled to acknowledge this year's celebration, for the planet was barreling ahead into the new millennium and the moon would not be full again at the winter solstice until ten years into it.

I played along because the food was gourmet and because we got to go down to the beach and have a bonfire, but mostly because I enjoyed spending time in Nancy's farmhouse. It was the closest thing to Johnson Road I ever got to in California. The peeling paint, the arched front gate grown over with a flowered vine, the creaking floorboards, the goats, the dried herbs hanging in the kitchen, the straw hat on the peg – I never told Nancy about Johnson Road. I suppose I should have. Then she'd have understood why I always seemed strangely fascinated with everything about her home.

◊

"Did you all remember to bring something to throw into the fire?"

"What? What is she talking about?" I asked the person nearest me.

"You were supposed to bring a representation of something you want gone from your life, and throw it away in the fire."

"I was? Oh, dear." I didn't have anything I needed to rid myself of, let alone something to represent it. No guy, no bad habits, no guilt, no regrets, no secrets.

Then it struck me.

Racing up the sandy path to the house, I rushed so I could get back before the ritual commenced. Spying a pencil and a fragment of note pad on the table next to the telephone, I scribbled out what I knew I needed to be

Walking away

done with. Returning to the beach just in time to close the circle, I followed everyone's lead and placed the offering at my feet. Photographs, bits of clothing, a wilted rose, a letter, a pack of cigarettes, a key – the assembly, suffused with retrospect and anticipation, no longer felt pagan but like a simple gathering of friends publicly sharing a break with the past and making a communal turn toward the future. Our guide (I shall not say sorceress), arms adorned with ringlets of silver, reached high above her head in praise of the night before instructing us to, one at a time, bring our forfeit closer to the bonfire, throw our burden into the blaze, and say what it was we were giving up. Unwanted pounds, excess baggage, dead weight – all things heavy became light in the presence of this fire.

It was no different when it came round to me. "I'm giving up a friend who's turned out to be dangerously bad company." Carrying my donation into the heat of the embers, I threw in the scrap on which I'd written the words, *My Walking Story*. It caught in the updraft of the flames, hovering, almost stationary, before it made its cradle-like descent, a leaf in a fiery wind. I could feel how the glow of the fire must have looked on my face, for I saw how it looked on the faces of the others.

With the electric shock of terror felt when suddenly we realize how perilous life can be, I comprehended what holding onto that daydream had almost done to me. I'd met secretly with my friend and accomplice, night after night, in a clandestine and selfish place forbidden to all but the two of us. To whom would I introduce such a friend? I knew then that the comfort I derived from my preferred plot line was a thick buffer masking the beast and, unlike a toreador who continues to provoke the raging bull, I needed to get away from this fiend as quickly as my legs would allow.

    That night, the darkness of my bedroom, the blackness before me, was the same as always. The way my body felt as I sank into the mattress, the way the covers draped over me as I curled into my sleeping position, and the way I sent the world outside away – all was as it had always been. Not until the next morning did I realize I forgot to tell the story.

> Distracted. That was a hell of a word.
> – Laurie R. King, *The Language of Bees*

21 The JMT

With minor exceptions, Y2K went off without a hitch; Silicon Valley's apprehension receded into nothingness, and the twenty-first century was soon just another day. Winter quarter began at UCSC. It was my last, but with preparations for student teaching well under way, I remained confident that the magic of these years would not taper off until I landed a job and stepped into my new life.

As Austin had astutely noted, mine was not the only commencement to take place that year. To celebrate his, I suggested we combine his Christmas, eighteenth birthday, and high-school graduation presents by sending him off on a four-day, all-expenses-paid weekend snowboarding trip to Mammoth Mountain. He was stoked (his word) by this. "Sick!" he added. Then I realized I may have spoken too soon. Mammoth Mountain was a six-hour drive in summer. This was winter.

"Chill, Mom. I know how to drive in the snow. I made it to Kirkwood in three hours once in a white out with no chains. It's easy."

"When did you do that?"

"Last year."

"Oh, brother." I looked into booking a flight.

It was not a simple matter, as I was forthwith to uncover. The airport at Mammoth was not big enough for the major carriers to fly into, and the small service outfit had stopped landing there "just last season," according to the girl who answered the phone. "Not enough crazy people willing to do it," she warned. "Besides, the weather conditions could make such a trip impossible."

Four or five discouraging phone calls later, the gal at the local airport just south of Santa Cruz piped up with, "Hey, wait. You know, there's a new guy in town. I talked to him this morning. He might take you over the mountains. Would you like his number? He appears reputable."

A mother averse to disappointing her son, I made the call, figuring the dangers of flying in a small plane over the mountains with an experienced pilot surely paled in comparison to those of a teenager who saw himself as Mario Andretti driving over them.

But pity the poor pilot! "Don't worry, Ma'am, I've been flying for a living for ten years. I won't risk carrying passengers in bad weather. Is there flexibility in your schedule? Your son and his girlfriend may have to stay in Mammoth a few extra days. No, I won't charge you for that time. I turn around as soon as I drop them off. Then I'll go back to pick them up." It took three days of responding to worried mother talk before he thought of what to say to mitigate my fears. "Would you like to come along for the ride?" I booked the flight.

◊

December's snowy peaks looked close enough to reach out and touch from the Cessna 310 we found ourselves safely strapped into. Boundless and inviting, the sweeping views got me thinking about my own graduation and the summer between it and the rest of my life.

The JMT

I remembered how I used to think that someday I'd like to hike the Appalachian Trail. *Maybe that's what I could do to ice this cake of mine,* I thought, as I took in the magnificence of the aerial scene. *But the Appalachian? What's here in the west? Oh, yes – the John Muir Trail. I'll hike the John Muir. Look at all this! That's what I'll do! I wonder how many miles it is?*

The decision to do the hike solo took all of a millisecond. That's not true. The thought to invite somebody else *never* entered my mind. Why would it? It was a hike in the mountains I wanted, not the company of others. I wasn't afraid. If I planned carefully and wisely, what could happen? All I was doing was going for a walk, and with the John Muir Trail on the short list of the world's most well-traveled pedestrian pathways, I'd have plenty of company. How difficult could it be?

Online research was not second nature yet, so except for some bookstore browsing which led to a set of maps and a small handbook devoted to the JMT, I used my own experience to prepare. I decided that the 219-mile span would be done optimally in late July, after the snow melted and the water receded but before the flies started buzzing. Taking the north-south route sounded more appealing than coming up the other way. I was familiar with Yosemite, and Mt. Whitney, at 14,500 feet, would be easier to climb after three weeks of hiking and acclimating to higher elevations. It would also make for a triumphant finish. However, this was the generally preferred route, making wilderness passes for this direction more difficult to procure. I sent for mine in February.

My concern was weight. That, and bears; but bears, I soon determined, though a necessary consideration, need not occupy much more than a passing thought. This is how it went: *What do I know about bears? Other than being furry and lumbering, they have an excellent sense of smell. They like free food. But as with Santa, they like their cookies and milk left out and will probably not stop for a visit unless the likelihood of such a snack presents itself. Therefore, I will put no cookies and milk out for Yogi and Boo Boo's California cousins. Being afraid of bears is along the lines of being afraid of getting struck by lightning. Take a few precautions, and it's doubtful it'll happen. Don't sleep with your food. Don't sleep near anybody who is. Don't become a lightning rod. Simple. Problem solved.*

Walking 219 miles while carrying everything I'd need to subsist, though, was a feat at sea level for a fifty year-old, let alone at the elevations I'd encounter. Concluding that I did not need to cook, make a fire, wear underwear, or have more than one change of shorts, t-shirt, or socks, the reality of the adventure began to take hold. Fleece pants, a pullover, and a nylon rain jacket would subdue the early morning chill and resist the occasional thunderstorm. I would shop for the lightest possible tent, backpack, and boots and use the reverse side of my maps for a journal. I would bag up one-pound packages of food – one for each day I was to be out – and . . . what else? A Band-Aid or two, a compass, two bandanas, a water filter, some toilet paper and a trowel, and I'd be set. Forget the tent stakes. My belongings would be ballast enough, and I could see no reason why my book light couldn't double as a flashlight.

On the off chance that I didn't go through with my ambitious resolution, I didn't tell anybody my plans until I received the passes that April. When, at Shirley's Easter Egg Hunt and Potluck Champagne Brunch, I revealed them, someone asked what I was doing to train. "Train? I don't know. Do you think I need to? I bicycle or walk whenever I can. Have for years, and if lugging two little boys around for half that time is evidence of a strong

The JMT

back, I'm well trained for that part, too. Nah. I'm good on getting in shape."

◊

I departed from Happy Isles in Yosemite on the morning of July 16, 2000. Turning to smile good-bye, Sean, who accompanied me as far as Little Yosemite Falls, reassured me that we would meet again in a week at the Vermillion Valley Resort on Lake Edison so he could hand off the very carefully arranged and precisely weighed out replenishment supplies I had placed by the back door of the kitchen.

◊

Day 1. High Sierra Camp. 14 miles. I felt a twinge of loneliness as I left Happy Isles. It lasted all of two seconds. I arrived at Sunrise Camp at 6:30 p.m. Some of the ascent was difficult. I was unsure of the way a few times, but I kept on. Some great views today. The mountains are so majestic, they're scary. My little campsite here is stupendous. Looks out over lush Long Meadow and across to the High Sierra. Full moon.

Day 2. Near Evelyn Lakes. 16 miles. Already the day and date have little meaning. Sitting in a lovely spot by a creek where I washed. Hanging clean (sort of) set of shorts and socks from backpack so they can dry while I walk. Hope to be off by 7 a.m. tomorrow. I am reminded of my camping days at Sugarloaf; my bandana, the all-purpose answer for everything. Easy hiking today. Meadows and wildflowers. Lyell Canyon is lovely. Birds, marmots, ground squirrels, and deer. Today I am thankful for the many footsteps in front of me I use as a guide when the path is not clear.

Day 3. Below Island Pass. 12 miles. Fourteen if I include the two I spent in a large snowfield searching for the trail at Donahue Pass. Where are those footprints I was so thankful for yesterday? I waited for others to help. Now I sit in my tent trying to wash with drinking water because the mosquitoes outside are so thick. I wish Austin and Sean could see the beauty through which I walk. It's 8 p.m. I'll be asleep by 8:30.

Day 4. Gladys Lake. 11 miles. Grueling but beautiful. Mosquitoes at dusk again. Presently in my tent to get away from them. The view through my netting is of the lake, trees, sky, and trout jumping. Dozens of trout jumping. I'll go out and stash my bear canister when it's dark and colder, and the bugs can't see me. Feeling raw, dirty, and sunburned. Yesterday, I thought of going home at Vermillion and tending to things. Today I got my head on straight, and this is what I have to say about it: I want to hold a place in my memory bank to make a withdrawal from when I'm ninety years old. When I'm walking – shuffling – very slowly, barely making it, half-inch by half-inch around the house or down a sidewalk or on a street that everybody's waiting for me to cross, I want to remember how I walked ever so slowly, barely making it – shuffling – up the ascents of the JMT for miles and miles when I was young.

Day 5. Deer Creek. 15 miles.

Yes. Then came Day 5, the day that made the trip a life-changing experience. My starting point, Gladys Lake, was but a few hours from Devils Postpile, where I stood and observed the long columns of this natural configuration for about a quarter of an hour. Then I went into the diner at Reds Meadow and ordered the fattest hamburger they had. I sat at the counter, placing my backpack on the floor next to me. There was an elderly lady, in her seventies I surmised, sitting at the table nearest me. She was by herself, eating an ice cream sundae. She was kind

The JMT

of dumpy, but there was something soft about her spirit that drew me in. She asked if I was hiking through. We talked. Our lives passed. I could see she hadn't fully applied her wisdom to her own life yet, but she was ahead of me and showed me a little of the way. I asked her questions about her life. She asked about mine. Our conversation then turned to speculations of the metaphysical and the "What's it all about?" complication. Something, her humble advice, her mild persona, or seeing how content she was, made me not so afraid of the second half of my life, which, at fifty, seemed to have just begun. I finished my lunch, tightened up the shoulder pads on the thirty-five pound pack I was becoming intimate with, waved, and headed out the door.

Within a half hour, I was hopelessly lost.

I don't know what happened. Somehow I got on a trail that took me into a very large, desolate, burned-out forest. I have since learned it was the remnants of the Rainbow Fire of 1992, and although the John Muir does get into that area for a mile or so, I somehow got on a footpath that put me in it for most of the afternoon.

Nobody had to tell me a firestorm went through here. The amount of devastation left no doubt. For hundreds of acres, the ground was sandy and hot, dry and covered with ash. There was nothing green. I was like a red ant on a Monday morning, stumbling over the rubble of the weekend's campfire. What was left of the trees – standing corpses, blackened sticks – was the vacant trace of an ecosystem, a community that had thrived without the help of men. Yet, there was a human quality to the spectral silence, a reminder of the sanctity of life. It was mid-afternoon, the sun beat down, there was no cooling shade, and it was the only day of the entire trip I hadn't checked my water supply. I ran out – an unthinkable mistake. My throat became as parched as the earth over which I dragged my body uphill for three long hours.

A distinct line ran between where the burn stopped and the live forest began again. Because it was at the top of a long rise, this destination could not be anticipated until the last hundred paces. When at last I reached it, I turned to survey the place where I had been.

"My God!" I cried aloud. Emotion welled up inside as immediate as the realization that accompanied it. I dropped my pack, oblivious to its heavy thud as I, too, dropped heavily to the ground. Tears filled my eyes, spilling over with a flash flood of understanding. I stood up, but could not yet turn away, for the symbolism of the scene was shockingly evident. All I could do was stare.

As I'd walked, lost for a day, through a desolate, burned-out forest, I'd symbolically traversed the desolation that was my close call with serious depression. *My Walking Story* had been a walk toward death – not the death of my body, but of my will to live. The decision to hike the JMT was a decision to walk toward life.

Turning to the living forest I was about to step into, I descried the lag between the subconscious awareness of the meaning of that decision and the now conscience realization of its meaning that came when I looked back at the remains of death.

Five hundred yards in on the now level earth, the fir and lodgepole pines made a sheltering canopy for the verdant woodland. Birds sang; chipmunks chirped; bugs hummed. Oxygen was in the air. Coming upon a flat, open intersection of trails, there stood a woman. She was not as old as the tender matron I'd met at Reds Meadow, but she seemed wiser. She wore a Western-style shirt with cowgirl embroidery and pearl snap buttons. Her silver belt buckle, a large oval set with turquoise, fit well

The JMT

on her rounded frame. We greeted each other. I asked if she knew how to connect up with the JMT and where the closest water might be. She said that if I continued in the direction I was going, I'd end up at Mammoth, but if I went to the right and down, I'd get back on track and find plenty of streams to quench my thirst. She drew a map in the dirt showing me how. I was about three miles off, far enough away that I had to go over the route with her several times to get it firmly in my head. As we were parting, I remembered to look back and thank her, but she had vanished in such a fashion that she has forever since been endowed the title of fairy godmother.

The next week presented proof that I had chosen to walk toward life. Each day saw me a stronger hiker. I was now acclimated to the altitude, little inconveniences did not perturb me, and the amenities of home were unimportant. When, on Day 6, I lost my wristwatch after I slipped crossing a stream, the prospect of using the sun to tell time did not unduly distress me. Food meant less and less, but my sense of taste seemed to have become more acute. A week without processed sugar allowed the sweetness of natural sugars to emerge. I never knew how much pleasure could be derived from a carrot!

The wildflowers were awesome; the sky, miraculous; the bespeckled steel-white of the granite, uncompromising. Water was everywhere – rivers, creeks, lakes, ponds. And there were the mountains. Lord, Lord, the mountains. I was slowing down. My mind was nearly depleted of its running commentary, the dearth of which is foremost in residing in the present.

I reached Vermillion on Day 8. Through-hikers coming down from Yosemite look forward to this day because it means a home-cooked meal, a cold beer, and a bed. It also means the last convenient link to civilization until Whitney Portal, 136 miles away, so it is here most hikers re-supply. Some mail a package to the resort; others have a friend or relative bring it to them. Some buy junk food at the camp store, because the friend or relative forgot the re-supply box by the back door of the kitchen. This last option was the one Sean apparently thought I wanted.

The horrified look on his face as he approached me from the car made me think his brother must be dead or the house burned down. "Shall we go back and get it, Mom? I'm so sorry. You weighed everything so carefully in all those one-pound packages. We could drive all night and be back by tomorrow morning. Or tell us what you need, and we'll drive to Fresno right now and get it."

My poor Seanie. I could picture him, in high spirits, feeling privileged to be entrusted with Mom's new Honda Accord. I could picture his buddy, Mike, with his guitar in the passenger's seat, pressing his bare feet against the windshield, idly strumming a Beatles song or maybe experimenting with some jazz lead line he'd recently learned. Then, four hours into the drive, the, "oh shit" moment.

"Wait a minute," I could hear Sean say, panic in his voice. Without explanation, he pulls over, pops the trunk open, jumps out and goes to the rear of the vehicle. "Where is it?"

Mike sticks his head out the window. "What's goin' on?"

"I forgot the food box. I can't believe this. Mom's going to be so pissed."

They stare at each other. A nanosecond later, they realize they're each seeing the same thing: the re-supply box by the back door of the kitchen.

"Oh shit!"

The JMT

I re-supplied at the camp store.

◊

Day 10. Somewhere near McClure Meadow. 16 miles. Today was great. I keep saying that. Followed rushing rivers almost all day. No bugs until this evening. I'm not in the best campsite, and I'm afraid of Muir Pass tomorrow. I hope I find somebody to do it with. I am dirty even though I wash. I am getting into high country and am afraid of snow and a thin trail.

Day 11. LeConte Canyon. 14 miles. What a day! Got up early hoping to pass hikers heading for Muir Pass before they got started. Found two still in their tent, so I felt better knowing people were behind me. Up I went until I got to Evolution Lake. Beautiful! Washed clothes and self. 10,500 feet and no bugs. Then up I went. At Wanda Lake, there were two sections by the shore with horrendous little flies. I had to run – run, mind you – carrying the thirty pounds I have left. Above that, there were the most delightful little white and red 'bell' flowers. Then on up to the Muir Hut. The path was clear. What was I frightened of? There were two couples in the hut enjoying lunch. We hiked down together. It's a good thing because there was a lot of snow melt, and the trail was difficult to cross or even find. I was the designated guide! Little did they know how glad I was they were there to corroborate my decisions. We said good-bye at a lake above LeConte Canyon.

◊

I met Ranger Jane on Day 13. I had hiked Mather Pass in the morning. There was no one anywhere, but after two weeks out, I was feeling capable. The high country did not intimidate me and daily tasks were not daunting. I decided to go for Pinchot Pass that afternoon.

This meant descending from 12,000 feet to 8,000 and then climbing back up to 12,000. I was somewhat apprehensive, because telling time by the sun can be deceptive. I knew there were enough daylight hours left to get over the pass, but I wasn't sure how far I'd have to walk on the other side to get to a campsite before nightfall.

The approach to the saddle where the trail crossed, or "passed," to the other side of the mountain consisted of a series of rocky switchbacks, all well above timberline. Each turn created a "U" and each "U" got tighter and steeper. It was difficult to tell where the top lay, because the trail was cut like a giant's spiral staircase, with the railing made up of stones piled head-height and each step – the trail – the lateral incline. Hiking upward, this stone wall "handrail" started out on the left obscuring everything above it, but to the right, the valley below was in full view. When at the dip of the "U" I had to switch back (thus the term) to the next "step." Now uphill was in the opposite direction. The open valley was to the left and the rock wall was to the right, still hiding what was at the top. Hopefully not the giant, but I did start to wonder.

Not for the first time on the trip did I experience the meaning of the phrase "long and laborious" and not for the first time did I speak – out loud – encouraging words to myself. "Don't worry, girl. You're gonna make it. It can't be that much farther. You can do it. Just a little more. Keep on a-truckin'."

"Yes, you're almost there. You *can* do it."

Her voice came out of nowhere. Her words were very close.

Thinking I'd gone mad, I plodded around the curve of yet another switchback when I saw her. She was sitting atop a cliff, looking out over the wide open spaces of the other side. She was as close as a whisper in your ear. Suddenly, I reached the top.

"Hi, I'm Jane. I'm a ranger. How are you doing?" I could tell by her smile she knew what she was about.

"I lost my watch a week ago and was guessing at what time it is and how far I have to go before it gets dark."

"You're doing fine. It's only 4 o'clock."

"Really? Wow. I hiked Mather this morning. Thought I might as well take a shot at Pinchot. I could have sworn it was at least six."

"You hiked two passes today? Good for you! Where'd you start your trip from?"

"Yosemite."

"Superb. Shall we walk awhile? I'll show you a good camping spot."

"That'd be great." We began the descent into the Twin Lakes region. "How do you like being a ranger? My name is Lois, by the way."

"I love it. Being out here is the best part of my year. It frees me up and gets me rolling again. It reaffirms who I am," she explained.

"I feel like my brain is totally emptied out."

"Funny how it works, huh?"

"Last night, I was thinking about how hiking the JMT reminds me of working in a factory."

"How's that?"

"Well," I told her, "I've worked in a box factory, a sardine factory, and a plastic molds factory. Only a few months in each, but what I learned was that by performing routine, automatic motions, your mind is free to do nothing but think. After a while, stuff you haven't thought of in forever pops up. My friend, Cory, and I worked in the plastic molds factory together and somewhere a week and a half in, we marveled at what our brains came up with – memories from when we were kids. I remembered a story from the cloakroom in kindergarten. I could see the hallway-size closet in detail, an image I had no idea was anywhere in my head. Cory remembered a particular day at her aunt's house, what was going on and the room she was in. The thing was, her aunt had long ago moved out of that house."

"So, are you getting images from your childhood out here?" Jane asked.

"No, but my brain is flat lining, all right. And there's nothing more coming in to bombard it. I'm free to just be me."

"That's what I'm talking about," she said. "Isn't it great to have no phone, no newspaper, no radio or television? We live in a world of constant distractions, but you don't understand how many until you get away from them."

"I'd say we're away from them. No advertisements or commercials. No billboards!"

"No spouting off," Jane added.

"You know, you're right. Not one person I've run into has tried to push opinion on me."

"Yes, there's nobody out here telling us how we're supposed to think."

"Or how we're supposed to be," I stated. "It's difficult to put into words."

"The world is too small, with too many people on it," Jane continued. "There's too much to know; too many avenues to go down. How can we help anybody if we keep getting hit with *every*body's pain? Know what I mean?"

"Yep. It's enough dealing with the distractions of our own lives, let alone what everybody else is doing to keep themselves from themselves."

"Is it really ourselves we're avoiding?"

"Don't surround yourself with yourself," I said, reciting a few of the famous lyrics of my generation.

"Move on back two squares." Jane knew the lyrics better than I.

"That's such a great song. But aren't we talking about doing the very thing it admonishes us to stay away from? Isn't getting back to who you are the same as surrounding yourself with yourself?"

"I don't think so," she conjectured, "I think 'Move on back two squares' means to ease off, stop, and discover the real you."

"I never got that line. What's it mean to go back to squares?"

"No, no. *Two* squares. One-two. Go back *two* squares, like you can go back in chess or Parcheesi. The song means to say, 'Get away from the you surrounding you that's keeping you from the real you. Step away from being surrounded by your ego.'"

"Oh, I get it. Step back. Take a look at all the junk of you surrounding you, so you can see you." We laughed.

"For all the words in the dictionary," Jane continued, "the English language sure does fall short. Do you think stepping back two squares could be a penalty?"

"I suppose. Uh-oh. Now we're in trouble," I teased.

"Send that Instant Karma to me. Initial it with loving care. – What? You don't like my singing?" She had such a great smile.

"No, no. That's not it. I like your voice. It was the *Instant Karma* made me laugh."

"What about it?"

"Oh, just a story from my life, is all."

"It's amazing how we're nothing more than a bundle of experiences."

"Our encounters. Every day. Every minute. They're all in there."

We laughed again as we cried out, "Our distractions!"

Good humor and the downhill run put a light-hearted cadence in our step. Soon we reached the pond near Twin Lakes that Jane wanted me to see.

"Here's your campsite," she said.

"Wow. It's fantastic. Thanks."

"You're welcome."

"You're not staying?"

"No. There's a ranger station a little farther."

Unstrapping my backpack, which was now another couple of pounds lighter, I watched her disappear beneath a cleft in the sprawling terrain, the pocket image of a hiker. Jane was not someone who needed a good-bye.

Turning toward the pond, I wondered where the Greek gods and goddesses were, and the nymphs dancing in and out of the emerald green and white of the plants and stones that encircled its banks. *Now this is what I wish we could always surround ourselves with.* The water was clear and warm. Settling my gaze on its depth, I was astonished to see that it was filled with tadpoles and frogs at every stage of development. Like a nymph at play, I darted back and forth from shore to shore for the sheer enjoyment of seeing how many there were. There were hundreds and hundreds, and they seemed to be staring up at me. "Hey, froggies!" I shouted out to them. "I climbed over two passes today. Two!"

After pitching the tent on a hill a short distance from the water's edge, I lay in my sleeping bag, arms folded to make a headrest. I wanted to continue thinking on the things Jane and I had talked about. I wondered. *Is there anybody who's not distracted?*

The JMT

In this quiet time, when we bring our thoughts home, the answer came: my mom. My mom was never distracted. She never had to find herself, nor did she veer from who she was to spend years bumbling about trying to get back from the person she wasn't. Her struggle was in remaining focused and not allowing herself to become sidetracked. Her hand was steady; her aim on center. My dad's were, too. I mentally theorized. *Is this why they're the "greatest generation?" There was nothing distracting about World War II. It validated a belief system and a concrete set of values. It was who they were. This was their stability. And their greatness?*

The sun was setting. I needed to eat, but I did not want to abandon my speculations, so I set about the evening meal in that wonderfully mechanical way kitchen tasks have of performing themselves. Reaching for the bear canister, I continued my questioning. *How about the Vietnam War? Now there was a distraction – a big, fat one that my generation had to right, and Kent State was my personal part of it.*

Thoughts persisting, I sighed. *I wish it were that simple. How do things get so off kilter? The difference between right and wrong was so clear-cut for our parents. We, well mostly the vets – what hubris to think it was "we" – were left to pick up the pieces from the fallout of the Vietnam War that exposed the clear-cut for what it was: an uncertainty.*

While preparing dinner, which consisted of taking out a plastic baggy and opening it, I carried on the argument. *But then the eighties came along and people kept up the facade of distraction with the same thing those idiots at Rutgers did after the shootings when they booed me off the stage. They dismissed listening in order to create their own truth. That's how distractions dominate. It's easier to take the pontifications of some news analyst or pop psych guru and repeat them as if they're your own.*

I picked out a slice of dried mango and held the sliver of fruit to my lips. *The eighties were a reaction to what might've been the outcome of the sixties and seventies, if it'd been allowed – the Age of Aquarius.*

I bit down. *Was it Sean who commented that my generation had the lofty visions his generation has the technology to transform into reality? Maybe the ideas of those years were too close to the truth of where we came from. Are distractions merely deceptions by the self to maintain the individual? How many thousands of years ago did we begin separating from the animals? What was that book by Erich Fromm?*

I thought about it for a minute. *The Art of Loving. Yes, that's right. So if we acknowledge everything is just one thing, will we lose the awareness of self? I don't believe so, but we're too afraid to find out. The individual is a lonesome soul. Those magazines that started getting published in the eighties — what were they called? Self? You? Good Lord!*

I was worn out with questions that lead to more questions, but one last one nagged at me. Plumping up a pillow of clothes, I wagered, *How about Mom's affair? Wasn't there a clear-cut difference between right and wrong there?* I wasn't sure. She understood the deficiency of human nature in its attempts to adhere to its own high standards, but she firmly believed it was possible to punch through and preserve correctness by ignoring the officiousness of frailty, even as we submit to its inevitability.

Did the interference of Mom's affair distract me from being me? That wouldn't be fair to say, but in order to be me, I had to tend to the part of me that was her, and to the feelings her unhappy marriage left me with. How sorry I feel for people who have such monstrous deterrents to happiness that they must pile on more layers of distraction to alleviate the pain. I don't pray much, but that night I fell asleep thanking God for my health and my easy life.

The next three days flew by in a sweet, sweet blur of sky and sunlight and fresh air. I walked on and on, experiencing long periods of bliss without an iota of fear. I did, however, have a craving. Two, in fact, but even desires I could not satisfy made me smile. I wanted a frothy, ice-cold, root beer and a manicure. The root beer made sense, but why I imagined a manicure, I'll never know. I'd never had one – never wanted one – but the thought itself made me all the more joyful to be alive.

The John Muir Trail is a prime example of the metaphor of life as a path. The trail is steady and true. Many people have prepared the way. When you think you've lost sight of it, look out, and you'll see the path just a short distance ahead. Trail workers, an amazing bunch, pack in their tools, dig and pound and shovel, scratch their heads and measure as they work hard to keep the trail free of obstacles. Other hikers leave behind a footprint or a stick arrow, a log barrier or a cairn to act as guides. You'll invariably get off track a number of times, but the path, if you trust it, is there for you to find again. There are many annoyances that can't be ignored (like bugs!), but you wouldn't have missed any of it for the world – and all along and every where, the beauty of nature overflows with an abundance unwavering and a peace that abounds.

Day 17. Dow Villa Hotel, Lone Pine. 18 miles. Hiked 3,800 feet up and 6,000 down today. Wowee. Woke up in

the night to a thunderstorm – nice! Lots of people today. Getting to the junction for Whitney was endless, but hikers leave their packs at the point of the final ascent, which makes summiting feel as free-floating as a ride in a hot air balloon. It was another thousand feet up, and then the long push down to Whitney Portal. Boy, did I smell. I bought a shirt at the gift shop, washed my armpits in the bathroom there, and threw away the shirt I was wearing. Even then, the poor folks who gave me a ride down to Lone Pine had to open all the car windows.

And now, here I sit writing my last entry. On the time line, my life goes from my birth to three weeks ago, and again from now until forever.

The pilot who flew Austin to Mammoth came in the next day to pick me up. This time he was in a Cessna 172. "It's a Skyhawk," he said, "my private plane."

> Look, the trees
> are turning
> their own bodies
> into pillars
> of light
> – Mary Oliver, "In Blackwater Woods"

22 Walking toward life

I started teaching in August. During the four years I was in school, housing prices shot through the roof, so instead of buying the house I'd hoped to fund from the last of the Boat Rentals' reserves, I bought another condominium. Austin was off on his own, taking classes at the community college, trying to figure out his life. Sean was in high school, very serious about it and about his music. I was inundated with the demands of a first-year teacher, making the pair of us passing ships in much the same way my parents and I were when I was in high school. One afternoon, when he was coming into the kitchen as I was going out, we stopped. We had both noticed we were humming, but more than that, we noticed we were always humming whenever we met in this shipping lane of ours.

"Doesn't everybody have a song?" he assumed.

"I don't think so, honey. Just us musician types. Did you know you were humming?"

"Kind of. It's like having the radio on in the background. Sometimes you turn the volume up, but mostly, the music keeps you company. What'd you have going right now, Mom?"

"Umm. Sonny and Cher. Must be from when I was in the supermarket today. How about you?"

"Chick Corea."

"No fair!"

We came up with a game. Anytime, anywhere, either of us could stop the other and ask, "What song's playing?" If you didn't have an answer, you lost. Neither of us ever lost, but the asker got to sing.

◊

My mom called sometime in late September to see if I was coming home for Christmas. Dad still wasn't in pain, but the cancer was progressing.

"OK," I said. "Maybe I can have lunch with Ron while I'm there." Ever since broaching the topic two years before, I had periodically tried to get her to arrange a meeting with him for me.

"No dice. And stop asking me!" Her words finally cut through, and I heard what she'd been trying to say all these months: It wouldn't be proper to meet with Ron. Leave it at that.

"Sorry. I won't ask anymore."

"Good. See that you don't. It's your father you should be thinking about."

She was right. We knew Dad was dying. Maybe I could orchestrate some sort of closure over the holidays. It was highly doubtful this would come in the form of a conversation, but possibly sitting next to him while I prepared lesson plans and he watched TV would spark a word or two.

Walking toward life

◊

A week into the visit, I tried it. No sparks. I wasn't the least bit interested in his television show, and he wasn't the least bit interested in my work.

We toughed it out though, ignoring each other, my lesson plans spread out all over the coffee table, his coffee cooling, counting out the minutes in its usual place in front of him. It was frustrating. We were both uncomfortable, but I, obdurate I, let the situation continue. I could have moved to the desk or to another room, or put everything away and gotten into his TV show with him as I had oh so long ago, but I didn't. Too bad there weren't any Tastykakes in the cupboard.

I trusted silence would prevail. It did. I relaxed. This was my dad, and it was all right. It was our moment. It was what it was, and except for in the hospital, when the grip of death's ambassadors held firm, it was our last.

◊

When, after five years, I put this story to thought so it could become words on a page, it came into view from a different perspective. To break from writing and from the bright screen of my laptop, I bicycled from my downtown apartment to Golf Club Drive where I entered Pogonip, my favorite city park. Leisurely climbing up the sloping meadow, I paused to take in the day. There was a warm wind of the kind that invites you to forget yourself. Its breath, as light as the wisp of a butterfly, brushed my cheek, and I returned to the Christmas scene. My father's place on the couch became mine, and I became my father. I saw strange books and papers laid out every which way. Every few minutes, my college-educated daughter tapped her pencil, flipped pages, looked out the window, and then wrote as quickly as anybody can. This was no business of mine, because I never went past the eighth grade. What was there to talk about? What question could I ask?

My dad never read a book. I never saw him open a novel. How supercilious of me to think I was generous to him that day. Had I learned nothing from what I taught? "I'm sorry, Daddy," I said aloud, in tears, as I walked down to my bike, ready to turn my thoughts, the expected and the unexpected, into words.

When we were on the couch, he still had command of his body. When he obstinately refused to ask me about my work, he still had his dignity. In the hospital, he'd been stripped of both. Only now did I see that I might have also stripped him of his honor if I had insisted on pulling him into my world at a time when he would soon have so little left of what allows a man to stand tall. Thank heaven I knew enough to keep silent.

◊

As a child, all I ever wanted was to see my parents happy. Looking back over the years to find when joy shone through, only three moments come to mind. One is of my mom, one, my dad, and the third is of the two of them together.

I'll always remember my mom bouncing up onto the bed, rejoicing, on the night she got home from her weekend in New York City – before she told all. I beam just as she did whenever I think of it. I think of it now.

When I was fourteen, Daddy took me on a ski weekend to Vermont. He must have been thirty-eight. During après ski, he went off with some friends while I stayed in the room with a girl my age. On my way to get us a Coke from the restaurant, I heard what sounded like lots of fun coming from the lounge. Glancing in that direction, I saw my dad in a way I'd never seen him before and would never see him again. He was seated in a large cushioned, half-circle booth, filled with guys and gals. He was in the center, being thrown back by laughter, a drink in his hand, flirting with the girls – one girl. I think I know who. He was happy, genuinely happy, the happiest I'd ever seen him. So I was happy, too. I remember how good it made me feel inside. He saw me. A flash of parental concern swept over his brow, but I waved so exuberantly that he knew it was all right and went back to enjoying himself.

I saw my parents happy together when I was about nine years old. Daddy was smoking back in those days. My mom hated his smoking. But this time, she let it be. Holding smoke in his mouth, he teased her by sneaking up from behind for a kiss and then blowing the whole mouthful down her throat as she stretched her neck to accept his affection. Her explosive cough turned to a radiant smile. She gave him a girlish *whack!* as he twisted her around in his arms for a real kiss. They laughed a dazzling laugh, and the happiness they shared was enough to fill a childhood.

Epilogue

My father died in the spring of 2001, less than a year after I became a teacher. Robin was at the funeral. Sometimes you hear about somebody marrying his or her high-school sweetheart forty years later, after their respective spouses have passed away. I thought about this as we chatted, but I don't think it's in the cards for Robin and me. It's good to be friends with someone from your youth, though. That's a certainty, and that's why, when Corrine made a surprise call three years ago to ask for money, my heart sank.

Mom and Ron married in 2004. She was eighty; he seventy. Ron continued in his refusal to make contact with me until the wedding day. Then, as casual as pie, he said, "Long time, no see."

They built a house together. It's the one my mom's always wanted. Hers is a fairy tale come true. She tells me she keeps pinching herself to make sure she's not dreaming. But she hasn't forgotten my dad. "Ron is so good about it when I call him Austin."

Since his death, thoughts of my dad come often. I think of the innocence of the soldier. I remember the hug we shared. I see him in my actions and in my words. I can't decide if what she did was right or wrong, selfish or compassionate. I only know that I've relied on her my whole life, and she has never turned her back on me.

And how about me? Through the miracle of the World Wide Web, I recently found *Richard Hittleman's Yoga 28-Day Exercise Plan*. It was in a used bookstore in Illinois. So here I am, thirty years later, doing yoga again.

I'm also getting ready to take a position I've been offered at the middle school across the street from where I teach English. I'll be organizing a music department there, and over the summer, I'll pick out music and practice how to lead a school band. I bought a conductor's baton just yesterday. This is *my* dream come true.

Oh, and the other part of me? The part that would like a sweetheart? I will tell you what Tom tells Ruth near the end of Charles Dickens's novel *Martin Chuzzlewit*.

"You think of me, Ruth," said Tom, "and it is very natural that you should, as if I were a character in a book; and you make it a sort of poetical justice that I should, by some impossible means or other, come, at last, to marry the person I love. But there is a much higher justice than poetical justice my dear, and it does not order events upon the same principle. Accordingly people who read about heroes in books, and choose to make heroes of themselves out of books, consider it a very fine thing to be discontented and gloomy, and misanthropical, and perhaps a little blasphemous, because they cannot have everything ordered for their individual accommodation. Would you like me to become one of that sort of people?"

"No, Tom. But still I know," she added timidly, "that this is a sorrow to you in your own better way."

Tom thought of disputing the position. But it would have been mere folly, and he gave it up.

In the Pillared Dark was first printed in the autumn of 2013 as a limited edition of 100 signed and numbered hardcover copies. The body texts of that edition and this softcover version are identical. Both editions were designed by Barbara Hauser at Pelican's Way Press. The body typefaces are Iowan Old Style, designed in 1990 by noted sign painter John Downer. The titling faces are Niagara Engraved and Niagara Solid, designed in 1994 by Tobias Frere-Jones.

www.ingramcontent.com/pod-product-compliance
Lightning Source LLC
Chambersburg PA
CBHW022033290426
44109CB00014B/845